THE LAST ATTEMPT

THE LAST ATTEMPT

THE TRUE STORY OF FREEDIVING CHAMPION AUDREY MESTRE

CARLOS SERRA

Copyright © 2006 by Carlos Serra.

Library of Congress Control Number: 2006909196
ISBN 10: Hardcover 1-4257-3840-0
Softcover 1-4257-3839-7

ISBN 13: Hardcover 978-1-4257-3840-2
Softcover 978-1-4257-3839-6

All rights reserved. No part of this book may be reproduced or transmitted in any form or by any means, electronic or mechanical, including photocopying, recording, or by any information storage and retrieval system, without permission in writing from the copyright owner.

This book was printed in the United States of America.

To order additional copies of this book, contact:
Xlibris Corporation
1-888-795-4274
www.Xlibris.com
Orders@Xlibris.com

CONTENTS

Acknowledgement 9

Prologue 11

Chapter 1: Doomed from the Beginning 17

Chapter 2: Audrey's Pathway To Death The Daily Report ... 26

Chapter 3: How Beauty Met The Beast 40

Chapter 4: The Report Continues 51

Chapter 5: Countdown Goes On; Minus One-Week 70

Chapter 6: A Record-Setting Dive 87

Chapter 7: The Divorce Request 96

Chapter 8: Countdown To A Tragedy—Minus One Day 104

Chapter 9: The Day When Time Stood Still 115

Chapter 10: The Aftermath 137

Chapter 11: The Worst News A Parent Can Get 143

Chapter 12: Watching The Video 149

Chapter 13: Facing Audrey's Parents 160

Chapter 14: Back To Miami 165

Chapter 15: The Investigation Begins 173

Chapter 16: Profiting from Audrey's Death 183

Chapter 17: Hollywood Wants the Story 190

Chapter 18: Putting The Pieces Together 199

Chapter 19: The Beginning of the End 203

Chapter 20: The Point Of No Return 216

Chapter 21: A True Master Speaks Out 229

Chapter 22: In The Mind of a Master of Deep-Ception 238

Chapter 23: The Final Report—What Really Happened 250

To Audrey
1974-2002

Acknowledgement

After parting from my former partner; a person to whom I granted candid and blind friendship, I kept debating my options. When the legal alternatives were unfeasible, my inner circle of friends and family immediately supported the idea of writing a book as a way to expose the awful reality of what truly happened to Audrey. To them I want to express my deepest gratitude.

To my ex-wife Adriana, for Alexander and Christopher, our two wonderful kids. Also for your patience and sixteen years of having to deal with this adventurous right brain, but I still make you laugh and you miss my cooking, don't you? You're the greatest mother my kids can have.

My mother, whose courageous battle against cancer made me realize how insignificant my problems were. My love and admiration goes out to you.

My stepfather Basil, whose support helped me accomplish a dream; start my own business. Your advice against partnership, however, wasn't attended and you were right all along. My next book may be based on your culinary skills; keep cooking!

Carlos LoBosco, my brother at heart and Alexander's godfather. Our conversations over the Internet during those troubling times opened a window to a more pleasant reality. Unknowingly, you lowered my stress level; at least for a while.

Frank and Nestor Palmero, president of Scuba School International/Latin America and Vice-president of Oceanic Worldwide, respectively, and former owners of Dixie Divers, for believing on this newly-arrived, non-English speaker with the instructor-training division of your business back in 1993. Eternally grateful I am to both of you.

Matt Briseno, your support and friendship are priceless. Aloha, friend and please, don't send me a bill, I did say priceless, okay?

Daniel, the psychiatrist whose knowledge of the human mind was like freezing water splashed in the face of a dormant idiot. Thank you for the wakeup call.

Juan Carlos Caraglia, who conferred me with friendship I didn't deserve. I can only ask for your forgiveness and hope that one day you'll recover ten folds the money you lost. Sadly, there is nothing I can do for you to regain your faith in your former sport hero, but if it is of any consolation, we are rowing on the same boat of disillusionment.

CARLOS SERRA

Carlos Llantada, who, like Juan Carlos, lost a little fortune invested in their love and passion for the sport. Although I can understand the reasons for your initial allegations against me, I hope you realize now how incorrect they were.

Ricardo Hernandez, whose initial allegations were nerve-racking, to say the least, but turning out to be partly correct. Although I was already aware, I appreciate the additional information you provided in regards to those other mysterious incidents.

Angelo Cordero, whose pictorial collection on Audrey's event is a decisive tool on proving the story. As you'll see, you are getting the credit that was stolen from you before. Nothing we can do; that's the way "he" is; isn't he?

Eduardo "Wiky" Orjales; you were a pivotal point in revealing the truth. By speeding me out of Cabo San Lucas you probably even saved me from dead-serious troubles. We may never know for sure but that's good, because finding out could have been a surprise to die for. Thanks!

Christian Cano for his initial proofreading and for keeping my voice and accent present. However, I take full responsibility for the editing of this book. I've learned English only few years ago, but small criticism will be gladly accepted if written on a $20 bill. For larger complains, please use a $100 bill. That way I can afford a professional editor.

There are also those not so close but very supportive, nonetheless. Their objective and constructive counsel gave me the strength needed to complete this project. Writing about Audrey's demise was a painful but mandatory journey through sad memories.

Dr. Joe McInnis, whose recommendation to come out with the truth and nothing but the truth, added fuel to my inner spark. I started writing the day after your visit, doc. Thanks for your books, too. And your latest work, Aliens of the Deep, is a wonderful work. Maybe one day I'll write as well as you do.

Dr. Samuel Vaknin, for the insightful information found on his website (http://samvak.tripod.com/siteindex.html) and excellent book, Malignant Self Love—Narcissism Revisited. Thank you also for gently allowing me to quote your findings. When it comes to Narcissism, you're the man!

Maurizio Candotti Russo, Vice-President of Idelson-Gnocchi, for kindly allowing me to include excerpts from Jacques Mayol's book, Homo-Delphinus: the Dolphin within Man; a beautiful work from a true master of freediving.

Steve McCulloch, Director of the Marine Mammal Division at the distinguished Harbor Branch Oceanographic Institution in Fort Pierce, Florida, for the perceptive comments and quotes from his beloved friend, Jacques Mayol.

Paul Kvinta, for the excerpts from his article "Is Time Running Out for the Mythic Man Fish?" In only days, you saw the man for what he was; it took me much longer.

Umberto Pelizzari, for allowing me to include his insightful description on freediving. The best depiction I've ever read about our beloved sport, given in few words. Thank you also to your sister Stefania. Dinner is pending; my debt and treat for both of you.

Last but never least, Jacques Mayol, for saying exactly what my partner was made of. Sorry for not believing; you were right all these years. Please take care of Audrey, up there where you both are. May God bless your souls!

Prologue

OCTOBER 12—COLUMBUS DAY
TIME: 2:25 P.M.

There she is, floating in the middle of the ocean, surrounded by a circle of boats packed with curious natives. We are the show of the day. They all want to take a close look of the event for which Audrey is the central figure. While standing on the edge of a large Catamaran, I use a megaphone to keep those little boats and their threatening propellers away from her.

This Catamaran is normally used to introduce tourists to the tropical setting of the south-eastern coast of the Dominican Republic, but this day it's being used as the central quarters for an event of international magnitude; a world record attempt in the extreme-sport of freediving.

Over Audrey's head spreads a sinister and intimidating overcast sky, which only minutes before was roaring like a thousand angry lions in unison. Beneath her feet lies a lightless abyss of silence and desolation; the ocean and her usually enticing beauty, but today she's more daunting than inviting.

The stormy weather is passing, but the remnant of nature's power is still dragging its tail of darkness and gloominess over us. Not the best day to be plunging into the dark blue and claim records of depth while holding your breath; much less when the target exceeds—by many meters—what any human has done before.

Even a dolphin looking at Audrey descending to such depths may ask, *"Are you out of your mind?"* She wouldn't understand the dolphin, of course. Maybe one day, as researchers continue to study our marine cousins, we humans may decipher how they communicate, but I doubt they will ever understand humans, as only insanity can rationalize such endeavor.

Audrey is not in her best state of mind, in any case. She's feeling as gloomy as the day. Less than thirty minutes ago she was sobbing and reflecting on leaving her husband, and for an enterprise that requires the concentration of an elder Tibetan monk, thoughts of divorce are quite disrupting.

For the last two weeks Audrey has been enduring her husband's never-ending list of irrational actions and oddities. One of those oddities is, in fact, having Audrey perform her record attempt when the weather isn't ideal. He's not only Audrey's husband, but her coach and the current record holder, as well. And although I'm the president of the company we both own, the one organizing this event, when it comes to this record attempt, he's the decision maker.

That's him, anyway. That's the way he is, and that's the way he'll always be. He has made of that kind of behavior his trademark. He's well known for that. He is impetuous, imprudent, and what it is worse, nobody contradicts him.

At this point I've had a good share of clashes with my business partner, but feeling lonesome on a pointless one-man crusade to lodge common sense into his mind, and keep under control his hotheaded nature, I stopped arguing. Instead, I settled for performing the duties of a damage control manager, cleaning-up the mess after his stormy personality passes over. He's like a bullet-train in motion; you either sit down and buckle-up for the ride of your life, or bail out and risk the cost, but never get in his way, because the consequences can be upsetting.

That's his wife Audrey on the sled, in which she'll plunge to one hundred and seventy-one meters of darkness and crushing pressure. It's like jumping off a balcony located on the 57th floor of a high-rise, only that the building is submerged into the ocean.

This category of freediving consists of riding a weighted sled along a vertical line towards the bottom of the sea. Once the sled reaches the end of the line to a predetermined depth, the athlete disconnects the bottom (weighted) section, and rockets himself up to the surface by inflating a lift bag attached to the sled's top section. Compressed air coming from a small scuba tank is used for this maneuver.

Due to the water pressure offering resistance, your fall is agonizingly slow, and you can't breathe, not until you reach the end of the cable and return back to the surface. At the bottom you must withstanding the crushing pressure of the ocean. Your lungs are squeezed to the size of an orange. Your ears, in piercing pain, are ready to blow. Not to mention the overwhelming desolation at the bottom, where there is nothing but darkness and silence.

You must also endure the low temperatures of a place where warm-blooded creatures are not meant to be. And then, before your body collapses to the extreme environment, return to the surface, now riding in opposite direction the full extend of 57 floors, once again. And you're still holding your breath.

More than three minutes will pass before she inhales what we all take for granted; the life-sustaining air. By voluntarily holding her breath, Audrey must resist the urge to inhale. That happens when the brain emits an order to the diaphragm to expand the lungs and breathe, but if she does, she'll drown. Three minutes will seem like an eternity.

It'll be a constant battle between the brain, with its instinctive reflexes, and Audrey's conscious mind. The strong contractions of the diaphragm, commanded by the now persistent and oxygen depleted brain, are a demand for the lungs to expand and breathe, but they must be ignored to avoid drowning. That's as agonizing as receiving a punch

THE LAST ATTEMPT

right on the solar plexus from a heavy-weight boxer, again and again. Meanwhile, you're suffocating.

Life waits for you up at the surface, but while beneath the sea, you are flirting with death. Not an easy task, but he's the world champion and so is she; they both know better, I hope, but I still don't like it.

Few days back I was dreadfully concerned about Audrey's wellbeing. By now, I'm more than just her husband's partner; I had become one of her closest friends and confidant. I knew her well; I knew how fragile her amended spirit was. But I also knew how determined she could be to prove her worthiness to him.

At the risk of paying with her own life, Audrey kept accepting outrageous increases of depth during training. By adding tens of meters to her previous training dive, he had been pushing her too hard and I was the only one stopping him from sending Audrey even deeper.

This is a category of freediving foolishly called *No-Limits*, because there is a limit, after all. But determining where the limit lies can be a venture to die for.

My stress level was at a sky-scraping high, especially since Audrey was, passively, accepting her husband's drastic increases of depth. But as I stood up firm to him, his eyes turned into the soulless stare of the tiger; the icy gaze of a predator. That's a familiar look. I knew I had stepped outside the train and placed myself on the tracks ahead.

My plan was to stop him and it worked this once. After another strong argument he agreed to add only one meter—not ten—to Audrey's last training dive. The official record attempt would be one hundred and seventy-one meters; not one hundred and eighty as he wanted. My stress level is now within manageable parameters.

While watching Audrey climbing on the sled, some of the aforementioned circumstances are crossing my mind, but I need to focus; I also have a duty to perform. As the event's arbitrator, I have to watch the two chronometers that would time Audrey's descent and posterior ascent.

To give her some reasonable silence to concentrate, I have to keep the spectators quiet, but holding their boats within a safe distance proved to be a challenge.

Audrey looks at me; I look back at her. Her expression shows the depressive state in which she's already submerged. I plan to offer a shoulder to cry on, as I've done many times before, but not now. We have an international event to fulfill. The pressure is too much. Reporters from different parts of the world are on-site and waiting to wire the news, good or bad, to their respective headquarters. Audrey's shaky state of mind will have to wait.

Assenting with her head she gives me the signal. I start the countdown. In fives minutes she'll be plunging into the ocean. This countdown helps her establish a rhythm with her pre-dive ventilations, but it also helps coordinating the safety divers as they sink into the blue to protect her.

At minus five-minutes she starts her ventilation pattern. At minus four-minutes the divers will initiate their plunge and position themselves along the guiding cable. The most crucial of these divers is Pascal, the deepest one of all. He'll be at the end of the line. If there is anything to go wrong, that's the location; the farthest place away from the surface.

There are only few people in the world capable of diving to such depths; but Pascal, French native just like Audrey, is the best. If the sled's disconnecting mechanism fails to release the upper portion of it, which contains the balloon to be filled with air, just as it happened three years before in Spain, she could retrieve a regulator from Pascal and breathe from it. She should be safe down there.

Above Pascal, located at ninety meters, is Eduardo Orjales. Calling him by his name, however, won't do. He responds quicker to his nickname of Wiky.

Born in Cuba, Wiky is another prolific diver and very fond of Audrey. Although they aren't next of kin, they call each other niece and uncle. Wiky has been supporting Audrey on her world record attempts for the last five years and her husband's attempts for more than fourteen.

I'm also concerned for him. He's at ninety-meters breathing air instead of the safer mixture of blended gases called Trimix; the same one Pascal uses. But the night before Wiky was denied of such possibility. Why? Not many divers in the world would dare to such depth breathing just air. Not many divers in the world would dare to such depth, period. But the always trustworthy Wiky accepts his assigned post with resignation.

At minus one-minute all the divers must be already in place, including the ones remaining at the surface, the freedivers. They are also essential for Audrey's safety. The most likely scenario for Audrey's body to succumb after having reached the bottom is near the surface. Just like a car running out of gas, the brain could have exhausted its oxygen at this point and stopped functioning. This condition is called shallow-water blackout, and without the swift assistance of the freedivers, she could drown.

Now another concern arises; my partner has taken two of the safety scuba divers away from their protective duties and assigns them to videotape instead. Why? We did all the filming needed the day before in two simulated dives to only fifty meters. This way all the divers would be focused on protecting Audrey. But once again, that's him, my partner and his logic-defying actions compromising safety for no apparent reason.

I don't argue the point. If anything should happen, it's more likely to occur at the end of the line or near the surface, and both places are covered. These two divers were commanded by my partner to film between thirty and sixty meters of depth and nothing ever happens in that range, or so I thought.

As my countdown comes to an end, Audrey takes one last gulp of air. Like a heavy duty wet-and-dry vacuum machine, she sucks in forcefully. Since that would be her last mouthful of air for a while, she must inflate her lungs to capacity. She extends her left arm up and grabs the valve of a small scuba tank situated on the top of the sled. In the diving industry this undersized cylinder is known as pony-tank.

With her right hand Audrey pinches her nose and blows, creating a positive force inside her mouth. This maneuver is called *Valsalva*, in honor of the Italian anatomist *Antonio Maria Valsalva*, who discovered the benefits of this pressure equalization technique.

THE LAST ATTEMPT

It consists of attempting a relatively forceful exhalation with mouth and nose closed to compensate from the inside, the pressure being exerted over the tympanic membrane from the outside. This maneuver must be done continuously while descending; otherwise, the immense pressure of the ocean will burst her eardrum, causing uncontrollable vertigo. She may even fall off the sled.

With her lungs filled with air, now Audrey closes her mouth and assents with her head. That's a signal for her husband and coach, who while floating on the water next to her, grabs a short rope with a clip at the end. By pulling it, he will disconnect the sled from the mechanism holding it on the surface.

He pulls once—nothing happens. He pulls twice—and she remains on the surface. It's as if her guardian angel is tampering the mechanism to stop Audrey from plunging; a heavenly sign, perhaps?

"What's wrong?" I ask myself. *"He never fails to free the sled after the first pull. He's wasting time!"*

Audrey is already holding her breath at this point, consuming oxygen and wasting precious seconds that can make the difference between doing the record and suffering a shallow-water blackout. As per international rules, fainting at the surface would invalidate the attempt.

He pulls a third time, and finally, the sled is free; Audrey is on her way to conquer glory by beating her husband's own world record. Only once before, thirteen years ago when it happened, a woman has broken a man's record. After only three minutes she should be back and we'll be all celebrating.

Once she reaches the maximum depth, opening the pony-tank's valve will allow her to release compressed air into the lift-bag. Then she should rocket back to the surface with the tube to which the lift-bag is attached, brushing against the vertically extended cable serving as a guide.

Except that two minutes have passed and I don't feel Audrey's ascent. On board the catamaran I'm holding the cable through which the sled is going. An improvised crane has been made using one of the ship's booms and I'm grabbing the cable just before the point where it's tied.

I've always done this. The brushing of the sled against the cable sends distinct vibrations along its extension, allowing me to feel her descent. I can also feel the impact of the sled thumping at the end of the cable, and the more intense shudder on the way up.

She should be rocketing back by now, but more than three minutes have passed and there are no signs of her. I already know; something has gone terribly wrong!

He is on the surface, cursing, and requesting a scuba system already preassembled for him. That's something that got my attention before. Why ask for a scuba unit to be ready for him? He's more critical as a freediver, not as a scuba diver. But now I'm glad he did, so he can go and see what's going on.

With minutes stretching like hours, through the water I see a blurred yellow figure coming up. That must be Audrey's wetsuit. Next to it is another blurred but dark figure; maybe that's his black wetsuit. Bubbles are breaking the water surface, so she must be breathing safely from a diver's regulator; perhaps her husband's own. The record attempt is a failure, yet what really matters is that she's fine. But when two heads pop out of the water, the vision is terrifying.

After 8 minutes and 38 seconds exactly, Audrey breaks the surface without receiving air. That's an impossible time for any human brain to survive. He's holding her from behind but no regulator had been placed in her mouth. I had hoped to see her breathing from a regulator but she wasn't. The bubbles I saw were his.

A bombshell explodes in my mind; Audrey's motionless body presents no signs of life. I was hoping that she would be just unconscious; a blackout maybe, but then I see a horrible sign. A foamy fluid is coming out of her mouth and running down her chin. She had swallowed water; her lungs were filled with it. The amount is overwhelming.

For few seconds I'm speechless; I'm contributing to the absolute silence that reigned for a while. Maybe it's me, in such state of shock that can't hear a sound. But swiftly, reality strikes me, harshly. Seeing him attempting an ineffective mouth to mouth, brings me back from this surreal state of perplexity.

"Bring her here," I yell. *"Bring Audrey to the boat!"*

Ten minutes after initiating her descent, Audrey is pulled on board and laid down on the side of the vessel. Kneeled behind and over her shoulders, I'm holding Audrey's head with both hands. I open her airway as she gasps to breathe, but spurs of bloody foam keeps coming out of her mouth and running down my left hand. No air can make it through the massive amount of pink-colored foamy fluid she's expelling. The ocean had flooded her lungs.

"How is this possible? Why so much water?"

I check her carotidal pulse and it's strong; that's a good sign. She's attempting to breathe, and that's another good sign. Her eyes are semi-open, and as I extend her airway, she seems to be staring at me. Her pupils are not dilating and I already know what it means; the brain gave up, but by God I swear, I hear a screech coming out straight from her soul. Her eyes want to talk, to tell a story, but what's the story?

"How's this possible? Oh, God, what happened?" The answers, however, would become evasive for a long time.

"This can't be real. Audrey, please come back!" But that's heart contradicting reason. Audrey's condition is irreversible, yet I refuse to accept it.

He's next to her, silent. He stares at me and I don't like what I see. I don't know what to make of it. Yet, I try to comfort him with the good news about her pulse, but the news won't hold for long.

Her until now strong pulse starts fading; breathing also dies away, and although few of us worked intensely to bring her back, it was a done deal. She was beyond hope. This last attempt concluded Audrey's life prematurely and brought her dreams to an end, but for some of us, the nightmare had just begun.

Chapter 1

DOOMED FROM THE BEGINNING

MIAMI INTERNATIONAL AIRPORT
SUNDAY, SEPTEMBER 29, 2002
TIME: 7:25 P.M.

"*I wish I could be a dolphin,*" said Audrey seemingly contemplative. Seated next to each other, the roaring of airplanes either taking off or landing, along with constant announcements of flight numbers, embarking doors, and safety tips, kept interrupting our conversation.

"BIENVENIDOS A MIAMI. ASEGURESE QUE SU EQUIPAJE DE MANO..." continued the loud female voice of the airport's public announcer. But ignoring the recurring message, I asked intrigued,

"*Why's that? Why a dolphin?*"

"*Because, they swim freely throughout the ocean... they have a strong social structure... they hunt together... they are playful... they are smart and...*"

"*... and they are highly sexual,*" I interrupted. "*They mate all year round with multiple partners, and their mating ritual consists of ninety-five percent foreplay, but the actual copulation lasts only seconds. They are also excellent freedivers but intrinsically unfaithful.*"

Having said that, I looked around to see where Pipin was. Oblivious to my conversation with his wife, he was seated about five yards away chatting with Tata and Angelo (two of our helpers).

"*I guess that makes Pipin a dolphin,*" teasingly, I added.

"*Okay, now you've ruined it.*"

"Why? You two are married and he already has most of dolphins' innate characteristics," I joked.

"No!" she exclaimed with an unusually firm tone. *"I've just said that I wish I were a dolphin because I want to escape from him. And now you're ruining my fantasy by saying that he's a dolphin. So I don't have a way out?"*

"Hmm, we're not feeling too happy with the big guy, are we?"

"Carlos, I'm so tired of these records. For him everything is about breaking records, records, records! And Pipin's worst side comes out every time we have an event."

"Yeah, tell me about it. But the event is now with you, so I expect him to be more relaxed this time."

"I don't know, Carlos. I hope you're right because I can't . . ."

"SU ATENCIÓN POR FAVOR," interrupted the airport's public announcer once again. *"MEXICANA ANUNCIA LA SALIDA DE SU VUELO NUMERO TRES-CERO-TRES CON DESTINO A LA CIUDAD DE SANTO DOMINGO. SEÑORES PASAJEROS, POR FAVOR PRESÉNTENSE EN LA SALIDA . . ."*

"Okay, Audrey . . . that's us. Dominican Republic, here we come."

"We'll see how it goes," she added with resignation.

"C'mon, Audrey, let's hope for the best."

"You're omitting 'prepare for the worst'. Don't you always say that?"

"Indeed, that's an old axiom I always use, but I figured that when it comes to Pipin, there is no way to prepare."

Audrey heaved a deep and heavy sigh, got up the chair and went to Pipin, leaving me behind with an increased reservation about her emotional stability. A world record like the one she planned to break requires absolute mental equilibrium, but Pipin's overpowering personality seemed to be finally breaking her already shaken spirit. But on the other hand, only minutes before our conversation, she was seated next to Pipin, posing and smiling for some pictures. Accustomed to the scrutiny of a public life, they always present themselves as a loving pair in front of the lens. Besides, no matter what, Audrey was in love with him.

"Hmm, they are a couple, Carlos," I reflected, *"stay out of it."*

30 MINUTES AFTER TAKEOFF

"Ladies and Gentlemen," announced the captain. *"Unfortunately, we are unable to continue our trip to Santo Domingo. We have a warning light in the cockpit that just went off. For safety reasons, we are heading back to Miami!"*

Like jumping naked into the frigid waters of an Alaskan river, sudden blasts of cold wrapped my body. Not to mention how this kind of announcement can surface your spiritual side and renew your faith in your maker. Although not necessarily in the most appropriate fashion, I admit, because *"Holly shit!"* was my immediate and devout reaction.

THE LAST ATTEMPT

"¿Que pasa, Pipin?" asked an alarmed Audrey. She was seated by the window, next to Pipin and right behind me. But ignoring his wife's question, he echoed her inquiry to ask,

"Carlos, what's happening, chico?"

Pipin apparently didn't understand the captain's announcement and neither did Audrey.

"Damas y Caballeros," interrupted the captain with the same announcement but now in Spanish, and that made it clear; we had an emergency going on.

Even though the flight had been shaky for the last few minutes, not many cared to obey the *Fasten Seat Belt* signs lit in bright red. In fact, some people were just standing in the hallway chatting with others. But as an immediate effect to the captain's announcement, not a soul remained standing and numerous clicks sounded simultaneously.

"When are we Latins going to learn?" I muttered.

Eventually the rumble of voices flooding the cabin hushed in an instant. It was quieter than a crypt, literally, a tomb with over one hundred prospective corpses if the crew couldn't manage to keep the screws attached to the plane.

"This piece of shit is going to crash!" exclaimed Tata interrupting the stillness. That's Pipin's loyal safety diver for most of his freediving world-record attempts over the last fourteen years.

"Shut up, Tata," was Pipin's forceful response. *"Estas hablando mierda . . ."*

"I'm not talking shit, Pipin. The captain said something about going back to Miami, and look at this thing shaking like a blender. This is serious, man," insisted Tata and that was unusual, because whether it was out of respect or fear, Tata always followed Pipin's command as a voiceless and obedient servant.

On the way back to Miami the aircraft continued its unsteady flight. The shaking was nonstop and so were the chills all around as everyone knew this type of tremble wasn't caused by atmospheric reasons. The problem was coming from within.

As minutes progressed, and now recovered from the initial shock, some passengers broke silence and voiced their own conclusions,

"Must be the flaps," someone said.

"I think the landing gear is not working," somebody else assumed. Meanwhile, a guy with a distinctive Argentinean accent also gave his connoisseur's opinion:

"Yeah, I knew it, during takeoff the airplane was moving kind of weird . . . I almost asked the flight attendant to let me speak with the captain."

"Oh, shut up you idiot," I muttered with my forehead pressed against the window. It was pitch-black outside. The aircraft took-off from *Miami International Airport* around eight in the evening and at thirty thousand feet, the chances of seeing something are somewhat limited.

"What are we going to do now, Carlos?"

"I do not know, Audrey, but for the moment praying would be adequate."

"No, I mean . . . we have to make it to Santo Domingo for the record attempt and all . . ."

CARLOS SERRA

"Well, we can take another flight tomorrow, but let's just hope this flying martini stops shaking and makes it in one piece to Miami."

"Don't worry, chico," interrupted Pipin. *"My saints are going to protect me."*

"Okay, just tell your saints to protect us all; not just you," I replied with acerbic tone.

Pipin is a firm and openly admitted believer of the Santeria cult, which incorporates animal sacrifices among some other witchcraft-like rituals. I've never been particularly inclined to believe in it, but what bothered me was his branded ego coming through in a moment like this.

Nevertheless, that's always the case with my business partner and friend; it's all about him and that's why, even though I cared for him as a brother, we had been clashing quite often, lately.

Pipin, whose real name is Francisco Ferreras, is a living legend of freediving. Breath-hold diving, skin diving or apnea diving—as it is also called—is not a mainstream activity like basketball, football or baseball, but with an exceptional level of fanatic devotion among its practitioners, it is more a cult than a sport. Pipin and Audrey are both top athletes in a division of breath-hold diving called, *No-Limits*.

After many years of being considered one of the top *No-Limits* freedivers in the world, Pipin is used to be the center of attention from the specialized press and fans alike, and that can awake the inner egotistical monster on anyone. So I've learned to deal with that fact and for the most part, we both got along well.

Pipin and I share similar backgrounds that helped bond our relationship despite some distinctive differences in social issues, upbringing and moral values. For instance, we both got enticed early in life by the enchanting call of a captivating señorita called the ocean.

Also, and given the lack of it in our respective countries, we migrated to the land of opportunity. We both showed our entrepreneurial spirit by establishing our own businesses within few years of arrival. We were forced to learn a new language and like most Latinos in the United States, we both struggled with certain degree of discrimination coming from those who believe that speaking with an accent means that you also have it when you think.

These elements of coincidence allowed us to overcome most of our differences. Even so, Pipin is not the easiest person to deal with. His corpulent body, above-average height, and shaved-head, originates the intimidating combination of a malicious wrestler. But besides his rough facade and his by-now notorious self-centered stand, it is his unleashed hostile nature what frightens people around him.

That's the case of Orlando "Tata" Lanza, his trusty safety-freediver, whose loyalty towards Pipin resembles the one of a fearful slave to his master. When Pipin is in a pleasant *Dr. Jekyll* mood, Tata can be loquacious and even participates in the jocular conversation that other members of our team may have. But when Pipin brings *Mr. Hide* out, Tata can turn into the quietest and most withdrawn person of all.

Tata is a slim, shy-looking and low-profile fellow who like Pipin, is also Cuban. But in contrast with his timid appearance, he's also one of the most exceptional freedivers

THE LAST ATTEMPT

I've ever seen. Being in his mid-forties, when it comes to freediving, he can stay longer and go deeper than much younger, professional-level apneists.

Next to Pipin was Audrey, a good-natured and attractive French-born young lady, whose youth and beauty made her more fitting to be a model than an athlete. Her long and fine hair, cascading downward like a waterfall over her shoulders, framed her slim face and enhanced an equally slender figure. Despite being a *No-Limits* freediver like Pipin, Audrey's initial formation and involvement with the ocean started as a scuba diver.

Contrasting with Pipin, she was formally trained as a compressed-air breather and respected the laws of physics with the devotion of an obedient pupil. Pipin, on the contrary, is a real calamity when it comes to the use of scuba. And as for the laws of diving, or any other law, Pipin is not particularly inclined to follow them. But the contrast between the two doesn't end there.

Audrey is one of the most introverted, peaceful and gentle personas anyone can find. Next to Pipin's rudimentary appearance, which includes Goofy-like gapped teeth, along with a forceful personality and his well-known egotistical behavior, the two of them are the living representation of *Beauty and the Beast*, both metaphorically and literally.

Still looking out the window, we could finally see something; the lights of the city where we live. Miami, the cross-roads of the Americas, had become our point of departure and arrival, as well.

"At least we made it back," said Angelo, a skilled photographer accompanying us to Santo Domingo. His task was to document the event for our company. Seated next to Tata, he remained uncharacteristically hushed.

"Yeah, but the worst part is now the landing," I responded. But Angelo was right; at least we were in Miami and not somewhere in the Caribbean, where any rescue effort in the middle of the night would have been more complicated and less promising.

The thought brought a sense of relief somehow, but it didn't last long. Entering the city from the east, the airplane had passed Miami completely. It was pitch-black outside the window, once again.

"What's happening?" a passenger asked alarmingly. *"We are not landing in Miami!"*

All the passengers shared the same concern. We were flying over the everglades. Out the window we could see nothing but darkness, but since the everglades' swampy topography covers the entire west-side of Miami, we all knew; we were flying over Alligator-land.

A wordless Tata, with his eyes ready to pop out, had the universal expression of terror reflected on his face. Probably the same one we all had. The same with Angelo, who for the very first time since I met him two weeks ago, couldn't utter a word.

Angelo seemed to be a great guy, but he has the remarkable ability to turn a group conversation into a monologue. Understandably, he wasn't too talkative this time. If surviving the crash, we now had the prospect of becoming a feast of human flesh for the gators.

Then the aircraft started to turn left and at the distance, the lights of Miami were visible once again. Few minutes later we all realized that the airplane was dumping gasoline over the everglades before making the final approach to *Miami International*. It's a standard procedure for a plane in emergency, we were told by one of the flight attendants.

With the airplane now aligned with the runway, a dead silence invaded the cabin, once again; no more theories, no more conclusions; we were all immersed in our own undeclared fear. To make matters worse, I turned around and saw one of the flight attendants at the end of the hall, firmly strapped in her chair, with eyes as wide as Tata's and her flesh color blending with the pale *Formica* panel behind her seat.

Looking back out the window I recall seeing the face of my son Alexander. But I guess I was looking inward into my thoughts. The prospect of a child under three years of age to lose his daddy in a plane crash could be overwhelming, especially since I was that daddy.

Finally, a harsh impact, accompanied by the screeching sound of the tires notified us of a rough landing. But we didn't crash, and that's always a plus. Then the thunderous roar of the engines in reverse, as power-assisted brakes, reduced the speed of the aircraft. The shaking was finally gone; so was our stress. We were safe.

With the jet still moving on the runway, flashes of red and blue lights flooded the cabin. Out the windows we could see the emergency vehicles surrounding the plane. Fire trucks and ambulances were all around and running next to us. And even though it gave us a sense of protection, it also brought a deeper concern at the same time, because a defective coffee-maker couldn't have caused the type of mobilization we were witnessing. *Mexicana Airlines* flight number 303 definitively had a serious problem.

After a couple of hours repairing the aircraft, an empty stomach, cramped legs and blood-infused eyes, we departed from Miami once again. As for the warning light, we never had a clue. They never shared the information with the passengers.

At least the flight was uneventful this time, but it took much longer than expected to get to Santo Domingo. With hopes of eating and resting at our resort, we reached our destination point around 2:00 a.m. but we all had to pass immigration, clear customs and deal with a two-hour ride to our resting spot. The capital city of Santo Domingo is located on the southern edge of the island, while the resort is located east; passed the city of La Romana.

ARRIVING TO THE DOMINICAN REPUBLIC

Remarkably, our old friend Eddie Matos, a former officer for the Santo Domingo Police Department, had waited for us. Eddie was exceptionally helpful, particularly with Customs. We traveled to Santo Domingo with over fifteen hundred pounds of weight distributed in over thirty pieces of luggage and we were only five people. If it wasn't for Eddie, it would have taken much longer to clear Customs.

Eddie is a short and plump guy, whose expression resembles Al Pacino in *Scarface*, yet his harsh-looking face conceals his altruistic nature; he's loyal, accommodating and supportive. In times of need, he's always there. Diligently, he assisted us getting the whale of luggage through customs and loading it later into the mini-bus sent by the resort to pick us up.

THE LAST ATTEMPT

SEPTEMBER 30, 2002
4:30 A.M.

Looking like zombies wandering around the crop-fields of neighboring Haiti, we finally arrived at the *Viva Dominicus Resort*. Even so, the lobby of the hotel invigorated us with a visual infusion of Caribbean decor. It was a pure tropical setting made with finesse and class.

The lobby was designed as a wide open area with no walls; therefore, no doors and no windows, only lots of vegetation and a combination of rattan and wicked furniture. The upholstery had the imprint of palm trees and flowers blending harmoniously with the surrounding vegetation.

The floor was made of stone and the lack of walls allowed the air to impregnate the place with the fresh smell of oceanic breeze. The staff wore colorful and informal, yet stylish shirts, and the only wall was right behind the check-in area. Audrey and I went straight there to sign everyone in.

"Are we in the Dominican Republic or in Hawaii?" I asked Audrey.

"Carlos, you've been here before, remember? For Patrick's event."

"Yeah, but I still love this place as the first time we came. It reminds me of Hawaii, and you know how much I love the Aloha state."

"Are you going to move there," she asked smiling.

"One day I will. But anyway, I only hope we don't go this time through the same predicaments as before."

Indeed, we were in the Dominican Republic for a second time. Last time was back in April of the same year 2002, when we coordinated another world record event for Patrick Musimu, a Belgian freediver of exceptional capabilities.

That event was a nightmare that lasted for about three weeks due to Pipin's jealousy over Patrick's incredible performance underwater. Except for technique and body motion beneath the surface, areas in which Pipin is one of the most stylish and graceful freedivers in the professional circuit, Patrick's breath-hold capacity and stamina was far greater than my partner's. That was something that Pipin's ego didn't handle too well.

Actually, the day after the event concluded, with Patrick setting a new world record in constant ballast, we were all together as a group at the airport ready to return to Miami when Pipin asked Eddie Matos if, as a former cop, he had drugs in his car to plant on criminals he wanted to arrest.

"No, Pipin, of course not," an astonished Eddie replied immediately. *"But why would you ask me that?"*

"To plant drugs on that arrogant black guy's luggage," responded Pipin while pointing towards Patrick, who thankfully, wasn't close enough to ear what Pipin had in mind.

"Carlos," asked me Eddie, *"is he asking seriously?"*

"Of course I'm serious," interrupted Pipin. *"I want to give that Negro a lesson of real power and keep him here in the Dominican Republic; in jail."*

"Pipin, you better calm down right now," I replied without hesitation. "And you, Eddie, if you do that, you better put me in jail, as well."

"Carlos. Are you crazy? First, I don't carry drugs with me, so I don't know where Pipin is getting this idea from. And second, I would never do something like that, anyway!"

"C'mon, Eddie, I'm sure you can get it somehow. Call one of your cop friends; let's do it," insisted Pipin. That's when I turned around in disgust and went to check my luggage by the airliner's counter.

Audrey, who was checking her luggage already, asked me why I was so upset. After narrating Pipin's drug-planting plan, her answer was a disdainful,

"Pipin is like a little kid. Don't pay attention to him."

"No, Audrey; he's more like a big bully, and the fact that he can come up with such idea, really frightens me."

But now, with no other athlete—except for his own wife—attempting a record, Audrey and I were hopeful that Pipin's temper would be restrained this time.

Glancing around first, to make sure that Pipin wasn't nearby, Audrey whispered,

"Don't worry, Carlos, I guess you were right at the airport. Except for me, there is no other athlete this time to piss him off. Pipin should be okay."

"Hmm, now I'm not so sure anymore. With Pipin's temper you never know. If you end up breaking his record, he won't be a happy camper."

"Yeah, I know," Audrey said while looking down, probably remembering some previous experience dealing with Pipin's unsettling side.

Having completed the registration, the bellboy guided us throughout multiple three-story buildings comprising the hotel. Spread over hundreds of acres of neatly cut grass and Eden-like gardens, the place was a fantastic setting that helped us rapidly forget the tremulous adventure we just had with the airliner.

Walking right behind the bellboy was Pipin, always leading the pack. Tata and Angelo, looking like automatons, followed him. Audrey remained a little behind and kept walking next to me.

In the background we could hear the waves breaking peacefully against the sandy beach.

"Oh, I love the sea breeze on my face," Audrey said inhaling deeply.

To which I replied with a blunt, "What I need on my face is a pillow." She turned around, looked at me and smiled.

"I would smile back at you, Audrey, but the muscles of my face are not responding. They are numbed with tiredness."

"Carlos, you never stop joking, ah?"

Like a big brother with his little sister, Audrey and I shared a strong bond, although occasionally, some people would think in different terms. In this particular area, and despite his possessive nature, Pipin never showed a hint of jealousy over me. I was one of the very few people he could accept been so close to Audrey, while on the other hand, Audrey would take advantage of my longer experience in life and ask for the occasional counsel in personal matters. And in this regard, she had many issues afflicting her.

THE LAST ATTEMPT

Following the bellboy through a concrete path between two buildings, we stopped by the entrance. Audrey, Pipin, Tata and Angelo were to stay on the building to the left; I would stay on the building to the right.

"Your room is in the second floor, sir" said the bellboy handling me an envelope with the key inside. I almost fainted right there. Having over three hundred pounds of personal luggage and no elevator, carrying the heavy load upstairs was a crusade I wasn't looking forward to. The bellboy immediately started to help Pipin, Angelo and Tata with the remaining twelve hundred pounds of gear. Audrey had crashed on her bed right away. I was on my own.

Searching for energy to pull my belongings upstairs, my Venezuelan roots brought out a nasty but rather familiar expression; *"Coño de la Madre!"* which kept coming out while pulling the wreck of the *Titanic* upstairs.

To make matters worse, the room had an unbearable mildew smell and the stench had impregnated the bed sheets, making it impossible to sleep. So I decided to turn the TV on, but the set didn't work. I got off the bed and with my bare feet I felt the sogginess layering the tiled floor.

"Carajo, I wonder if the room was used by the Swamp Monster," I recall saying.

After that, I tried taking a hot shower to relax but the shower head broke and the drain was clogged. Getting out of the tub I slipped, grasped the shower curtain to avoid landing horizontally over the toilette, and that's when the pole, holding the curtain, landed on the back of my head.

"Jesus!" I exclaimed loudly. *"What's the room number they gave me, six-six-six? This freaking room is possessed. Now I only need to see Linda Blair levitating over the bed and twisting her neck,"* I kid myself.

Then, somehow, I ended up collapsing over the bed well after 5:00 a.m. to die for a couple of hours. But my last thought before embracing the pillow revealed my innermost concerns,

"Nothing seems to be going well. I hope this event goes fine and nothing happens to Audrey, because this is a bad start."

Chapter 2

AUDREY'S PATHWAY TO DEATH
THE DAILY REPORT

It was few days before, during Audrey's initial training sessions in Miami, when I started writing the daily journal. Filled with anecdotes, the report became quite popular and the swell of visitors to our website, climbing the numbers into thousands of additional cyber-guests every day, proved it. Even our Internet Provider forced us to increase our storage capacity and bandwidth to cover the demand.

Being written within a positive context, for the most part, and with a hint of humor, very little did I suspect of the negative and devastating tribulations waiting ahead.

Also unexpected is how these reports would eventually become a crucial element in unwrapping the complex factors that lead to those tragic difficulties to come. Not even in my wildest dream or darkest nightmare, I could have envisioned the life-changing events approaching us, swiftly, menacing, like a tsunami of tribulations, from this point on.

The following is an expanded assemblage of those reports but without the self-imposed censorship given to the original versions.

MONDAY, SEPTEMBER 30, 2002

After a quick nightmare with *Freddie Kruger* and a late breakfast, I went to the front desk to complain and ask the maintenance department to repair the shower, change the TV set, replace the sheets, and send the local priest with a gallon of holly-water to exorcise the room.

As an alternative, and to compensate for the unbearable experience, the resort offered another room. They sent me to the *Viva Dominicus Palace*, the newer and more luxurious wing of the hotel adjacent to the east.

In fact, there are two distinct hotels under the same ownership and sharing the same beach. *The Palace*, however, is classier and the room they gave me had a magnificent ocean view. From the balcony I could see the beach and the pool, as well. The nauseating smell of mildew was replaced by the soothing and stimulating scent of the Caribbean. And as a bonus, room number 5643 came with the relaxing sound of waves, the lyrical squawk of sea gulls and *HBO*. Things were starting to look better.

Later that day Pipin and I met with Bill Stromberg, a Swiss freediver who competes in the Freediving World Championship. He had come to see the record attempt after receiving an invitation from Pipin. Well, Bill paid his own expenses, but Pipin had given him the okay to assist.

On the other hand, I wasn't particularly thrilled with Bill's visit; I know how Pipin spawns into something sinister with another athlete around. He becomes very unpleasant to deal with, and since Audrey was the only one to attempt a record this time, I was hoping to enjoy the trip. Pipin, however, wanted to show off with a member of the rival organization, *AIDA,* based in Europe.

Pipin and I owned the *International Association of Free Divers* (IAFD), and *AIDA*, which its French acronym translates to *International Association for the Development of Apnea*, was not in the best of terms with ours. Although both organizations had the same general goals—the promotion of the sport through events and education—we had different approach to achieve each organization's goals.

Despite being in his mid-30's, Bill looked much younger. He was a judge and athlete for *AIDA,* and after the formal introductions, shared with us some of his background information.

As Bill continued chatting about his performances in the championship, his personal-best in the water and so forth, I started to observe Pipin's reaction a bit closer. I knew he could blow like Saint Helens volcano any time if Bill would continue stating his athletic achievements.

For Pipin, Bill was trying to impress him and attempting to diminish his legendary status. But the truth is that by being in the presence of a living legend of the sport, Bill is the one who was impressed. I had seen that same reaction before with some other athletes. It's like looking up to a master to tell him about your good deeds and how fine an apprentice you are. It's a natural reaction.

It even happened to me once after having met renowned Hawaiian marine artist *Christian Riese Lassen,* when the famous painter visited my dive shop in Key Largo. I kept on telling him about my other passion besides diving and how much I loved to paint marine landscapes with dolphins and whales using oils as a media. I wasn't trying to impress Mr. Lassen, who through his art is an inadvertently master for me. I couldn't even dream of doing such thing. Subconsciously, I only tried to convey that my admiration for his work was so much that I wanted to imitate him.

Christian Riese Lassen, with a smile on his face, responded to my irreverence by making a phone call to his studio in Hawaii. The following day I received a package containing multiple posters of his work and one of his books; an autographed Limited Edition which I treasure to this day.

But I knew Pipin's reaction wouldn't be as gracious, as his internal pressure kept building up. Bill was, innocently, in danger of having a clash with his admired freediving hero. I had also seen it before in the worst way. Actually, Pipin have had conflicts with every single one of the high profile athletes he has worked with or just met.

"Get this dick-sucker away from me before I kick his ass," Pipin told me in Spanish and that was my cue to intervene, change the subject, and take Pipin away with the excuse that we needed to see the boats we would be using for Audrey's training. Luckily for Bill, Pipin's patient lasted long enough to avoid a serious confrontation . . . for now.

The rest of the day was invested getting acclimated to the one hundred and ten percent humidity level and the oven-like heat. Then we spent time greeting people we already knew from the hotel and unpacking the diving gear. Audrey was barely seen, but I guessed she had remained in her room recovering some sleep.

TUESDAY, OCTOBER 01, 2002
8:00 A.M.

We gathered for breakfast at the *Dominicus Palace's* restaurant, where a great buffet with at least a hundred different choices charmed our hunger. For those who enjoy the culinary arts, the place offers a permanent temptation for indulging yourself, and if not careful, it'll be easier to leave the place rolling instead of walking.

An amazing example of strong will in that regard is Pascal Bernabe, the deep safety diver for most of Audrey and Pipin's record attempts. Pascal is a short but strongly built guy in his thirty's, who like Tata, comes across as shy in nature and seemingly timid in his interactions with Pipin.

Being a world-class technical diver and one of the deepest scuba divers in the planet, Pascal also carries tremendous amount of luggage. I only wished that a bar of soap and deodorant was part of it.

He had arrived directly from his native France the day before, and was eating fruits for breakfast with the local birds flying around him asking for their share.

The restaurant, while roofed, is open all around, allowing the winged creatures to fly inside the dining area.

"These birds are going to shit on my food," said Pipin while scaring a bird away waving his hand in the air.

Except for a couple of bloodcurdling encounters with the local fauna, I enjoyed it greatly. Around the landscape I had seen from a supposedly harmless snake, to a monster-size spider. And even though I come from a country where the local eight-legged, furry creatures inspired the movie *Arachnophobia*, and our local Anacondas have the spotlight in every related documentary the *Discovery Channel* shows, I could never get used to having neither one near me, so I kept my distance. As for the Dominican gardener who told me that the snake was harmless, I disagree. If that slimy and slithering thing would have gotten any closer, I would have suffered a heart attack.

Just before entering the restaurant, there is a lagoon with geese, ducks and dozens of flamingos claiming it as their property. But the birds share the enchantment of the pond with a huge iguana that resides on the grassy area around the pond and which anyone can pet. I didn't pet the lizard; it reminded me of a documentary I had seen in the *Discovery Channel* where a Komodo Dragon was eating the kids of a local village in an Indonesian island. The Iguana was not a Komodo but it was too big for comfort. Oddly enough, I prefer sharks.

Photo Credit: Carlos Serra

The hotel's beautiful setting was peaceful and the local fauna enhanced the Eden-like scenery.

Audrey, like Pascal, also had fruits for breakfast and spent most of the time talking with her countryman in French. She wouldn't miss the opportunity to speak in her native tongue and they were good friends.

After the morning meal, the day's activities started with Pipin, Tata and Angelo loading the boat with the sled, the cable, the weights, ropes, buoys and the entire paraphernalia needed for Audrey's first practice dive. Meanwhile, Pascal was waiting for the gases he needed to prepare his breathing mixture for a planned one hundred and fifteen meter dive.

Avoiding the heat I remained in my room becoming familiar with the features of the camera I would use underwater, a high resolution digital *Nikon* encased in a waterproof housing. As part of my duties, I was one of the two people designated to take pictures of the event for the Internet report and for the memories. The other photographer was Angelo Cordero.

Soon after I left my room, and while walking towards the boat, I saw Audrey. She was seated in a beach lounge chair with a palm tree protecting her from the relentless Caribbean sun. A sleeveless navy blue t-shirt with a pair of matching shorts and a pair of sunglasses comprised her entire attire. She seemed relaxed, so I decided to tease her as I normally would.

"Audrey, get out from the shade and take some sun; you are so pale that you remind me of my grandma when I saw her last week."

"Why? Is she pale, too?"

"Kind of . . . she's a ghost . . . she's dead."

"Carlos! Have you not respect for dead people?" she said holding her laugh.

"I do, but my grandma has no respect for living people; she's the one who appeared."

Unable to hold herself any longer, she chuckled.

Audrey was in good humor and that was a good sign. It normally meant that Pipin was also in a good mood.

Only steps away by the shoreline, Pipin, Angelo and Tata were still working on the boat, so I approached them to take pictures for the daily report. Once they finished attaching a metal frame to the vessel from which the sled would be hung, Pipin wanted to depart immediately, but we had to wait for a few industrial size cylinders of oxygen and helium to prepare Pascal's breathing mixture of gases called, *Trimix*.

Trimix is a combination of oxygen, helium and nitrogen, and the idea is to substitute a large amount of nitrogen in the mix with helium. By doing this, the narcotic effect of nitrogen is minimized. In addition, helium is about eight times lighter (or less dense) than nitrogen, and this attribute allows for a safer and faster off-gassing during decompression.

The moment after Pascal received the cylinders and mixed his breathing cocktail, we departed. The diving spot was located only few hundred meters away from the hotel' beach, but the depth, however, was already unfathomable.

Pipin, as always, took immediate command of the sled's rigging. After all, no one knew the sled as well as he did. He designed it and even welded it together. The sled was his love and devotion; the source of fame and recognition. Therefore, he was very protective with anyone trying to mess with it. I knew it, so I was always reluctant to touch it.

The sled was being held by a piece of tube extending horizontally about three feet away from the boat. The tube itself was welded on top of a double "A" frame that was secured to the boat with ropes.

Photo Credit: Angelo Cordero

Pipin never allowed anyone to touch the sled without his direct supervision.

With usual jealousy, Pipin controlled the entire setting; the placement of the sled in the water, the cable through which the sled would ride down and come back up, and the filling with compressed air of the pony-tank in the sled. The needed amount of weight in the lower portion of the sled had been added by Pipin before departing from shore.

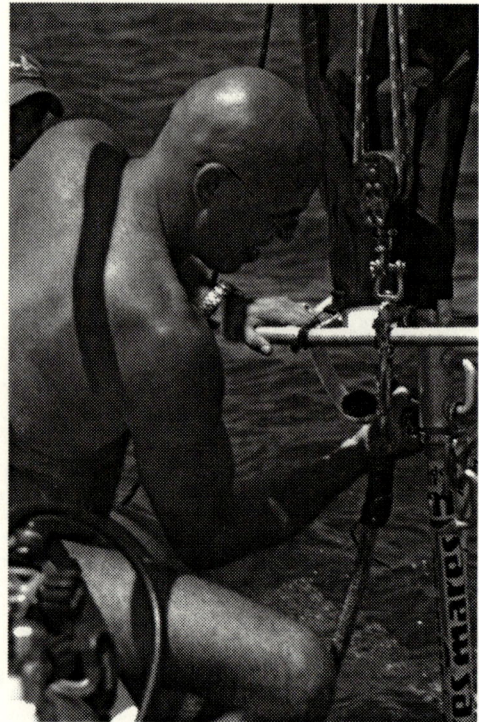

Photo Credit: Angelo Cordero

The same applies to the filling of the pony-tank with compressed air. Pipin was always in absolute control of it.

With everything in place, Audrey got her wetsuit on and entered the water. Pascal had arranged his equipment as I helped him to put it on. He required assistance ever since he carries a lot more gear than any of us.

Besides Pascal, the safety divers were Pipin and I underwater, and Tata at the surface as a freediver. Bill came as an observer, because in spite of his freediving capabilities and his heartfelt interest to cooperate, Pipin didn't allow him to participate. That was not too smart from Pipin's part. The rest of the team was not in the Dominican Republic yet, so this first dive was done short on support.

Audrey initiated a sequence of "warm-up" shallow dives by pulling herself down the line to eight or ten meters. She did it to activate her *mammalian diving reflex*, a natural built-in condition in all mammals—including humans—that allows for the brain and body to adapt to extended periods without breathing.

It is a condition in which the brain decreases the consumption of oxygen by slowing down the heart rate, restricting the flow of blood to the extremities and rerouting it to the brain and other essential organs in the upper body.

But without letting Audrey finish her acclimation process, Pipin commanded her to climb on the sled and get ready to dive.

"But, Pipin, I haven't finished," complained Audrey.

"You have done two descents already; that's enough. Vamos, vamos, vamos; we don't have time to lose!" insisted Pipin seemingly impatient. Compliantly, she climbed on the sled and initiated her pre-dive ventilations, but he was rushing her for no apparent reason. We had plenty of time.

As Pipin descended to check on something with the cable, I took a picture of Audrey. She was over the sled and I was already geared up and in the water surface. But as I saw Audrey's face through the viewfinder, I noticed her melancholic state. So I handled the camera housing to Bill Stromberg and approached Tata, who was seated on the edge of the boat, to joke around,

Photo Credit: Carlos Serra

Audrey's palpable sadness motivated me to joke with her to lift her spirit.

"Hey, Tata, when Audrey comes up in blackout thanks to Pipin's rush, make sure you ventilate her through her big nose. That way she'll get a lot of air."

Accustomed to my jokes in reference to her nose, Audrey chuckled right away, but seemingly baffled, Tata asked,

"Blackout? Why blackout? She's going to blackout?"

"I'm just kidding, Tata . . . relax, just kidding. But, hey, keep an eye on her anyway, okay?"

"Okay, man, okay, but don't say blackout; no blackout!"

Tata's overreaction extended Audrey's laugh, and seeing her cheerful is all I wanted. When I turned around to get the camera housing, I noticed that Bill had taken a picture of the moment. Then Pipin surfaced and had Audrey ventilating.

Photo Credit: Bill Stromberg

Bill captured the moment when Audrey laughed after a joke I made about her nose.

Seeing Audrey ventilating before the dive was a spectacle by itself. With a torso that could snugly fit a small-size t-shirt, I could only marvel on how her lungs could accommodate so much air. Inhaling, she sucked air like an industrial-size vacuum machine.

Exhaling, she would become a blood-powered, heavy-duty blower with the capacity to gust away leafs from a sidewalk on an autumn morning. After all, she needed to charge her brain with enough molecules of oxygen to last for about three minutes being devoid of breathing.

Photo Credit: Angelo Cordero

Audrey had an exceptional lung capacity.

Tata provided the five-minute countdown for the dive. At minus four minutes Pascal went down. He plunged early since he takes longer to reach his post. He would go all the way down to one hundred and fifteen meters. Pipin and I went down at minus three minutes, almost simultaneously. However, I stopped at fifteen meters to take advantage of the natural light and to take some pictures of Audrey on her way down.

When Tata released the sled with Audrey on it, she seemed fine, very relaxed. When she passed by me she was pinching her nose to equalize the pressure being exerted in her eardrums.

Credit: Carlos Serra

Audrey, seemingly relaxed, equalizes the pressure exerted over her eardrums.

As she progressed into the blue abyss, I checked my watch to take the time. Based on previous dives, I had estimated how much time she should take to reach the bottom and come back up. Then I grabbed the line to feel the vibration of Audrey's sled brushing against it as a rudimentary, yet effective way to feel her dive.

On the way down, the vibration created by the friction of the sled against the cable would be softly dissipating as she went deeper, approaching the end of the line. A twenty-five pound plate from the gym, used to lift weights, was tied-up at the end of the cable as a safeguard to protect the sled from going any deeper. Then a harsh pull of the cable would indicate that she had reached the end.

For a few seconds I should feel nothing. That's because Audrey is disengaging the top part of the sled from the weighted lower section and inflating the lift bag. Then I should feel the vibration, once again, but much stronger this time. The rate of ascent is much faster, thus generating a stronger friction between the sled and the line.

But suddenly, much sooner than anticipated, I felt the vibration. She was ascending so rapidly that forced me to 'jump' away from the line, barely on time to avoid a collision. Her lift bag was bursting up, leaving behind a nuclear-like cloud of bubbles with her body hidden within.

THE LAST ATTEMPT

Credit: Carlos Serra

An explosion-like swell of air bursts out of the lift bag. Audrey is inside that cloud.

"*That was too fast,*" I recall thinking, "*Something must have happened.*" But I looked up and she seemed fine. A moment later she was climbing on board the boat being assisted by Tata. As the only person in the team with medical training, I remained close to the surface just in case.

Knowing that she was alright, I descended to fifty meters to check on Pipin and Pascal, and after receiving the okay signal from them, and making sure they were ascending safely, I went up to decompress and exit the water. Once I climbed on board . . .

"*What happened, Audrey?* I asked puzzled for the briefness of the dive, "*that was too quick.*"

"*I think I hit somebody with the sled,*" she said alarmed. "*Are they okay down there?*"

"*Yes, don't worry, Pascal and Pipin were only ten meters below me when I left the decompression line; they are both fine.*"

"*Did you see if Pipin is mad?*" she asked nervously.

"*No, besides his usual cranky face, he seemed okay. Why?*"

"*I hope it wasn't Pipin; he's going to get mad at me,*" she said fearfully; visibly shaken.

"Why, Audrey? You go through the line; you have no control over the sled's direction. Whoever you hit was in your way, and by now, he should know better."

Audrey was visibly concerned about Pipin's possible reaction, but when he came out of the water, he seemed contrite. Obviously, it was him who got in the way. He was okay, but as a result of the impact, Audrey had released the bottom part of the sled, grabbed herself to the upper section, opened the tank's valve to inflate the lift bag and rocketed to the surface before reaching one hundred and fifteen meters.

Only on the way up she realized that she hadn't reached the end; that instead, someone got hit. Her final depth was only eighty-some meters; quite short from the target. Surprisingly, Pipin even apologized to Audrey but even so, Audrey seemed disturbed about the incident. Perhaps, she remembered how Pipin had held her down at depth few days ago during training back in Miami, for no particular reason.

After returning to shore, we all went to our rooms for a quick shower and a nap. Well, the nap part didn't apply to me, because I had to write the report. Besides, I can't sleep during the day. But for Pipin, a siesta is a must.

In the evening, we met at the pool to listen to Pipin's briefing for the next day activities. Having finished the briefing, we all got up from the plastic pool table and headed towards the restaurant for supper. Pipin was held up by Bill, who wanted to chat some more about his one and only subject; freediving. Angelo and Tata remained next to Pipin, while Audrey moved faster and placed herself next to me.

I was leaving the group behind for two reasons; I was starving and the topic of conversation was starting to get on my nerves.

"It seems like Pipin found his equal on Bill. That guy can't stop talking about freediving, records, competitions, and so on," I said to Audrey.

"Yeah, but at least he talks about freediving; Pipin only talks about himself."

"Well, isn't that the same? Pipin is freediving . . . or so he thinks." Audrey looked at me and smiled. At this point her frustrations with Pipin's egotistical side were more palpable.

Between the pool area and the restaurant, there is a small wooden bridge that divides the lagoon where the Flamingos and the Komodo Dragon reside. We were just crossing it when I decided to ask,

"Audrey, how come we are not seeing you much, lately?"

"Well . . ." she paused and sighed. Then, after looking over her shoulder, maybe to check where Pipin was, she continued. *"Pipin wants me to remain in the room."*

"Why is that?" I asked, looking over my shoulder, too.

"He wants to avoid distractions for me, or that's what he says," claimed Audrey in low voice.

"Are you sure that's what it is?"

"What do you mean?"

"The way I see it, he's tightening his control over you?"

"I don't know, Carlos. Except for training, going to the gym and eating, he's not letting me out of the room, at all."

THE LAST ATTEMPT

"But that's not even healthy for the attempt, Audrey. You need to get out that room, breathe some fresh air and distract your mind; otherwise you'll end up getting crazy."

"I already am. I feel asphyxiated, but what can I do?"

It was puzzling to see how Audrey, being a well-educated woman from a developed country, submissively accepting such treatment from a person whose education level was far inferior, if any, and from a country where a 1959 Chevy is the latest model.

"Get out and breathe some fresh air, Audrey, for God's sake," I repeated edgily. *"Just open the door and tell him that you're going out for a walk. It's that simple."*

"I can't do that. He doesn't want me out of the room. I have to stay there," she said somberly.

Chapter 3

How Beauty Met The Beast

As a shy, exquisite and educated woman, it's hard to understand what Audrey could have seen in Pipin. He is a very basic human being, packed with flaws that he either doesn't try to hide or he's just unaware of them. In some occasions he is charming and loving, but in some others he is nothing short of an evil bully; hostile and creepy.

He proudly admits his worship for the occult and rejects the notion of God. He firmly believes that loyalty must only exist in a woman's heart, while as a man he's entitled to have multiple lovers. Machismo is not a reprehensible stigma, but a rightful principle to which adhere with pride. And when it comes to achieving self-gratifying goals, he's like a bullet in motion; to be safe you must never cross its path.

Although Pipin is broadly flawed and his behavior is at times cruel and aggressive, he is also a natural charmer with the perfected talent to convey friendship, tenderness and affection, if needed. Whether he means it, or it's just a theatrical performance to obtain a calculated objective, he can charm his way through anyone's principles and values and appear as a big but innocent kid in desperate need of attention and direction.

That's what really got me to work with him in the first place. He needed someone with the ability to manage a business, think with logic, and to apply fairness to the staff, while on the other hand, I provided protection against the consequences of his own illogical and irrational actions.

In Audrey's case, however, it went beyond a mere sense of mother-like protective love or a humane natural commitment to save a "lost soul". Besides been dependant, she seemed to embraced his rudeness and use it as a protective cocoon against the world. Actually, she was in fact attracted to the rough and savage-like side of him, and even Pipin acknowledged and exploited this dependency.

THE LAST ATTEMPT

"Without me, you'll be a lost pendeja being eaten alive by the world," he said to her in front of me more than once, and Audrey was infatuated with the powerful image he projects. This became evident after the sobremesa chat we both had in a *Boston Market* nearby the office, in North Miami.

SIX MONTHS EARLIER

Pipin had just departed to Mexico, and Audrey was noticeably depressed after being bawled-out by Pipin. So I decided to invite her for lunch at the *Boston Market* restaurant where the juicy roasted chicken, flanked by steamed vegetables and macaroni and cheese, had become her favorite dish. But for some reason, she wasn't fond of the corn bread, so I always got double pieces and I loved it.

Apparently, she was upset for something related to another woman, some German lover Pipin had, but she didn't give me the specifics and I wasn't too keen to hear it, anyway. I already knew about Pipin's double life and preferred to stay out of it.

"Audrey, just out of curiosity, what did you find attractive on Pipin? Because for me, he's uglier than a car-crash with dead people, and when it comes to personality, he is so unlike you that it's baffling."

"I don't really know, Carlos, but I know it happened before I even met him."

"How is that?"

"I was in love with his body, his face and his performances. I don't know; I can't explain it."

"Hmm, then you are like a groupie."

"What is that?"

"An admirer, a fan; one of those crazy girls madly infatuated with rock-stars. They even chase them from concert to concert for a chance to meet them; sometimes intimately."

"Intimately?"

"Yes, Audrey, as in going to bed and have sex."

"Ah, actually, it was kind of like that," she admitted while her face showed a bit of blush.

"So, there is a wild animal hiding inside that introverted sheep costume after all, ah?" I said teasingly.

"In fact, I wrote everything that happened that day when I met Pipin. I'll give you a copy when we get back to the office."

Back in the office, Audrey gave me a floppy disk in which a diary-like letter describing that first encounter with Pipin was contained. She had written it with the intention of providing the content for the script of a movie project we were working on, and she wanted for me to edit it and translate it from Spanish to English for the same purpose. But she also expressed her intention to share her feelings with me about Pipin. At this point I had become her confidant and our conversations included very personal and sometimes, painful issues.

"Are you sure you want me to read this?"

"Yeah, it's not a big deal, but if you consider that we should cut the end, just do it. Maybe it is a little bit strong."

Then I inserted the floppy disc on my computer, opened the file and went directly to the end of the letter, and after a glance to its final part, I jokingly said,

"Audrey, why don't we send this to Penthouse magazine; they have a forum section where they publish pornographic and grotesque stories like this."

"Oye," she exclaimed with a smirk, "that's not pornography, and why grotesque?"

"Well, if involves Pipin naked, sweating and moaning like a frantic creature of the darkness, it is grotesque."

While still laughing, she commanded, "Come on, Carlos, read it. Maybe you'll understand why I fell for him."

Audrey grabbed a chair and sat next to me while I started to read her letter.

AUDREY'S OWN WORDS

29 of February of 1996. It is four o'clock; I'm in front of the Melia San Lucas, in Los Cabos. It's hot, it's steamy. Perhaps I will see him. Eight months of work about his lungs to prepare my thesis creates curiosity and fascination. I am anxious but I have hope. I believe in signs, until now they haven't failed me; they cannot fail me now.

I was born the 11th of August of 1974, In St. Denis, only 12 kilometers to the north of Paris, France. My maternal grandfather transferred me his love and passion for the ocean and diving. Ever since I was born, three months a year I'm with him, in his tent in one of the beaches to the south of France. Freediving, swimming, play in the waves, admire the sunset and sleeping are the only occupations I have and the only ones that pleases me. I accompany my grandpa to hunt fish but with my young age, I spend more time holding the buoy that he pulls than helping him.

The rest of the year I have to just accept the pool near the house. My father and my teacher struggle to make me swim. They want for me to learn different styles, but I am only interested for what's happening below the surface. Down there I feel well; I feel peace and tranquility, security and protection.

At age 13, I discover the tanks. With air bottles in my back, my dreams become reality. I imagine that I am a fish and I struggle to look like one. I observe the marine life around me and try to imitate it, how the fish swims, how they move, the attitudes they adopt, their behavior. This passion becomes a drug. I need it, it gives me strength and courage, and it relaxes me and soothes my rage.

At age 18, this very same passion separates me from my family. It has been three years since my parents move to Mexico. This is why I speak Spanish. I have just finished my preparatory and passed my high school. I'd selected a science career because the numbers don't lie; words do.

I have now to choose the university and what I'm going to study. In reality, I have been waiting for this moment for years, and years ago I had chosen to study Marine Biology.

THE LAST ATTEMPT

What else could it be? But for that I have to pay a high price; a price to high for me. I have to leave the house. The only university offering Marine Biology is in La Paz, South Baja California, to the north of Mexico, near the border with the United States. Or what is the same, about 2000 kilometers from my parents in a country other than mine.

For a long time I blamed myself for this; for my selfishness and pride. Because I wanted to pursue my passion, I broke my parents' heart. I will have to learn to live with this guilt; with it and with my loneliness.

Throughout my career I realize that some subjects fascinated me more than others. That is the case of physiology and marine life. In general, physiology subjects are quite boring, like: 'What is the oxygen consumption of crab Y when compared to a lobster X?' Not too exciting at all. I wanted something new, something unforgettable that would captivate the attention and interest of the whole world; but why?

I took a month and a half to respond that question, until one day, by coincidence, I read an article about Pipin. Being the world champion in freediving, I knew him for a long time through magazines, just like I knew about Jacques Mayol, Enzo Maiorca, Umberto Pelizzari, among others. This article got my attention.

After few experiments, some scientist from Buffalo University, in New York, reached the conclusion that at high pressures, Pipin's lungs filled with plasma to avoid pulmonary collapsing. In other words, while he is descending, and he is exposed to increasing pressures, these pressures will squeeze the gases like the air contained in the lungs. To prevent a potentially fatal lung collapsing, the brain sends the order to the arteries and veins in the periphery of the lungs to pump plasma inside of them. Because liquids are not affected by pressure, the pulmonary membranes will remain apart regardless of the depth.

> Author's note: This phenomenon is known as *Blood Shift*, and even though Audrey mentions the experiments done over Pipin as "reaching a conclusion", for the sake of historic accuracy, I must clarify that *Blood Shift* was discovered by scientists in the mid-seventies when Jacques Mayol offered himself to test a theory he had, after studying the corpses of Dolphins at the *Miami Sea Aquarium*. Until then, this natural ability was known to occur on marine mammals—dolphins, seals, whales—but not in humans. Consequently, it was discovered with Mayol, and *all* deep-water mammal freedivers, human or otherwise, benefit from this phenomenon.

The reason why it is plasma which fills the lungs and not blood is because white blood cells, red blood cells and platelets cannot be filtered and remain out of the lungs. When returning to the surface, the hydrostatic pressure is reduced, increasing the volume of air to its natural amount inside the lungs and passively pushing the plasma outward. This is what I wanted to prove and demonstrate. This would be the subject matter for my thesis. The next problem was to define how I would do that.

Alter so much time reading about Pipin, his deeds, his pictures, his interviews, his training, goals, passions, everything that was happening inside of him, his physiological changes and his problems, it became all familiar and got incorporated into my personal life. I lived with him, slept with him, dreamed with him, I only talked about him. Pipin became my second passion, my newest obsession and obviously, after few months I bored everyone with my only talking subject: Pipin!

By February 11, 1996, a whole month had passed since I presented my project, which became a success. In parallel with my studies, I passed the test for scuba and went to receive my certification as a diver, and when the instructor gave it to me, he also gave some good news; Pipin was in Los Cabos, in Mexico, where he was training for a new record. I could not believe it. The same person, who got into my life in such unexpected way, is only 250 kilometers away from me. Without a second thought, I decided that one way or another I had to see him, even if it was from the distance. Right at that point, Pipin would become my platonic love.

The following day I called my parents to tell them about the presence of Pipin in Mexico. They knew how significant this was for me. They followed my work closely and immediately supported me to go and see him. They even send me money for me to go to Cabo. In the afternoon, I went to the diving center where one of my friends works, and with emotion and happiness, I see that he brought for me a poster of . . . Pipin!

Five minutes later, that poster was hanging on the walls of my room. Perhaps this is a shocker and an absurd, but I talked to this poster as if this printed image of Pipin could hear me. There was not a night that I would not say good night to it before going to bed, with him; with the hope that one day we would meet each other.

Now back to February 29 of 1996; it's five in the morning and I haven't been able to sleep. I have this fixation in my head that I can't remove. I can't stand these emotions any longer. I gather my diving gear, a short and a t-shirt and take the first bus heading to Los Cabos. I have to find out if I can meet him or not, to finally stop thinking about this. I'm seated between country people, between roosters, packages, dust and sweat, but I don't mind. I'm closer to him with every second that passes.

Throughout the four hours of travel, I see before my eyes, the thesis, the first picture I saw of him with a long curly hair and glasses with a heavy prescription. I must admit that at first, he wasn't my type. The only thing that got my attention was his lips, thick and meaty. Some lips that I could easily imagine caressing my body, feeling them against my skin, sweet and softly, whispering in my ears, go down on my neck and along my back.

I am now in front of his hotel, standing outside for 15 minutes and I still haven't decided to get inside. This is ridiculous, I'm already here and maybe he's not there. I get in. I go directly to the pool area but there is nobody. Then I see a shack on the beach. I move towards it, but he's not there. Inside, there are only two shoeless Mexicans, tanned after working under the sun. Suddenly, I see a guy, young but with a funny face. In the cartoons of Disney, he would be Mickey Mouse. After meeting him, I get his name, Charley, and according to him, Pipin is not there, he went out. In any case, I sign up for a dive the next day to see Pipin descending with his machine.

This guy Charley seems like a shameless womanizer. After 10 minutes of conversation, he invites me to dinner in one of the restaurants in the harbor. If I accepted to go out with

THE LAST ATTEMPT

this guy is only because I had no more money to eat and I'm always hungry. It amuses me to see how convinced he is that I like him. He probably imagines that after the restaurant, I will end up in his bed and about this point he is really mistaken.

It's 8:00 p.m. and Charley is waiting for me in my hotel's parking lot. Of course, it is not the same as Pipin's. Mine is away from the downtown, in a street without pavement; therefore, much cheaper. We arrive to the restaurant and very courteously, Charley rushes to open the door for me. We walk through the entrance and there are a lot of people waiting. To impress me, Charley asks me, 'How about if you meet Pipin now?' I respond not to joke with this type of things.

Then my heart stops, my respiration falters, my hands are sweating and I have the presentiment that I am red like a tomato. I feel stupid. Here, in front of me; in flesh and bone is the person who influenced my life. Pipin is seated in one of the tables and Charley is walking towards him. 'What do I do now, what do I tell him?' Charley introduce me with him. I greet him.

His head is shaved; his eyeglasses are slim and round. He is tall, strong and impressive. The scent of his perfume reaches me; a strong smell but sweet at the same time. It's a smell that captivates; smells like him.

He introduces me with his girlfriend! She is much older than he is. She wears too much make-up, with nails too long and too many rings on her fingers and silicone breasts; a woman too fake. What are they doing together? I have no idea, but what I know is that they don't match.

We seat in the same table but in the opposite end. Next to me is another fascinating character; one of Pipin's divers, Pepe. He is even taller than him, with dark skin and incredible yellow eyes, like honey. On my other side is Charley, all happy about the impression he caused me.

Dishes come in and out and I don't even know what it is. I'm not eating, I'm not listening to the talks that everyone are having; I can't take my eyes off of him. I can't stop seeing him. He is handsome. How come I haven't noticed it before? He has an animal-like strength that fascinates me, that attracts me. He looks back and I cannot resist his eyes; it's deep. I'm afraid that he may read my mind through my eyes. This meal takes an eternity. I can feel my heart beating. I even feel as if everybody can hear it.

It's 10:00 p.m. and I haven't called my parents yet, and they must be worried. I already saw him and there is nothing else I could do. He has his girlfriend, his training, his fame and his life. I have to go back to reality; I have to go back to my life. When we finally finished, everyone get up and walk towards a cabaret. His girlfriend is shouting, laughing kissing him and showing to everyone that she has the key to his room. Therefore, I presumed that they have been together for a long time.

She's American and eccentric, and when we reach the bar, everyone seems to know her. This not my ambiance, I don't feel comfortable in this kind of atmosphere. It's late and it's better for me to go. I turn around to get out, but someone stops me by the shoulder. I look back and almost fainted, it's Pipin! He smiles and tells me, 'Why don't you seat next to me?' He must be kidding or I must be dreaming. Like hypnotized, without understanding what he was doing or trying to do, I go towards the table where everybody is installed.

Then Pepe takes a video-camera and starts to film. When he goes to Pipin's girlfriend, she grabs Pipin by the cheeks and starts to kiss him like a desperate. What's wrong with her? What is she trying to demonstrate? That she hangs with the champion? That she lies down and has sex with him? I feel that Pipin is a little embarrassed, but doesn't say a word.

When the camera finally got to me, I smile and turn my face away. Suddenly, and as if an army of ants had bitten his girlfriend, she gets up, walks to the stage and starts to sing. She's so ridiculous! Because of that, now Pipin has an empty chair next to him while he is to my left. I would like to start a conversation, but what do I ask him? An autograph? That is silly. Are you afraid of doing what you do? Of course not, or he wouldn't be doing it. What does it feels to descend? Based on my studies and readings, I already knew the answer. What goes on inside of him? That was the objective of my thesis. So, what do I tell him?

When I finally decided, I asked,

'Aren't you too stressed-out with so much responsibility and people depending on you?' He looks back and responds,

'Do I look stressed-out?'

How could I ask something so stupid? I swear to myself that I would never ask anything else. After 5 minutes in silence but looking at each other, he tells me,

'The problem with having so many people around is that you never know who your real friends are. I have had too many bad experiences, especially with the French.'

I could not believe what he has just said. He, without noticing, continued with his personal dilemma.

'The French are the worst race that can exist. They believe they are the center of the universe but they are only shit-eaters. I can't stand them. French food gives me repulsion, the same with their wines and pâtés . . .'

I wanted to cry; this cannot be happening. This cannot be happening to me. After a while, he finally stops, looks at me and asks me,

'By the way, from which part of Mexico are you?'

What do I do now? So I make one of my grimaces that he doesn't understand yet, I take a deep breath, smile and tell him,

'From no where, I'm French.'

Of course, he now feels stupid and doesn't know what to say. But then Pepe, who had been following the conversation, tells me,

'He hates the Frenchmen but not the Frenchwomen.'

'I think I better go,' I said. So I called Charley who was in the other side of the table and asked him to take me back to my hotel. I don't have any resentment for what Pipin has just said. Every country has some good people and some bad people, as everyone is entitled to have their own opinion. After that, Pipin is embarrassed and I don't know what to say; so is better that the night doesn't get any worse.

THE LAST ATTEMPT

The moment we are stepping inside the car, we hear some yelling coming out from a contiguous discotheque. Charley asks me if I know the place. Of course not; I have ever been here before. He asks me to get there with him, but I tell him that I have no interest; my mind is not into that right now. Right in that moment, Charley did the most stupid thing I have ever seen, but perhaps, the one thing that would change my life for ever.

He kneeled down and begged me to accompany him for just five minutes. It's 11:00 p.m. and I haven't called my parents. My mother must be all over, imagining that the worse has happened to me, and my father must be bringing her into reason. I said no to Charley, that maybe another day, that I have to call my parents, but he insists and continues with his knees on the floor. Then I think that it would be faster just to remain 5 more minutes.

'Okay, let's go,' and we get inside.

Then I receive a surprise but a disappointment at the same time. From the distance, I can see Pepe dancing along with the rest of the group. I head for the exit; it doesn't make any sense to continue to waste time. But just then, I see Pipin entering the disco, alone. I stop and tell Charley that I want to dance. From the corner of my eye I see Pipin heading towards the group, and consequently, towards me. I continued dancing.

Then I move and positioned myself in the middle of a corridor entrance. Now, every time someone has to make it through, like every other second, they bother me. Of course, that's what I have in mind. I'm hoping for Pipin to notice it, feel sympathy for me and call me to dance with him. Five minutes after, I feel a hand holding mine and pulling me back. I turn around and, bingo, it's him.

'Why don't you dance with me? Over there we have more space.'

I smile back. Every movement, every second that passes gets us closer. There are a lot of people. I'm out of control; in trance. Then I receive the final thrust. The song, "Lamento Boliviano" is playing and I can't resist any longer; I let go. I feel his torso against my chest, his warm abdomen against mine, his leg between my legs. I close my eyes and the world can come to an end right now, because there won't be a noise loud enough to wake me up. I feel his mouth against my ear as he says, 'Kiss me'. I open my eyes and we are entwined. I realize that I have gone too far and I have to stop what I started. I separate myself from him and pretend not to hear. He gets close to me and tells me again,

'Give me a kiss.'
'No.'
'Please.'
'I didn't come for that.'
'What did you come for?'
'I came to dive with you.'
'Tomorrow, I will dive for you if you give me a kiss.'
'I can't.'
'Tomorrow I will risk my life for you and in exchange you don't even want to give me a kiss?'

What else can I say? I couldn't resist him anymore, I tried, but even though my upbringing tells me to do nothing and to leave, another voice tells me that perhaps, there won't be another chance and I have to take it now. It all happened so quickly that I had no time to decide. Our lips were sealed in a passionate kiss, just as I had imagined it before . . ."

What happened afterward is something that doesn't require a wild imagination; therefore, no need to publish the rest of the letter. Pipin and Audrey spent that first night together and many more to come.

Only hours after this encounter, Pepe, the safety diver for whom Audrey also felt attracted, died in an inexplicable way while diving with Pipin during his training. Pipin alleges that his former roommate and intimate friend died from a heart attack produced by the venom of a scorpion that had bitten Pepe the day before.

There is only one problem with that conjecture; it's well known that scorpion venom is unlikely to kill a young and healthy person, and much less to cause a heart attack 24 hours later. Although deaths occur, immediate and evident signs and symptoms from the bite like a severe allergic reaction, anaphylactic shock and hypersensitivity must occur first. So I asked Audrey if she noticed anything abnormal in Pepe before he died.

"No, he seemed to be normal that day."

"Then what happened?"

"I don't know, Carlos; because whatever happened, it happened underwater."

"Well, based on your letter, you were attracted to Pepe, as well."

"And?" Audrey asked curiously.

"Maybe Pipin got jealous," I said jokingly.

One way or the other, Pepe's death remains a mystery and Audrey found herself taking his place in the water as a safety diver. That was an irresponsible move from Pipin's part. Placing an untrained diver—untrained for this type of dive—in depths beyond the limits imposed by recreational diving is simply reckless, but that's Pipin's nature and Audrey accepted it.

With Audrey still seated next to me in my office, and after having finished reading the entire letter, I told her,

"Audrey, you are pendeja. How could you fall for that old trick of, 'I'm going to risk my life for you tomorrow, baby, give me a kiss and open your legs.'"

"Oye, that's not what it says there!"

"Not literally, but that was his ultimate objective and he did get it in a flash."

Now seemingly embarrassed, she responded,

"That was silly, I know, but I was in love with him."

"Audrey, you were not in love, you were infatuated; obsessed maybe. Loves develops with time."

"You think so?"

"Do I think so? I'm certain of it, but I can see now why he controls you so well."

"What do you mean?"

THE LAST ATTEMPT

"Well, you showed how infatuated you were over him. Then you ended up in bed with him the very first night you met him. He placed you in the water in a hazardous situation when Pepe died and you accepted it, blindly. And after the record, you left college and came to Miami to live with him. He knew right there that he had found in you a submissive European beauty willing to die for him. I got to tell you; that's a dream come true for any guy."

"It was a dream for me, too."

"It was?"

"Yeah, now it's different . . . it's not a dream anymore."

"Of course, you didn't see his flaws in that poster hanging in your room, did you?"

"No, not at all," she said seemingly contemplative.

"You didn't know about his voodoo stuff either, right?"

"Nooo . . ." she exclaimed rising her eye brows.

"You didn't know about his hostile nature either, right?"

"No, he was actually very sweet in the beginning."

"That's because you got attracted to Dr. Jekyll and ended up having a ménage a trois with Mr. Hide, as well."

"Uh-hmm," nodded Audrey.

"You didn't expect him to be, ah . . . let me put it mildly; a damned womanizer, right?"

"Of course not, how would I know?"

"But what makes you believe that if he dumped his girlfriend the very same night he met you, that he would be faithful to you?"

"I never even thought about it. I just wanted to be with him, but now he cheats on me all the time. That's why he is in Mexico now."

"Listen to yourself; he even takes an airplane to cheat on you. The truth is that he cheats on you because you tolerate it."

"Hmm," she sighed with a sad grimace taking over her beauty. "Actually, I even had to wait in a lobby of a hotel once while he was in the room with another woman."

"Yeah, Pipin told me, and feeling proud about it, and even said that you were okay with it; that as Frenchwoman, you are open-minded and not jealous."

"That's not true. I don't like it, but what can I do? He is the typical Cuban macho."

"Okay, Audrey. It's your marriage and I'm just being too intrusive here. Pipin is my friend but so are you, and I just don't like to see that long face you have right now."

"I know, Carlos . . ." she said with a deep melancholic sigh. "I only wish things were different."

With her eyes becoming glassy, Audrey headed for the door to return to her office. But before she walked out,

"By the way, Audrey, you make it look as if Blood Shift was discovered with Pipin and as if Pipin is the only one who experiences this phenomenon."

"He told me that it was discovered because of him," she said seemingly disconcerted.

"That's another one of his crafted fables. It was discovered thanks to Jacques Mayol when Pipin was still sucking a pacifier and wearing cloth diapers back in Cuba. Check it out on the internet."

"I don't have to; I believe you. I know Pipin. I just can't believe how easy it is for him to lie that way."

"One more thing, Audrey; I've talked to Domingo Palma about the preliminary script he's working on for OceanWomen, and you told him about the two occasions when you attempted against your life."

"Yeah, what is it with that?"

"Are you sure you want that kind of information to be out in the open?"

"Yeah, why not . . . it's not a secret and it happened. Besides, Pipin says that it will make the movie more dramatic."

After giving me a timid smile and a sad *Princess Diana* look, she finally left my office.

The suicide attempts and the reasons for it, is something Audrey had told me before, and indeed, it was not a secret. But I also knew how dejected she became every time she spoke about the times when she cut her wrists open to put an end to her life.

Chapter 4

THE REPORT CONTINUES

WEDNESDAY, OCTOBER 02, 2002

  Like magma ready to erupt from his ears, Pipin's boiling blood forecasted a turbulent day ahead. Actually, it all started the night before during supper, when Pipin considered placing the decompression line and the sled's cable, simultaneously in the water. I interrupted Pipin to suggest setting the decompression line after Audrey had returned from the dive. I elucidated my point by saying that it was too risky to have a long line with scuba tanks hanging along the length of it.

  "Audrey could injure herself on the way up with one of those tanks," I dared to contradict.

  Pipin argued back saying that due to the lack of current, it wasn't necessary. He insisted that the lines should remain parallel and never get close to one another. That was a surprising statement from him. He knows, better than anyone else, that no one can predict which way the sled is going to surface. He has bumped his head against the bottom of a boat in more than one occasion and even fell unconscious once. And that happened under perfect conditions.

  Occasionally, the sled would ascend pulling the line away from its vertical axis with tremendous force; particularly when the amount of weight at the end of the line is lower than required. For some unknown reason, Pipin had been placing less weight than needed to keep the line tense.

  What's more, the two lines could encounter each other based on the boat's movements caused by the wind. Even without any current, the boat, being adrift, could get the lines dangerously close.

CARLOS SERRA

"Carlos, how many records have you done?" asked Pipin pompously.

The question took me by surprise. He had asked that same question many times to many people, but it was the first time to toss it at me. But with my temper level rising, I replied immediately,

"If you're referring to breaking records, I don't have a death wish. But if you're asking me about the organizational aspect of it, should I remind you that the few I have put together for you and Audrey, went flawlessly?"

"Well, yeah . . ." he hesitated.

And before he could put a phrase together, *"This is operational, and you are placing an additional element of risk in the water for Audrey, needlessly!"*

Meanwhile, Tata, Angelo and Audrey followed the argument silently, alternating a quick gaze between Pipin, their empty plates and me. Pascal, being the only one who had already served his food, also avoided getting involved by immersing his face on his dish. More likely, he was clueless about the subject, anyway. Pipin and I were having the argument in Spanish.

"Besides," I persisted while Pipin, looking down, deployed his peculiar signs of stress; frowning, rubbing his shaved head back-and-forth and biting his tongue with his front teeth. *"When it comes to scuba tanks and placing deco-lines in the water, I was doing that for my advanced-level students when you were selling fish on the streets back in Cuba. So spare me the 'how many records have you done bullshit.'"*

Pipin, however, finished the argument by saying that he knew what he was doing. He wasn't open to reason; so I stopped arguing the point. But in clear defiance I stood up and went to the buffet area before he had finished his briefing, and I know how much that pissed him off.

Minutes later, while filling up my plate at the buffet table, Audrey approached me. She came to serve Pipin's plate.

"Carlos, I agree with you, the decompression line can be set in the water after I've surfaced . . ."

"Of course," I interrupted. *"It's just plain logic. Tata can place the line down while Pascal, Pipin and I are still ascending."*

"It's true," Audrey admitted timidly.

"Yes, but I wonder why nobody backed me up in the table. Why is everyone so fearful to speak out?" I asked irately.

"Pipin has been very aggressive, lately," she replied. *"And you know that neither Pascal nor Tata will contradict Pipin; they are afraid of him."*

"Not just them, Audrey. You didn't say a word either and it'll be your head smashing against one of those tanks. It'll be your brain scattered all over the ocean!"

Realizing what I had just said, she promised that she would talk to Pipin after dinner, but somehow I doubt it. There were occasions when Audrey wouldn't mind telling Pipin what was in her mind, but with the increased anger he had been showing, I didn't think Audrey would attempt to exacerbate his temper any further.

THE LAST ATTEMPT

Now in the boat the following morning, we all witnessed Pipin's foolishness at its worse. It was a beautiful sunny day with calm seas and a gentle breeze, but the splendorous morning was rapidly spoiled by Pipin's grumpy face.

He seemed characteristically upset; maybe worse than usual. I was curious to find out if Audrey had asked Pipin to set the deco line after her ascent, but it didn't take long for me to realize that if she had asked, he hadn't listen. Perhaps, that was the reason for his madness; she had asked.

Once we arrived to the training spot, about a thousand yards away from shore, the first thing Pipin did was to throw the deco line in the water. It was a clear statement that things would be his way.

Then Tata, Angelo and Pipin set the sled's line in the water, but after only few minutes . . . Bingo! The lines were as I had predicted; dangerously close to each other. Now Pipin, with his rage-meter in the red zone, grabbed his mask and fins and jumped in the water while the rest of us just watched from the boat.

Acting frantically, Pipin took the deco line—which was hanging from the same side where the sled line was, the port side—and transferred it to the starboard side of the boat.

He asked Tata and Angelo to help him from the boat to pass the line around the bow, but it didn't work. The boat was too small to make a difference. The two lines were still too close.

In a sudden attack of plain silliness, now Pipin swam away from the boat pulling the line with him; he was trying to separate it from the vessel. But the moment he let it go, the line, predictably, went back down to set itself close to the sled's line, once again.

I couldn't help it, so that's when I looked straight at him, shook my head and said, *"Tell me, Pipin. How many records have you done?"*

That made matters even worse; I had just challenged his pride in front of everyone else. He looked at me with piercing eyes and, stubbornly, left the line the way it was. Audrey now had to descend with the two lines almost colliding with each other. Only that the deco line, in addition to the tanks placed along its length, also had a twenty-pound concrete block at the end of it as an "anchor".

With Audrey's ascent averaging between 1.5 to 2 meters a second (about 5 to 6.5 feet per second), a head-on collision with the "anchor" or any of the tanks would be like smashing a watermelon with a sledge hammer.

Audrey, who was still in the boat waiting for Pipin's poor display of common sense to end, was yelled at furiously,

"*AUDREY, you are not on vacation. Get in the water, RIGHT NOW!*"

"Pipin, I'm ready, I'm . . . I'm just waiting for you to . . ."

"Shut up and get in the water, NOW!" he yelled again. *"We don't have the whole day."*

Audrey, now standing next to me in the edge of the boat, was also on the edge of an emotional breakdown. While adjusting her fins and wiping her tears as well, and while I was gearing up my scuba equipment, she whispered to me preoccupied,

"What's going to happen with the decompression line?"

"Don't worry, Audrey," I said calmly while staring at Pipin. *"I'll be in the water pulling the line away from you."*

When Audrey entered the water, Pipin approached her and vigorously demanded for her to start to ventilate right away. She needed to execute, first, a series of descents without the sled as a way to activate her mammalian diving reflex. But after only a couple of descents, Pipin stopped Audrey, told her to climb on the sled and to get ready to dive *"immediately."*

Audrey wasn't ready, but she didn't say a word; Pipin would have blown a fuse on her, again. Before descending I spoke with Tata and asked him to be more alert than usual at the surface. The line situation was an unnecessary risk for Audrey, but I would take care of that particular problem.

Since Audrey hadn't finished her pre-dive routine, my concern was now the possibility of a shallow-water blackout. That usually happens towards the end of the dive when the brain doesn't have enough oxygen to keep running.

Then, out of nowhere, Pipin barked right at Audrey's face something I knew it was meant for me,

"You do as I say. I'm the only one in command in this shit, IS THAT CLEAR!"

Instead of discharging his wrath on me, the cause of his irritation, Pipin yelled at Audrey, increasing her stress even more just before the dive. In fact, when Audrey climbed on the sled, she was shedding tears. I even took a couple of pictures to show Pipin and argue later with him, his positive reinforcement skills.

Even Angelo reacted, *"Oye, leave her alone, man!"*

It was a disturbing and emotionally painful situation but I felt powerless. Therefore, I did the only thing I thought appropriate at the time, to descend and try to prevent an accident with the decompression line.

Before descending, however, I saw Pipin kissing Audrey on the cheek instead of her lips. She avoided it and didn't return it. Pipin's kiss, nevertheless, was a trademark for the pictures.

THE LAST ATTEMPT

Credit: Carlos Serra

A visibly gloomy Audrey prepares to dive and even Angelo, seated on the boat, yelled back at Pipin, *"Oye, leave her alone, man!"*

Once I positioned myself next to the deco-line, and as I kept timing Audrey's dive, I started to pull the rope away when she initiated her ascent.

Thankfully, the line was not an issue, but an accident almost occurred, anyway. Audrey was in a collision course with the boat when Tata, who was on alert, grabbed Audrey and pulled her away from the lift bag just few meters beneath the vessel; he caught her just in time to avoid a severe impact. But with the thrust she had, although slower, they kept ascending straight to the boat and Audrey ended up banging her head with the vessel. Luckily, it was not a hard bump, but if it wasn't for Tata's quick reaction, she could have suffered a neck injury or perhaps even died.

The lift bag and its holding aluminum frame also hit the boat underneath, hard, scaring the captain on board. He later described how he kept looking at the boat's deck expecting to find the Caribbean water flooding it, but with the exception of a scratch underneath, nothing happened.

Credit: Angelo Cordero

Audrey rubs her head after hitting the hull of the boat. Tata's quick reaction saved her from a potentially devastating injury.

I saw the incident from about twenty meters of depth, and after confirming that Audrey was okay, I descended to sixty meters to check on Pipin and Pascal. When I met him he avoided eye contact with me. So I checked on Pascal, who was just below Pipin, leaving the black abyss right under.

They were okay, so I went back up. My computer showed that I had to do a five minute deco-stop at 3 meters (10 feet). But when I was in my way up to decompress . . .

"Coño, what's going on?" I wondered in distress.

My regulator had been pulled out of my mouth leaving me with no air. I turned around in awe to see what the hell was happening and there he was . . . Pipin!

With the piercing eyes of a raving maniac he signaled me that he was out of air, but only after securing my regulator in his mouth. What resulted more shocking is that he had my tank already in his hand.

"How the hell did he take my tank and I didn't feel a thing?" I reflected. But without giving me much time for analysis, I saw Pipin descending back into the dark blue taking my air-supply with him.

"Great," I though, *"he runs out of air, but I should be the one drowning?"*

THE LAST ATTEMPT

I looked up; the surface was about twenty-five meters away. Audrey's silhouette was floating in the surface against the sun, looking down and witnessing the action. I even considered chasing Pipin down to recover my gear, but that would have been an unintelligent move. That's when I grabbed the sled line and hand over hand, I kept exhaling gradually to avoid lung overexpansion and to remove as much nitrogen as possible while surfacing slowly.

Raging in anger I climbed the boat, threw my fins and mask to the floor, and yelled a rather nasty expression in Spanish, *"EL COÑO DE SU MADRE!"*

Audrey climbed on board right behind me and heard my discontent lingo,

"You know, Audrey, he must be from Mars, where there are no signs of intelligent life."

Audrey smiled timidly for few seconds, but only until she realized I wasn't joking; not this time.

"What was that all about?" she asked.

"Your husband is a lunatic. He pulled my regulator and removed my tank off my back. He claimed to be out of air."

A speechless Audrey kept looking at me; she seemed bewildered first, but alarmed soon after. Then I added,

"Doesn't Pipin know that I have an octopus? I still had plenty of air left in my tank for the two of us." (In the diving lexicon an octopus is a spare regulator).

"Why didn't you take the octopus then?" Audrey asked.

"Because he took my whole gear and went back down right away . . . didn't you see that?" I replied. *"What did you want me to do? Chase him down to the bottom? It was either the surface or to drown . . . and I will not die like Pepe or Massimo."*

I referred to two divers who had died in the water while supporting Pipin in previous world records. Some people claim that Pipin is directly responsible for their deaths, and although I never believed that, now I was starting to wonder.

Then Audrey changed the subject and complimented my breath-hold capacity by saying,

"Carlos, I'm amazed. It took you almost three minutes to surface without air."

"Audrey, don't you think twenty years in diving gives proficiency to anyone? I started as a freediver. If you don't normally see it, it's because I don't want to challenge Pipin's ego. So with him around I keep a low profile."

"It's just that I don't see you freediving too often."

"That's because on the first class we ever taught, I rapidly learned about Pipin's jealousy."

"Why, what happened?"

"Do you remember Eduardo, the taxi driver friend of Pipin?"

"Yeah, I remember him."

"Well, I gave him an underwater demonstration in the pool of Florida International University during that class, to correct a wrong kick he was performing . . ."

"Aha," she nodded curiously.

"And it happens that when I came out of the water, Eduardo gave some flattering remarks for the distance I swam, the time I spent underwater and my kicking technique."

"And Pipin got upset?"

"Upset? He was furious. 'Eduardo, stop talking so much shit!' he yelled at the poor guy. So I learned, back in the year two thousand, that to keep a low profile was a good idea."

"But, Carlos, I've seen your demonstrations before in front of Pipin, they are really good and I haven't seen Pipin getting mad."

"Not really, Audrey. I always make conscious mistakes to give Pipin an opportunity to correct me, so that I don't awake the inner monster. I did that in Hawaii the second time when you went there; remember."

"Oh, yeah, I thought you were fooling around."

"No, I wasn't, but don't change the subject, Audrey."

Audrey's attempt to change the subject didn't surprise me. Even though Audrey and I were very open in our topics of conversation, every time I mentioned the deaths of Pepe Fernandez and Massimo Berttoni, she would evade the subject as the plague; as she did this time, too.

She was present in Cabo San Lucas, Mexico, when Pepe died few years back, and something in her evasiveness told me that she knew what had really happened. The disconcerting thing is that Pepe died while diving in support of a record attempt for Pipin, just like Massimo. And here I was, in another record attempt with my regulator being pulled out of my mouth by Pipin.

As I kept thinking about Pipin's outrageous behavior I also started to wonder why he didn't take my octopus. Accustomed to training new divers for years, I always carry a redundancy system for such eventualities, and he knew it. Besides, it's standard in the diving industry to carry a spare regulator. We could have shared air from my tank as I still had plenty of it, but instead, he removed my tank and ripped the regulator off my mouth.

This last point also brought an additional concern about the whole situation. A person who is desperate for air may go for the main regulator; that's expected, but when Pipin removed the tank off my back I didn't feel a thing, and he did it before ripping the regulator off my mouth. Not to mention that he abandoned me in twenty-five meters of water with no air.

While still chewing over about what had happened, I kept monitoring myself just in case any sign of decompression illness would develop, because for the first time in my twenty years as a diver, I had missed a decompression stop.

Pipin didn't come out of the water for another hour; he remained decompressing with Pascal. Only then I realized that bewilderment had affected my judgment underwater. On the way up, I could have taken any of the tanks from the deco-line but I didn't. I didn't even see the line which probably was only few meters behind my back. Shocked

THE LAST ATTEMPT

by the abrupt end of my air-supply and Pipin's behavior, I didn't consider the deco line as an option.

Once they both came up, Pipin wouldn't even look at me. So I decided to leave the argument for later, back at the hotel. But as we were on the way back to shore, another surprise would arise. With Pipin in the stern of the boat talking with Tata, Audrey quietly showed me her computer and asked,

"What do you think about this?"

I grabbed Audrey's hand to hold the computer closer, and what I saw, took me a moment to assimilate. Her computer showed 143 meters! In awe I saw Audrey, who gave me a shy and compliant grin. Then I look around to see Pipin, but oblivious to Audrey's interaction with me, he kept on talking with Tata in low voice.

That was thirteen meters deeper than the 130 meters planned the night before, and more likely, only Tata and Pascal knew the depth before hand. Tata had helped Pipin set the line in the water and Pascal had to blend his mixture to a precise proportion of gases based on the depth of his dive. He must have known, otherwise, Pipin was not only risking Audrey's life but Pascal's, as well.

Let's remember that Pipin had gotten in the sled's path during the last practice dive and interrupted Audrey's descent around eighty meters. So in the end Audrey did, not only thirteen more meters than planned, but sixty-three meters more than her previous dive.

When Pipin originally planned adding fifty more meters from Audrey's last practice dive (from 80 to 130 meters), I addressed my concern. Yet Pipin replied back claiming that Audrey was doing great in the simulated dives on land. But knowing that the total addition was an astonishing sixty-three meters, was disquieting, to say the least.

When we got back to the hotel, Pipin, Audrey and I gathered by the pool before heading to the restaurant for lunch. The rest of the team had gone to return and rinse down the diving gear at the dive shop, so we waited for them. Audrey sat away from Pipin with a long face, red eyes and a sad, evasive stare. Pipin was still visibly angry but I wasn't any happier, anyway. That's when I decided to take a picture of his grumpy face, for which I knew it would upset Pipin even more.

"Don't take pictures, Carlos," he jumped off the chair.

"Why not? We are all a happy family; aren't we?"

Then I proceeded to take a picture of both of them. As he's always been careful with the loving couple image he likes to convey, this picture shows otherwise.

CARLOS SERRA

Credit: Carlos Serra

Audrey's gloomy state is evident, prompting Pipin, always careful with the image of happiness he wanted to project, to stop me from taking the shot.

I was so upset that I even wrote in the report some of the disturbing actions that had happened. Although I would normally write a censored version of the events, I could not disguise my frustration this time.

Later that day Pipin came to my room; he had read my report, which I had given to Audrey to send it via email to our office in Miami. Her room was the only one with Internet connection. Pipin asked me why I had written about what happened that day,

"Because it's true; because I'm pissed, and because somehow you have to listen to reason," I said heatedly while finger-pointing him.

"Come on, brother, relax . . . nothing happened . . ." Pipin said condescendingly.

"Yeah, thank God for little miracles, because what I saw today is the most flagrant and reckless display of stupidity I have ever seen, and I've seen quite a few from you by now."

"Carlos, brother; take it easy."

"Take it easy? Today you could have killed Audrey or me, and you want me to take it easy?"

"Carlos, what are you talking about?"

"Oh, now you don't know? First, the lack of common sense with the line; second, taking my air away, and third, sending Audrey to one hundred and forty-three meters just like that. What is it with you? Are you trying to kill her?"

"Hey, she did it, right? I knew she could do it."

"So, you are going to keep pushing her until one day you find the limit, is that it? One day she may not come back alive. Have you thought about that?"

Pipin, now seemingly apprehensive and probably noticing my edginess, persisted that Audrey was doing great with the training and that he was confident she could do it. On the other hand, I kept debating on the possibility of going back to Miami.

In the evening, at the diner, Audrey approached me while I was serving my food at the buffet. She was, as always, serving food for Pipin, who remained seated at the table.

"Why can't Pipin serve his own food?" I asked her.

"Well, you know, he is the typical machista."

"That's because you let it happen, Audrey. Today he treated you like crap for something you had nothing to do with."

"Of course," she said looking down and visibly gloomy. *"He won't tell you anything, so he discards his rage on me."*

"I've told you before; that happens because you let it happen."

"But," she paused, *"what can I do?"*

"You could start by telling him to be a gentleman and serve his own food and yours, as well."

"Who? Pipin? He wakes me up in the middle of the night to bring him water to bed. You think he's going to serve his own food, or serve mine? That's how he was raised."

"If you don't get the water for him, he would have to get up and get it himself, right?"

"Carlos, I tried the first time and he pushed me off the bed. Then he yelled at me, 'go and get me water!'"

"Audrey, you must be the last of your kind, because dumb women like you doesn't exist anymore; not among educated people. You are a lost case."

"That's the way he is, Carlos. We are not going to change him. You know he'll never change."

"Perhaps, Audrey, but something I can change is my own ticket. I'm going back to Miami."

"What?" she exclaimed visibly alarmed. *"Don't leave me alone, Carlos. Without you around he'll be out of control."*

"Hey, look what he did today. He's already out of control."

"No, please, don't go. Only you can keep him in line."

"Audrey, he pulled my regulator out of my mouth, and you know that an inexperience diver could have freaked-out and possibly drowned. Not to mention sending you to one hundred and forty-three meters. That's totally insane!"

"Yes, but if you leave, who's going to stop him from sending me to two hundred meters tomorrow?"

"How about you, Audrey?"

CARLOS SERRA

"Oh, Carlos, you know he won't listen to me."

Deep inside I knew Audrey was right. She was powerless against Pipin. His control over her was already absolute and her willingness to overcome that situation was null.

"Did you ask him last night about the deco-line?"

"Yes, I did, and look how he reacted."

"Hmm," I sighed with resignation. *"Okay, Audrey, I'll stay, for now. But I'm doing it only for you, because I've had enough of his madness."*

Then we added the final scoop of food to the plates and headed to the table where Pipin had interrupted his chat with Pascal to stare at Audrey and me. He had piercing and inquisitive eyes; the icy eyes of a predator, as I call that gaze.

As a challenge, I returned the stare and asked, *"What; is there a problem?"* Without replying, he turned around and renewed his conversation with Pascal.

THURSDAY, OCTOBER 03, 2002

After the stressful events of the day before, this day was quite different. Pipin seemed to be in a better mood and had decided that Audrey would rest. Eduardo Orjales, who is another loyal assistant of Pipin for about fourteen years, had arrived from Miami last night. Just like most Cubans helping Pipin, Eduardo would respond quicker to his nickname of "Wiky" than to his real name.

Unlike Tata, Wiky's anatomy is built like a fighting-bull. He's also much more talkative and extroverted than the first. In fact, Wiky had a natural tendency to standout as the comedian of the group. But the contrast doesn't end there; Tata is a great freediver but a poor scuba diver. Wiky on the contrary, is a diving instructor with ample experience and skills.

Even though they both had been working with Pipin for the same length of time, Wiky is much more outspoken with Pipin than Tata would ever be, and this situation had actually stirred up many confrontations between Pipin and Wiky.

Along with Wiky, a good friend, Matt Briseno, had also arrived, but his home is much farther than Miami. Matt is an always-cheerful, middle-age accountant who lives in Kona, Hawaii, where he practices his profession and freedives on a regular basis with the wisdom of a middle-age man and the energy level of a kid.

This day the whole team, except for Audrey, went out to the ocean for some fun dives. We left the front beach of *Viva Dominicus Resort* around ten o'clock. The plan was simply to enjoy the day, which was partly clouded and with the heat indicator reaching the *"Welcome-to-Hell"* zone.

Once we made it to the spot, Pipin set the line for those who were freediving: Bill, Tata, Matt and Pipin himself. Meanwhile, Wiky was providing some scuba training to Angelo while I kept photographing the underwater session for our website's daily report. It was a much needed relaxing session which made me forgot how close I was from packing my luggage the day before and return to Miami.

Credit: Carlos Serra

Bill Stromberg shows his world-class skills during this descent.

On the way back, under the captain's supervision, Angelo took control of the boat, but not realizing where he was heading, he took us farther than supposed and we ended up in another resort's beach located to the east. Except for Angelo we all laughed; he wasn't aware of his mistake. From the whole group he stood alone as the only not aquatically-inclined team member.

We decided, nevertheless, to anchor there for a while since Tata wanted to try a set of modified swimming goggles Pipin had received. The designer, a Canadian freediver named Eric Fattah, had sent a pair to be tested.

Due to the crushing pressure at depth, deep-water freedivers wear neither a diving mask nor goggles. The air trapped in the space between the lenses and the eyes gets compressed by the ambient pressure, causing a very painful and dangerous squeeze over the eyes. This new goggles' design avoids such problem by allowing water between the lenses and the eyes while compensating for the blurred vision the water in contact with the eyes always causes.

Curious about the goggles' performance, Tata got in the water with them, but he immediately came back on board shouting,

"Man, with these goggles you don't see shit!"

Pipin, Matt and I laughed. For the goggles to work they must be flooded with water, but Tata was not aware of that simple and rather significant detail. That's when Bill asked,

"Are those the 'Fluid Goggles'?" That's the name Eric Fattah had given to his clever design.

Pipin, Matt and I looked at one another and decided not to respond just to see what was coming next. To test the goggles, instead of getting in the ocean, Bill took a bottle of water and poured the water in one side to try them out while remaining seated onboard the boat.

"Tata is right; you don't see shit with this," said Bill with disdain.

Pipin, Matt and I seemed to be the only ones aware. For the goggles to work correctly, they must also be used underwater. The goggles' design contemplated having water between the eyes and the lenses to avoid squeeze, and for obvious reasons, it also contemplated being used beneath the surface.

Credit: Angelo Cordero

A much better mood. From left to right (back): Bill, Tata, Wiky and Pipin.
(Front): Matt and Carlos

In the afternoon Audrey remained in her room reading, as it was becoming customary for her, nowadays. The rest of the team took the afternoon off and went out to tour a nearby town. Pipin and I met with Laura Gualazzi, the manager of *Viva Diving* and friend of Pipin, to set things up for an *IAFD* Training Center at the *Viva Dominicus Resort*. The meeting went very well. We were exited about the prospect of operating the first freediving training facility in the Dominican Republic. That was part of our plans to internationalize the *IAFD* even more.

FRIDAY, OCTOBER 04, 2002

This day an unprecedented event occurred; it was the second time in history that a woman, regardless of affiliation, made a *No-Limits* dive deeper than any man. The first one was Angela Bandini in 1989, when she broke Mayol's official record and Pipin's unofficial record, as well.

Today, Audrey reached 166 meters—four meters deeper than Pipin's last absolute world record—with a total bottom time of 2'44". It was a practice dive, but remarkable, nevertheless. Audrey had become, unofficially, the deepest freediver in the world. Despite the contentment for Audrey's achievement, a brawl that happened earlier between Pipin and Wiky caused a distressing situation throughout the training session.

It all started with a removable ladder that was always on board the small boat to allow the divers a safe climb back on. Pipin, just looking to punish Wiky after a previous altercate, left the ladder on shore before departing so that Wiky would have a real hard time getting back on board after the dive.

Without the ladder, the only way to board the boat was by extending the arms up, grabbing the topside and pulling oneself up with muscle power. Every one of us had to do the same, but Wiky, due to his heavier complexity, was struggling more than the rest of us.

"*Pipin, where is the ladder?*" I asked.
"*I left it on the beach.*"
"*But . . . why?*"
"*I'm giving Wiky a lesson. He's too fat; he's got to loose weight.*"

Knowing Pipin, I knew he was only *punishing* Wiky for having argued with him earlier. I have seen this type of behavior on Pipin many times before with the employees at the office, the safety divers, and even Audrey. It was indeed so common that I even had a name for it, *Concealed Punishment;* concealed because the target of Pipin's castigation was usually unaware of the action.

It was just a personal and self-satisfying vendetta, and this time it was no different; Wiky didn't know why the ladder wasn't aboard. But what it may seem like an inconsequential childish action, in reality was risking the scuba divers' health; including Pipin's own.

After the long decompressions that Wiky, Pascal, Pipin and I had to carry out after each one of Audrey's practice dives, we all needed to avoid exertion. We were making dives deeper than most divers in the world are willing to try; particularly Pascal, who was doing dives way below the 100 meter or 330 feet mark.

Even after decompression, a large amount of dissolved nitrogen remains in the blood stream and within the body cells that will last for hours before dropping back to normal levels. The amount of dissolved nitrogen is relatively safe assuming the diver avoids certain actions; like taking a hot shower—heat expand gases—and exercise. Exercising will accelerate the body's metabolism and convert the dissolved nitrogen into harmful bubbles that cause decompression illness. I tried, in vain, to explain it to Pipin.

But this last situation was not the only odd occurrence. While Pascal, Pipin, Wiky and I were decompressing, we heard a boat approaching. Right at that moment, Pipin surfaced without completing his decompression. That was a highly risky maneuver that left us astonished. There was no need for Pipin to take such a risk, but he seemed to be in a hurry.

I'd finished my deco before Pascal and Wiky, so I climbed on board trying to find out why Pipin didn't finish his decompression. To my surprise Pipin wasn't there.

An expected guest who was running late had just arrived from the capital city of Santo Domingo. His name, Johnny Ventura, is quite prominent in the tropical music circles all over Latin American countries.

Mr. Ventura is a Merengue-music singer, the emblematic Dominican rhythm similar to salsa music but with a more intense percussion beating. Actually, its beat and tune is for Latin dancers as gratifying as Meringue Pie to a sweet tooth. Our friend and loyal helper, Eddie Matos, accompanied him, as he provided protection services to Mr. Ventura.

The musician needed security not because of his artistic achievements, but because he was a former Mayor of Santo Domingo. He was also aspiring, according to the local grapevine, to the presidency of the country and that made him a potential target for radicals and prospective political enemies.

I understood then the hurry Pipin had. He wanted to attend Mr. Ventura. When I got out of the water, Pipin had already left in Mr. Ventura's boat.

Something that got my attention, however, is that Audrey was left behind.

"How come you didn't go with them?"

"Pipin left me here," she said with a cheerless tone. *"You know how he gets with a celebrity around."*

"Yeah, I know," rolling my eyes up. *"But he didn't even finish his decompression."*

"He always does that," she affirmed not too concerned.

"But it's still surprising, anyway, that he left you behind. He's not leaving you alone for a minute and aside from the training dives and eating, we don't get to see you at all."

"That's because Pipin is not letting me out of the room."

"I figured that much, but why is that? I don't get it."

"I don't know . . . He keeps saying that he doesn't want for me to be distracted."

"That's bullshit, Audrey. I'll talk to him."

"No, please," she tensely implored while closing her fist around my wrist. *"Don't talk to him, Carlos; just leave it as it is."*

Then she said that she had preferred to stay behind waiting for us to make sure we were all fine. That didn't make much sense since we were already decompressing safely and Tata, Bill and Matt were checking on us. Yet, Audrey's preference to remain behind to support us didn't surprise me; after all, before switching to freediving, she originally was as a scuba diver. She was well aware of the potential consequences our extreme dives could bring.

"And why did they leave?" I asked Audrey.

"Pipin invited Johnny Ventura for lunch and the restaurant is almost closing."

We were, indeed, running out of time for lunch, but Pascal and Wiky made it out of the water just in time. Pressured by us, the boat captain pushed the throttle all the way and just like an amphibian troop carrier on the beaches of Normandy in 1944, he ended up *landing* the small fiberglass vessel over the sand.

Resembling soldiers invading the seashore, we stormed our way through the resort. Our mission was to enter the diner before closing; otherwise, we would have to wait until dinner time and that wouldn't be good. If there is something diving does, is make you hungry. But mission accomplished; we entered the restaurant only one minute before closing.

Mr. Ventura, Pipin and Eddie were seated on one table for four, but when Eddie looked at us, he got the help of two waiters right away and added three more tables in a row to accommodate the rest of us. Audrey, Matt, Angelo, Pascal, Wiky, Tata, Bill and I joined them.

After the formal introductions, I got intrigued after seeing Audrey seating across the table, away from Pipin. That was a subtle sign of insurrection not common on her. Normally, she would seat next to him. Pipin, meanwhile, ignored Audrey and kept entertaining Johnny Ventura.

The meal was enjoyable and satisfied our after-diving enlarged appetite, but as we all kept our mouths busy, Angelo put his energetic tongue to work. He was visibly excited by the presence of the illustrious singer, and as an immediate effect, he turned on his vocal radio and kept on talking . . . and talking . . . and talking.

Pipin's frustration was becoming palpable. The rest of the team perceived that something was about to happen. But things turned from bad to worse when Angelo began to praise Audrey's recent performance. Being the novice of the team, Angelo wasn't aware of something the rest of us would avoid; to admire another athlete's accomplishments in front of Pipin, including his wife's.

Raising his cup, Angelo invited to cheer for the now unofficial deepest freediver in the planet,

"Let's have a toast . . . to the deepest woman in the world; even deeper than men. A true champion!"

Everyone joined the toast, but as Angelo continued praising Audrey, I saw Pipin's face changing from composed to fury in a blink of an eye. I looked at Wiky, then Tata, and they both raised their eyebrows realizing what was going on. They both have been with Pipin since his beginnings in Cuba. They knew Pipin's jealousy and temper, but they also agreed that it had been getting worse, lately.

A persistent Angelo kept adding high-octane fuel to the fire,

"Hey, Pipin, how does it feel to have your record shattered by your own wife, ah?"

And that was the last straw. With fire spitting from his eyes, Pipin yelled,
"Angelo, turn-off the radio y para de hablar mierda, RIGHT NOW!"

Angelo, shocked and embarrassed, remained with his cup raised for few seconds. He looked at Pipin, astonished, sat down and said no more.

Pipin must have been really upset to burst like that in front of Johnny Ventura. He would explode like Chinese fireworks in front of the staff, but never in front of someone he's trying to impress.

Yet Angelo was right, Audrey was now a deeper breath-hold diver than Pipin, but all he did, in spite of his good intentions, was to rub it on Pipin's face. Although Pipin was coaching Audrey, he never expected the river flow of attention she was gathering, and that exceeded the limited capacity his pride could handle.

For the next few days, many people would make comments to Pipin or joke in a similar fashion. And like Angelo, no one intended to diminish Pipin's realizations as a freediver.

Involuntarily, I also contributed a bit by hurting Pipin's wounded pride. Just before arriving to The Dominican Republic, I had published a glossy magazine, *FreediverPro*, as an *IAFD* sponsored publication. The magazine became an instant success and the words of praise came as a river flow towards me. I was not only the editor of it, but the writer of most of its articles.

Pipin's participation in the creation of the publication was null, and even the one article signed under his name was written by me. Audrey, meanwhile, not only supported me but wrote a couple of articles. The entire project was created by me with the aid of Carolina, our creative wizard who formatted the entire magazine and Barbara, my personal assistant who collected a large portfolio of advertising clients.

Along with the publication, I had also shaped the idea of creating our own line of freediving equipment under the same name, *FreediverPro*, and that's the only aspect of the project Pipin was inclined to help me with.

As challenging as the creation of the magazine was, most of my troubles orbited around maintaining Pipin's ego under control. While I was looking to expand and secure our business' success, he kept diminishing my efforts based on a simple premise; these projects were not his creation and they furnished too much attention towards me.

THE LAST ATTEMPT

I was very proud of this achievement

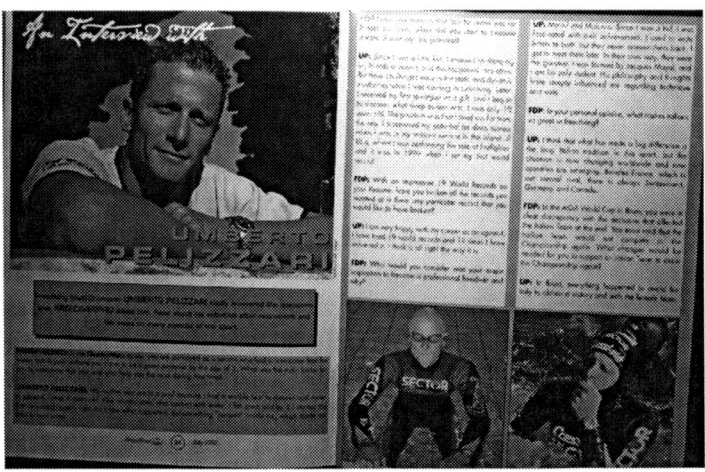

I even obtained an interview with Pipin's most reviled rival, Umberto Pelizzari.
But my partner evaded this project from the beginning.

So between the praise I received for the magazine and as the admiration for Audrey continued, along with the jokes, they kept pushing two wrong buttons; Pipin's branded machismo and his now unrestrained ego. That's when things started to spin out of control.

Chapter 5

COUNTDOWN GOES ON; MINUS ONE-WEEK

SATURDAY, OCTOBER 05, 2002

Exactly one week before the event, the crew had the day off. Some of them decided to visit nearby towns while the rest decided to relax by the pool; one of three pools, actually. A splash in fresh water was a tantalizing idea, especially since the heat index was in the *Gatorade-won't-do-anymore* zone. But Pipin and I were heading to the neighboring Bayahibe Bay to check on a catamaran for the event.

We were looking to rent a double hull vessel for added stability and someone had recommended one in particular, but the owner wanted so much money for a couple of days' rent that I proposed a longer lease to smuggle Haitians to Miami to collect enough money to pay him. The owner, who gave me the impression of being the result of a genetic experiment gone wrong, looked at me with a frown accentuated by his prune-like wrinkles,

"I thought we were having a serious business arrangement, young man," the senior chap said with a solemn *Darth Vader* tone of voice.

"So did I, boss. But when you threw that price I said to myself; this gentleman has a great sense of humor, because he must be kidding."

Pipin was inspecting the boat when I had the exchange of opinion with Mr. Bloodsucker, but he later got the quote from the owner. The visit came to an abrupt end. Afterward, I even joked with Pipin,

"You should have raised your hands, it was a robbery."

Pipin even managed to smile and then added, *"What is he, crazy? We are not looking to buy the whole boat."*

Actually, even one dollar was a dollar too many for Pipin. He wanted the boat for free in exchange for the publicity we would provide through the Internet and the international press. It was, indeed, a reasonable proposition. Those catamarans are used for tours, and they advertise in local newspapers and travel magazines to attract tourists. They have websites and booking programs in connection with travel agencies and hotels, so they spend a small fortune in promotion.

On the other hand, Audrey's event was being followed in Europe through our website, and Europeans were their main market. In addition, local TV Networks, *Televisa* from Mexico, and other international media were covering the event, too. Besides, it was low season for them and the boats were mostly available. Pipin was right this time, we should get the boat for free, so we kept searching.

In the afternoon, Tata, Wiky, Angelo, Matt, Bill and Pascal, joined me for a refresher CPR (Cardio-Pulmonary Resuscitation) course. Although I'm a certified Medic First Aid and CPR instructor-trainer, I wasn't giving a formal course.

To practice, we used a CPR dummy provided by Laura, from the dive shop. After a demonstration from my part, each one of them proceeded with their individual practice. But despite the importance of the improvised training, jokes made the session quite enjoyable; especially when Pascal initiated his mouth-to-mouth practice with the mannequin,

"Hey, Pascal," asked Wiky, *"is that what you call a French kiss?"*

To which Tata added, *"Oye, Pascal, I don't think you're supposed to put your tongue inside its mouth."*

"I think I'm going to take her to my room," was Pascal's response, referring to the dummy which we named *"Cindy"*.

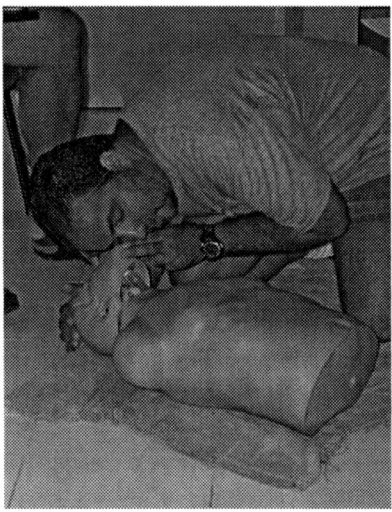

Credit: Angelo Cordero

Providing a CPR demonstration for the staff.

CARLOS SERRA

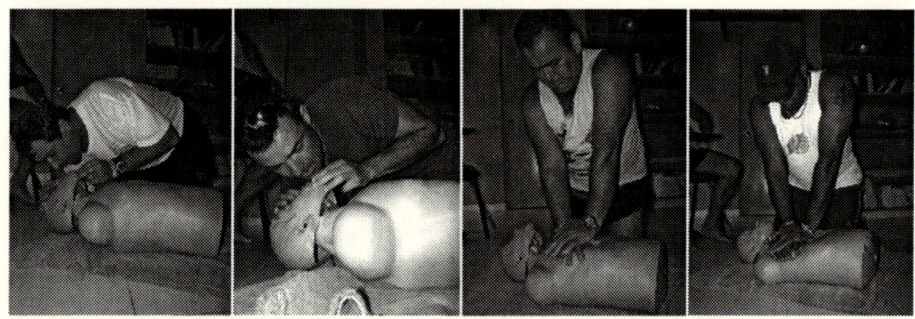

Credit: Carlos Serra

From left to right: Matt, Pascal, Wiky and Angelo

Besides covering the basics of CPR, I wanted to discuss some one-to-one essentials with Tata.

He was the official helper for Audrey on the surface, but had made some mistakes that could have caused serious injuries to Audrey, such as the day when Audrey hit the boat with her head.

Thanks to Tata the impact was reduced to just a light thump, saving her from a potentially devastating injury, but instead of immobilizing her, evaluating any possible neck or head injury, he lifted Audrey out of the water. Should Audrey had suffered an injury, Tata would have worsened it. He had the best intentions but not the best schooling.

That day, since I was working in the "medical area", I asked Pipin about the doctor for the event, to which he confirmed that Audrey's personal doctor would be there. I felt so relieved that even announced it later on the website report. I know how much Pipin dislikes doctors, so I was getting concerned about the possibility of not having one.

SUNDAY, OCTOBER 06, 2002

Another day off, yet we gathered for breakfast as usual at the *Dominicus Palace's* restaurant. While waiting for a Swiss cheese omelet with peppers, mushrooms and tomato being prepared by the chef at the buffet area, I saw Audrey coming out of the bathroom and heading my way.

Able to recognize her mood changes, Audrey's gloomy state became evident. I was adding an unhealthily delicious portion of hash browns and sausage to my omelet when she stood near me at the buffet table. While she prepared a sandwich, I decided to joke with her in an attempt to make her smile,

"Audrey, did you wash your hands or are you making a fish sandwich?"

Surprised by the unsophisticated nature of my comment she chuckled, but then a friendly recrimination followed.

"Carlos! That doesn't sound like you, at all."

THE LAST ATTEMPT

"I guess I'm letting Pipin influence my refinement."
Then she frowned and shook her head.
"Hey, but I made you smile, right? That's all I want."

She gave me another smile that lasted few seconds before it became a grimace. I did notice something odd and yet familiar in her reaction. Knowing her and Pipin, as well, I sensed something odd related to him or possibly linked to the upcoming excursion.

Laura, the manager of the hotel's dive center, had planned a day-off surprise; a trip to a nearby island, a paradisiacal place according to the brochure I've read.

"Are you two coming to Catalinita?" I asked Audrey.
"C'mon, Carlos, you know Pipin. He doesn't want to go," she said frustrated.
"Well, you come then," but that was a silly proposition from my part; Pipin never let Audrey go anywhere alone, as she immediately attested.

"If he didn't let me visit the Pyramids, you think he's going to let me go to that island?"

Audrey was referring to a trip to Egypt they had made few years back. The following story became an anecdote I had always used to tease Pipin every time he showed his disdainful nature.

Audrey, who was captivated by Egyptian mythology and history, had a nice view of the Pyramids from her hotel room in Cairo. To the western edge of Cairo and only 10 kilometers (6.2 miles) away from their hotel, is the most famous and the only surviving structure of the Seven Wonders of the ancient world; The Great Pyramid of Giza. Cairo also has one of the most outstanding museums in the world; Museum of Cairo.

Egypt is an incredible place to go, but when Audrey asked Pipin to visit the pyramids, his answer was a blunt,

"Who wants to see some old buildings full of dust and spider webs?"

Then Audrey asked to go by herself but he refused, vehemently. In consequence, Audrey never visited the Pyramids, the sphinx or the museum, even though she was a stone-throw away from any of those historical legacies.

The story would have been hard to believe if it wasn't that Pipin himself confirmed it. Besides, I have had a similar experience with his primitive side on another historical site. In our first trip to Hawaii in June of 2001, Pipin and I were invited by Michael Otsuji to visit Pearl Harbor. Audrey didn't come to Hawaii on this trip. Michael is a soft spoken and well-mannered native Hawaiian who had organized a freediving class for us, and knew of my interest for WWII history; therefore, visiting Pearl Harbor.

It took me a while to convince Pipin to go; he had planned to stay in his hotel room waiting for a female student with whom he was having a more in-depth instructor-to-student connection. Yet, he ended up coming, anyway. The student wouldn't arrive at the hotel until later that evening for her private lesson.

Upon arrival, and just after Michael had acquired the entry tickets, Pipin looked at a WWII-era submarine docked not far away from the ticket counters. Unexpectedly, his immediate words were,

"Well, we just looked at that old piece of shit over there; let's go back," referring to the rusty-looking submarine.

"What?" asked Michael astonished, "he wants to go back?"

"I'm afraid so, Michael," I said while staring at Pipin.

"But . . . we've just arrived."

"Well, when we have a chance, I'll tell you a story about Egypt, Pipin, Audrey and the Pyramids," I said, leaving Michael even more perplexed. Pipin gave a piercing glimpse.

With Pipin persisting, Michael drove him back to the hotel and promised to come back in the afternoon to pick me up, because I wasn't going back to the hotel. I wouldn't allow Pipin to stop me from visiting Pearl Harbor the same way he stopped Audrey from visiting the Pyramids. Eventually, it was Michael's lovely wife and his beautiful 5-year old daughter who picked me up late in the afternoon.

So Pipin not wanting to visit a paradisiacal island with sandy beaches, coconut trees, a soothing breeze, and the gracious company of the Cartoon Network—as I called the hilarious exchanges between Angelo, Tata and Wiky—was not a surprise. But it was quite unfair for Audrey to be dragged into Pipin's sordid world of disinterest. That's why I insisted,

"Let's go, Audrey. Leave Pipin here and let's go to Catalinita. You need a break."

"No, are you crazy? I can't do that."

"Audrey, Laura put this trip together to honor you. You should come."

"No, I can't. You want Pipin to kill me?"

"What are you talking about? It's a semi-deserted island with only coconut trees, a bunch of mosquitoes and few iguanas, and you'll be with us."

"Carlos, you have seen Pipin lately. He's worst than ever . . . I don't want to provoke him."

"Oh, c'mon, Audrey; let's stop this nonsense. I'll talk to him right now."

"No, no, no, Carlos, please don't do it," she pleaded while holding my arm. "It'll complicate things even more."

"Okay, Audrey, maybe you're right. I know how controlling he is. But you can't let him rule your life like a marionette. It's not healthy."

"I know, but he's acting crazy. I really don't want to provoke him," Audrey repeated lowering her head with a heartbreaking expression.

"Speaking of crazy, Pipin keeps on doing his decompressions by breathing from Pascal's oxygen tanks."

"You see? That's crazy. He knows that he is oxygen intolerant. Why is he doing that?"

"I don't know, Audrey. But I'll keep monitoring him, because one of these days he's going to convulse as if he had a high tension wire shoved up his . . ."

"Hey!" she stopped me.

"Audrey, what is it with you and bad words?"

"It's not the cussing. Is that you only use foul language when you're mad. Please, don't be mad. I need you to be rational."

"Okay, shoved up you know where; that spot where the sun never shines. That's what I was going to say."

"No, you were going to say something else, dummy."

After an abundant breakfast, we departed. Tata, Wiky, Angelo, Matt, Bill, Laura, Jen (Laura's boyfriend) and I headed to Catalinita. It was a thirty-five minute ride over smooth waters, but only few minutes into, Wiky and Tata started to make jokes to one another.

Credit: Carlos Serra

A group picture taken in a deserted island. From left to right: Matt, Wiky, Laura, Angelo, Tata and Bill.

Pipin's recent behavior had lessened the group's enthusiasm for jokes and improvised comedy, but since Pipin remained at the hotel, the group was having a well-deserved good time. The Cartoon Network was in action, once again. We concluded the trip with a horseback ride at sunset, along the beach. Audrey missed a magnificent day as we, most certainly, missed her. She would have enjoyed it greatly.

CARLOS SERRA

Credit: Angelo Cordero

While we were enjoying a delightful and mostly needed stress-free day, Audrey was kept in her room.

MONDAY, OCTOBER 07, 2002

No training dives for Audrey this day, either. And as it had become regular, she returned to her room after breakfast.
"Why is Pipin keeping her inside the room like a prisoner?" Wiky asked me.
"I don't know, Wiky."
"Hmm, there is something happening," he concluded.

The crew immediately went to the dive shop and spent most of the time working on last minute details, including, beautifying the sled by removing the old stickers and replacing them with new ones. The stickers had been sent by the sponsors for promotion.

Later, Pipin and Tata installed the video and lighting system with Matt's assistance. The system was attached to the bottom of the sled to videotape Audrey's descent. I kept taking pictures of the assembling process for the website report.

The main concern was the battery pack since we weren't sure if it would resist the crushing depth. This record would be the deepest ever made and the battery pack had never been tested to such depths.

But what it seemed to be another inconsequential and peaceful day, rapidly materialized into another one of Pipin's outbursts. Only this time, it was Bill Stromberg on the receiving end. Bill was also taking pictures to preserve a visual testimony of the event and post them in his personal album. Pipin, however, perceived Bill's personal photo session as "Industrial Espionage".

"What's going on with that come-pinga taking pictures of the sled?" Pipin asked me quietly but visibly exasperated.

"What do you mean? He's only taking pictures for his personal memoirs, I guess."

"No, I know he's taking pictures to copy the sled."

"Why would he do that?"

"Because he has never tried a No-Limits world record, but he wants to try it in the future and take my record."

Perhaps Pipin was right, but I doubted it. First, the sled is quite simple in design and doesn't take much to copy it. Second, the sled was accessible any time of the day without Pipin or any of us around, so why would Bill execute his "evil plan" in front of Pipin? Third and final, there are many videos in the market and pictures on the Internet showing the sled in great detail.

Even so, Pipin was attentive to Bill's alleged intentions and didn't like it. But a moment later, Bill, not satisfied with just taking pictures, started to ask specific and very technical questions about the sled. His gathering was going now beyond the visual documentation. For Pipin, Bill's direct approach was more than his short fuse was willing to accept,

"What the fuck are you doing? You think I don't know what you are trying to do? You think I'm an idiot?"

"What?" Bill asked visibly stunned.

"You're trying to copy the sled so that you can try to break my record."

"But . . . I'm . . . I'm just . . ." Bill tottered.

"Get this fucker out of here!"

With Pipin blowing fumes at Bill, I intervened as a mediator. I called Bill apart to explain why Pipin was so agitated. Bill, on the other hand, seemed genuinely surprised. He just wanted to take pictures, he insisted, and his questioning was a mere curiosity.

As I continued to perform my self-assigned duty as an *U.N. Blue Helmet*, the crew continued to assemble the sled. For a selfish but natural reason, they seemed amused. Pipin had discharged his anger on someone else outside the team this time. It's not that they were mean, but as the old American proverb says; *"Folks like the truth that hits their neighbor."*

In the afternoon, Pipin and Audrey went to the resort's gym. The gym visit had become customary. Every afternoon they would go to workout and Audrey seemed to enjoy it. Besides eating or training, that was her only way out of the confinement of her room.

I, on the contrary, wasn't too crazy about it. The stench of sweat inside the gym was unbearable, not to mention that at times I could smell the sweatiness emanating from unmentionable parts of the body. But at least the egotistical stand of the gym-freaks, infatuated with their reflection while exercising in front of the wall-wide mirror, was amusing.

"Hey, Audrey," I whispered while she stretched over a rubber mat. "Look at that couple doing the steps in front of the mirror."

"What is it with them?" she asked curiously.

"They are madly in love."

"And how would you know that? They may not even be together."

"Ah, but they are not in love with each other. They're in love with themselves."

Chuckling, she replied, "Oye, leave them alone. Why don't you do some exercising?"

"Oh, no, thanks. I do enough exercising by keeping people safe from Pipin."

"Oh, yeah, I've heard about what happened with Bill."

"You see? That was my workout of the day. Besides, none of these machines work."

"What do you mean?"

"Look that couple on the steps. They are climbing nowhere. And what do you call that machine over there?"

"That's a treadmill?"

"Well, that's a walking machine, but that lady on top keeps on walking and she's not moving forward."

With Audrey smiling while opening a bottle of water, I turned to a European-looking, fit lady in her early thirties, who based on her smile, had been listening to my conversation with Audrey.

"And I have news for you, lady. That bicycle is broken. You've been pedaling for the last ten minutes and you haven't moved at all."

Audrey almost choked with a sip of water and ended up spitting it on the mat. The European lady laughed, and with a distinctive British accent, she responded,

"Thank you for the advice, handsome. But I'll keep trying, if you don't mind."

"It's okay, keep trying. But you may want to put some wheels on it first."

Then I immediately turned back to Audrey to whisper,

"Did she call me handsome?"

"I think she did."

"She must be blind as a bat in a London fog."

Laughing along with the truly handsome British lady, Audrey hit me in the arm, instigating me to, "Stop it, Carlos, please. I have to workout."

That's when a grave voice came from across the gym, sucking the fun off the air. The voice reverberated as *Count Dracula* calling his bug-eater servant *Mister Renfield*.

"Carlos, come here." Pipin was seated down on a bench getting ready to pump some weights.

"Take few pictures of me for the report."

"What, you don't want pictures of Audrey?"

"No, Angelo and you have taken enough pictures of her already. Let's put some more pictures of me on the website."

"Pipin, do you realize that we have almost two hundred pictures of you in the website, already, and only about sixty of Audrey?"

"How do you know?"

"I counted them."

"Well, those are old pictures. We are going to change them."

At this point I knew that Pipin's self-absorbed side had surfaced, and some jealousy about Audrey being the center of attention continued to hurt his sense of self-importance. So I didn't say anything else. It would have been pointless.

Then he laid himself down on the bench, took the weighted bar and started to make faces as if he was lifting up the *Rock of Gibraltar*, but he had only twenty-five pounds on each side.

"Pipin, are you constipated or what?" I said jokingly. *"You only have fifty pounds there. Even my grandmother can lift that with one rheumatic hand."*

"Take a close-up only, Chico; it's for the website."

That's when I realized his intention. He was performing an act for the pictures; just like when he *"practices"* yoga. It's only a depiction, a pose. So, I took few pictures, including a couple of wide-angle shots showing the weights to compare them to his *"effort"*, just for my own amusement.

Credit: Carlos Serra

The effort doesn't measure up to the weight. Prolific when it comes to building an image, Pipin was just performing for the pictures.

Then I went back to Audrey. Pipin didn't like it but I couldn't care less. Her pictures should be the ones on the internet. She was doing the record, not him. Besides, Audrey had already told me about her frustration for Pipin's marked interest in announcing his upcoming record attempt when hers wasn't over yet. He wanted to announce his beating of Audrey's record; a record she hadn't done yet.

Later, Pipin and I met with the Resort's owner. The plan was to harmonize some details regarding a future plan to open the freediving operation at the Resort's location.

After the meeting, Pipin, Angelo and I went to Bayahibe Bay to check on another catamaran. The boat's name was *"Energy"*, a nicely maintained ship with capacity to accommodate our staff and the entire paraphernalia required.

The captain and crew were kind and willing to work with us in any possible way, and the cost was exactly what Pipin expected; zero. This vessel would be the one.

TUESDAY, OCTOBER 08, 2002

The team gathered in the back of the hotel's dive shop. The main objective was to link all the components needed for the sled to be ready. So far, Audrey had been using the sled without the lights or battery pack. The video-camera in its waterproof aluminum housing hadn't been used either. Pipin had the intention to attach to the housing, a pair of aluminum stabilizers shaped as wings.

The plan was to stop the sled from spinning on its axis while descending. Since I was the only one taking underwater pictures, I liked the idea. I had to position myself in a way in which I could take Audrey's front or her side. A picture of a frontal Audrey was by far better than a picture of her back. By having the sled descending in the same position without rotating, my job photographing Audrey underwater would be much easier. At this point a French photographer and reporter, Robert Margallan, had joined us.

To build the stabilizers from scratch, Wiky and Angelo went to the Resort's maintenance department once Pipin had finished giving them the specifications. In the meantime, Tata, Matt and I helped Pipin with the assembling of the lights, the battery pack and adding weights to the sled.

Later on, with everything affixed to the sled, Audrey came by. Incredibly, she had come out of her room by herself, because Pipin had been working with the rest of us for the last couple of hours. Actually, Pipin didn't look too happy to see her.

Before Pipin could say a word, I took the opportunity to capture some digital images of her observing the finished sled. Pipin, instead of greeting Audrey, walked away and got inside the dive shop.

While taking the pictures, I did notice Audrey a little depressed. I already knew of some of the troubles she was going through, so attempting to cheer her up, I approached her to joke around, as always.

"Now you have the video camera on the sled. It's been set in super-wide angle to get a shot of something other than your gigantic French nose."

"Hey, my nose is an asset, okay?"

THE LAST ATTEMPT

"Oh, yeah; you can smell Pipin from a mile away. That's probably how you found us here, ah?"

"Hmm . . ." grimacing, she mumbled.

"What is it . . . still struggling with him?"

"I just can't stand his attitude lately. I'm tired of it."

"Yeah, I've noticed how he's gotten green with envy ever since you did one hundred and sixty-six meters."

"Yes, I know. But why would he train me, then?"

"Audrey, remember, the initial idea was for you to break the female record; not his."

"It's true, but it's him who's sending me deeper and deeper . . . He wants me to do one hundred and seventy meters tomorrow. And for Saturday, who knows?"

"Wait! You'll do one hundred and seventy meters?"

"Yeah, that's what he said I'll do tomorrow."

"There is no doubt for me now. He's using you as a guinea pig for his new training method. You should know that. He hasn't done well lately, and before he attempts his overly announced two hundred meter dive, he wants to try with you first."

"Yeah, I've been wondering about that. But then . . . why is he getting mad if I do it?"

"Well, think about it. He hasn't done any solo-record since Cozumel in the year two thousand, and he suffered a blackout there, right?"

"Right"

"In La Palma, another blackout during training and canceled his attempt, so you had to do it instead, right?"

"Okay?"

"Before Cozumel, he had a blackout in Aruba, as well. And before Aruba, an even worse situation in Cayman Islands where he almost died, correct?

"Yeah, okay, but what's your point?"

"Don't you see all the improvements in the sled, the new cable, stabilizers now, and the new training program? And he's announcing his two hundred meter dive. But who's testing all that before he tries such an extreme dive? Just you, Audrey; it's only you."

"But I don't understand; in one hand he wants me to try the new stuff by going deeper, but on the other he gets mad if I succeed?"

"I know it sounds paradoxical, but that's exactly the problem; he's having a predicament."

"How is that?"

"He wants for you to attest that his improvements work, but at the same time his ego is suffering tremendously because you're doing better than he ever will."

"Carlos, I know Pipin has always been egocentric, but now it's too much. Why is that?"

"The problem is all the people praising and admiring you in front of him. Particularly when someone says . . . 'How does it feel to be second to your wife?' or 'Hey, Pipin, your wife is better than you man, are you retiring now?'... That's a hard situation for his ego to handle."

"Hmm," she mumbled.

"Look at it this way. You are in the dawn of your career, while he's on the sunset of his. He's yesterday's newspaper and people keep bringing that up."

Audrey nodded and then added, *"Can't they see how Pipin reacts? They should stop,"* she said irritated. *"What can I do now? Because, Pipin is taking it on me,"* she pleaded. Audrey seemed completely lost at this point.

"Not much, I'm afraid, Audrey... Just hang in there until this is over. It'll be over soon. Then he'll become the nicer guy we all prefer to deal with."

Audrey sighed while staring dead ahead.

"What is it, Audrey? Still not convinced?"

"No, it's just that..." she hesitated. *"Well, I agree; he's better when we don't have these events happening. But there are many things that I can't deal with anymore."*

"Like what? His witchcraft stuff, perhaps?"

"That's one of them. But there is also his cheating and the way he treats me in private. He calls me names, says that I'm ugly, or that I'm fat, or that he'll find someone younger because I'm getting old..." then she looked up to the sky as in search of a heavenly answer.

"Yeah, I was there in one occasion, remember? But, hey, you just turned twenty-eight and he's already... what, beyond forty?"

She assented with her head and gave me a glimpse that lasted only few seconds. Then she stared down, scraping the grass with her sandal.

Looking to distract her mind, I came up with something silly, *"Hey, are you looking for worms?"* But this time, she wasn't in a mood for silly remarks.

"I wish I could dig a hole and bury myself in it. I want to disappear."

"C'mon, Audrey," I said in a futile attempt to lift her spirit. *"The problem is Pipin, not you. His best years are behind him; yours are still ahead and that's his problem."*

"But what can I do to keep going?"

"The only thing you can try is to reassure his self-esteem. Remember, Pipin has two sides; the ordinary man we know and love and the egotistical monster we all hate, but the last one is the only one we are seeing lately."

"I wish I wasn't doing this record. I should have listened to my dad. He didn't want for me to do it."

"Yeah, you told me about how mad he got with you over the phone."

At that point Audrey's eyes became glassy with tears ready to flow down her face. I felt like placing my arm around her in support, but Pipin was nearby and that could have caused a delicate situation. I felt helpless, and her glassy eyes became contagious.

Later that afternoon, Pipin, with the help of Wiky, Angelo and Matt reassembled the sled back in the boat for Audrey's next training dive. They received a helpful hand from two of *Viva Diving* boat captains. They were locals and with an excellent sense of

THE LAST ATTEMPT

humor. Ignoring Pipin's grumpiness, Wiky and I enjoyed an unrehearsed exchange of comedy with them.

Tata stayed in his room recovering from some stomach problems. Meanwhile, Pascal was getting his equipment ready for his deep dive to 170 meters. Audrey was right; that's the depth Pipin announced for her next practice dive.

"Pipin, when are you going to stop?" I asked.

"She can do it," he said stubbornly.

"But we came here to break Tanya's record of one hundred and sixty meters. Audrey already did one hundred and sixty-six meters. Isn't that enough?"

"No, we are going to set the record so that that bitch will never try to break Audrey's record again."

Streeter is a blonde and slim native of the Cayman Islands and Audrey's toughest competitor in the *No-Limits* category. Her general looks is attractive, but what is really distinguishing in her physical attributes is her ample forehead. I used to make jokes with Audrey regarding Streeter's generous forehead and Audrey's elongated nose. Once, I even made a cartoon of what a clone of the two of them would look like, and even though Audrey wasn't good-humored when Tanya Streeter's name was mentioned around her, when I showed Audrey the cartoon, she laughed unstoppably.

Streeter had set the record in August 17, 2002. At the time, Pipin had made plans for three world record attempts for December 2002; a female *No-Limits* attempt for Audrey; a male *No-Limits* attempt for him, and a Mix Tandem record attempt for both. But due to Tanya Streeter's record, Pipin moved Audrey's attempt to October 2002. That was less than two months after Tanya Streeter's record and two months earlier than planned.

In consequence, it became a real headache in terms of arrangements and coordination. With only two months to prepare, getting sponsors, find the location, concur with the hotel, obtain the airline tickets, gather the support staff, and collecting the necessary funds, putting the event together was a challenge. It was an unnecessary rush, but it was Pipin's bullet-train in motion.

With Pipin now taking Audrey back to their room, I was left behind on the beach very concerned. But I was not the only one.

"*Oye, Pipin esta loco?*" That was Wiky, showing over his complexity the signs of what a tropical sun can do to the skin if left unprotected. He looked like a main dish at the local *Red Lobster*.

"He's going to send Audrey to one hundred and seventy meters? He's trying to kill my niece!"

Audrey wasn't his niece, but it was a reflection of his fondness for her.

"Carlos, you must stop him," Wiky insisted.

Next to Wiky were Tata and Angelo, but neither one of them made a comment.

"How can I stop him, Wiky? No one can."

"Hey, he listens to you. You are the only one he has ever listened to."

"He listens to nobody, Wiky."

"Carlos, I've known Pipin for fourteen years and you're the only person who has ever been able to bring some sense into his nonsense. Believe me."

"Maybe in the past, but I have been arguing with him too much lately. He's out of control, I'm afraid."

"But, papito, what are we going to do, then?"

"I don't know, Wiky. I honestly don't know."

Later, I coordinated with Laura an additional boat for the press; journalists from Italy, France and Mexico would accompany us the following day.

IN THE EVENING OF THAT DAY
7:00 P.M.

The staff gathered at the *Viva Dominicus Palace's* pool. We all sat around one of the pool tables and next to the bar. In addition to our regular staff, we also had members of the international press who had come to cover the event. Audrey sat down next to Pipin staring at the table and seemingly disheartened. Not looking particularly happy, either, Pipin provided the briefing for the next day's activities.

The briefing was, as always, Pipin style. It lacked of essential components to inform the staff of what to do and how to do it. In addition, the tone employed by Pipin was harsh and quite thoughtless, particularly with Wiky and Tata. They had made some inconsequential mistakes during the day while assembling the sled, but Pipin verbally smashed them like hot potatoes in front of everyone. Wiky reacted, and even quarreled back, but Tata didn't; no surprise there.

After the briefing, while crossing the wooden bridge over the flamingos-inhabited lagoon and heading to the restaurant, I told Pipin that he was quite rough with Tata and Wiky. That I openly disagreed with the terms he used like, *"sin cerebro"* and *"bobos".*

"To call your most loyal helpers brainless and dumb was inconsiderate and hurtful."

"What's more," I added. *"It was inappropriate to shatter them in front of everyone; the rest of the team and the guests, when in any case you should have reprimanded them privately."*

"I only wanted to remind them on who's the one in command. If they fear you, they listen and work harder."

But something that Pipin never understood is that intimidation doesn't make people work harder. I even reminded him about "positive reinforcement", something I had already explained to him many times before.

"C'mon, Carlos, that gringo shit doesn't work with Cubans," he said. "Look how Fidel has everyone in Cuba walking in a straight line."

"Well, just remember that I'm not Cuban, because if you ever try that 'Cuban shit' with me, I'll kick your ass so hard that you'll land in Havana next to your uncle Fidel," I said with a mixture of joking and yet serious tone.

THE LAST ATTEMPT

"You don't have to worry about that, you are not an idiot. Unlike Tata and Wiky, you have a brain."

This last comment left a bitter sensation in my *"brain"*. Tata and Wiky may not be Harvard graduates, but Pipin's education would surprise me if it ever made it beyond elementary school. Still, that doesn't make any of them brainless.

In fact, when it comes to ingenuity to fix mechanical problems they are extremely smart. Especially Wiky, whose dexterity to fix a marine diesel engine with a hammer and a roll of duct tape, reminds me of *McGuiver*, from the famous TV Show where the protagonist could build a machine gun with a pipe, a can of sardines and firecrackers.

Anyhow, they both had offered friendship and loyalty to Pipin since his beginnings as a professional freediver back in Cuba, thus they deserved some deference. That night, after this latest conversation with Pipin, I wrote for the Internet report the following,

"By the way, Audrey would like to send her word of appreciation to all the kind people who sent congrats messages through the IAFD's forum after her 166 meters training dive. And, on behalf of the staff, I would like to thank also those who sent their word of appreciation and concern for them. Without the athlete(s) there would be no event, but without the team to support the athlete(s) there would be no event, either. Like most things in life, it's teamwork. I'll pass your word along, that's fuel for the soul."

The truth is that no one had sent congratulations to the team. I just knew that Pipin would have Audrey read the report to him. So I used the report to send subliminal messages to Pipin attempting to induce a change in his attitude. Sometimes it worked, sometimes it didn't, and sporadically he would get irritated but discharge it with Tata, Wiky or Audrey; maybe with all three of them, at the same time.

WEDNESDAY, OCTOBER 09, 2002

We had a mixture of excitement and concern at the same time. Audrey was going to attempt 170 meters. No one had ever gone to such depth before, man or woman; not while holding their breath, that is. But after Audrey's great performance to 166 meters, and although Pipin was pushing it, we were all more confident.

Pipin had shown some reservations about the integrity of the battery pack that goes in the sled. The batteries provided energy for the two powerful lights needed to videotape in the darkness of the abyss. These two lights would be placed in the sled, side by side, with the camera located in front of Audrey at her knee level and pointing upward.

Before we boarded the boat, Pipin tested the housing and it was leaking water through a missing part. The housing would be used, anyway, to test the new "wings" attached to it as stabilizers for the sled, but no camera inside, of course. Wiky would fix the housing the next day even though he didn't have spare parts for it, but with his *McGuiver* skills, he should unearth some magic solution.

With everyone on board and before departing to the training spot, I've noticed how Pipin, once again, had left the ladder on the beach. Only this time I was expecting the action. So I took the ladder and brought it on board. Pipin, visibly upset, insisted on living it behind due to lack of space in the boat, but that's when I replied back,

"No, look here, it fits perfectly and it's out of the way."

I placed the ladder where it normally goes; in the stern/starboard side. Then I looked straight to his eyes,

"The ladder stays on board."

Pipin did not respond, at least not verbally, but reacted with a frown, biting the tip of his tongue and rubbing his shiny top.

For Audrey's dive, Pipin, Pascal, Wiky and I were the safety divers in scuba. In the surface as freedivers, Tata, Matt and Bill looked after Audrey. Yeah, now Bill was being allowed to perform such duty, and he was not only excited for the opportunity to participate but quite cooperative.

As a world-class freediver, plus the lack of support divers we had, not using Bill was a waste of resources, as I had addressed it to Pipin before. But as a key member of a rival organization, Pipin saw in Bill an intruder, a person to keep at distance to avoid the possibility of him *stealing* credit from an event that had to be 100% *IAFD*.

Now that Bill was permitted to play a part, he not only executed his duties diligently, but kept a lower profile; especially after his last encounter with Pipin. He learned his lesson, I guessed. And at least in that regard, that was one aspect for which I didn't have to worry any longer; finding Pipin strangling Bill in some dark corner of the resort, allegorically speaking, that is.

But many other aspects remained, keeping my stress level high, like Audrey's personal struggle, for example; because from this point on, her mood went from rolling down a hill to plummeting down a sharp ledged sea-cliff, and only the raging waves of a stormy ocean, breaking violently against the end of the precipice awaited for her, as I would, soon enough, find out.

Chapter 6

A Record-Setting Dive

WEDNESDAY, OCTOBER 9, 2002
MORNING HOURS

The ambiance was tense. No one talked. All the talking had been done by Pipin back on shore before departing to the training site. No one joked around. When the boat arrived to the dive site and the captain turned the engine off, the silence was nearly absolute. Only the ripples of water splashing on the side of the vessel, and the sporadic banging of scuba tanks swinging against each other with the rocking of the boat, could be heard. Everyone was focused on their specific duties.

Credit: Carlos Serra

Although he even admits his planning skills are not the greatest, Pipin must always be in command. Here he gives instructions to the team. From left to right: Tata, Wiky, Pipin, Bill, Matt, Angelo behind Matt and Robert Margallan.

This time we had an additional boat in case of an emergency requiring fast evacuation shall arise. Angelo was on board that second boat with his camera clicking.

On board our vessel, Pascal and Wiky—just like me—were assembling their respective scuba units. Matt and Bill were doing the same with their light gear, consisting of a wetsuit, a weight belt, masks and fins, only. They would linger at the surface as safety freedivers, the most important of all. If anything should happened it would be there, where the air meets the water.

A slim possibility, but a possibility, nevertheless, is for something to happen all the way down, but Pascal, one of the most prolific deep-divers in the world, had the end of the line covered and with redundancy of equipment.

Tata, as always, was assisting Pipin transferring compressed air from a standard 80 cubic-feet scuba cylinder into the pony-tank attached to the sled. Although the pony-tank had less than half the capacity of a standard cylinder, it was more than enough to fill the lift bag and rocket Audrey back to the surface, back to air, back to safety.

Except for the ladder issue, the uneasiness wasn't caused by Pipin, at least not directly. It was the extreme dive that Audrey was about to perform what kept us on the edge. But it was Pipin, nevertheless, who set the depth to such extreme.

While Audrey climbed on the sled, I noticed her sobbing quietly but I didn't know why. But whatever it was, it's something that made Wiky roar back from the boat at Pipin who was in the water.

"Why you have to put that kind of pressure on her? Give the poor girl some peace, chico!" But Pipin ignored Wiky.

Credit: Carlos Serra

Audrey, visibly depressed, climbs on the sled while Wiky recriminates Pipin, whose shaved head can be seen slightly above the water. *". . . Give the poor girl some peace, chico!"*

THE LAST ATTEMPT

The stress level was high, anyway. A plunge to 170 meters (557.7 feet) while holding your breath is not an easy task; otherwise, many others would have done it by now. After all, who in his—or her—right state of mind would ride a home-made aluminum frame to the bone-chilling darkness of the bottom of the ocean? That's a 340 meters ride (1,115.4 feet) if you consider that, with any luck, it's a two-way ride. There was only one person brave enough; one person with the guts and willingness to try it, but with his wife as the test subject.

Pipin kissed Audrey. It was part of his ceremonial gestures. He'll do it whether he's mad or not and had given instructions for pictures to be taken at that moment for the internet.

Tata gave her the 5-minute countdown, and by minus two-minutes we, the scuba divers, were all underwater. I positioned myself in about thirty-five meters to take pictures. The visibility was crystal clear, so I went deeper than usual. With the sunrays penetrating that far down, there was enough light for the pictures. But I had also planned, however, for the photos to come out a bit darker this time to convey a sense of depth.

Below me was Pipin, who had barely talked during the last minutes before submerging. Wiky was few more meters below him and Pascal at the maximum depth. We couldn't see him, he was too deep. We knew he was okay by observing the sets of bubbles emanating from his regulator, coming up and passing by us. Each set reflected Pascal's exhalation pattern, and the greater the distance between sets, the more relaxed he was breathing. At least that was my own unorthodox way to determine if Pascal was alright.

Even though I was keeping an eye on his bubbles, there is nothing any of us could have done to rescue him if anything should go wrong. Pascal was on his own. Normally, Pascal would bring his dive-buddy, Cedric, but he had died about few months ago while diving with Pascal on some deep-water caves.

When the countdown came to an end, Audrey took her last and deeper breath while Tata pulled the cord to disconnect the sled. Audrey was on her way to become, unofficially and for a second time within a week, the deepest freediver in the world.

When Audrey passed by me, she seemed in perfect shape. Her position over the sled was correct. Her hands placement was also adequate. The left hand was up, holding the valve of the pony-tank located inside the lift bag. Her right arm was *hugging* the vertical tube of the sled as her right hand was pinching her nose, equalizing the increasing pressure over her ears.

CARLOS SERRA

Credit: Carlos Serra

October 9, 2002. In perfect position, Audrey is on her way to set the deepest mark for any person; male or female.

Once she passed me, I closed my hand around the cable to feel the vibrations caused by the friction of the sled against the line. I also kept observing my watch. Her timing was good. By the time she reached the target depth, which I felt thanks to the thump produced by the sled bumping at the end of the line, she still had enough time to finish the dive under three minutes. That's what we were all hoping for, because anything over three minutes exponentially increased her chances for a blackout.

As I felt the now stronger vibration in the cable, I knew she was coming fast. For my own safety, I pulled myself away and kept looking down. I was looking to position myself in the best possible way for the picture.

With incredible speed, Audrey passed only a couple of meters away from me seemingly conscious, but I did notice her body a bit contracted and her hands tightly grasping the frame that holds the lift bag. That's usually a sign of a freediver who is either not relaxed, or fighting the urge to breathe. She was likely to be on the edge of a blackout. So I ascended few meters to be sure.

THE LAST ATTEMPT

Credit: Carlos Serra

Audrey's legs show the tightening of her body. That's a sign of suffering. At 170 meters, she was reaching her limit.

Looking up, I saw Tata submerging to meet Audrey at about ten meters of depth. At the speed she was going, Tata would have to react with lightning speed and so he did. He grabbed Audrey, pulled her away from the lift bag, and assisted her to the surface.

Bill and Matt were next to her, as well. When she was vertically at the surface, on her own, moving her legs as a sign of consciousness, I went back down to check on Pipin, Wiky and Pascal. I met Pipin at about 60 meters while Wiky was only a couple of meters below him.

Surprisingly, Wiky was the first one to signal me asking for Audrey. I outstretched my index finger up to the surface and then made a *circle* by joining the tips of my index and thumb; the international sign for *okay*. A muted, *"Audrey is fine."*

I looked at Pipin; he looked back, and then kept on swimming up along the line. I remained down waiting for Wiky and observing Pascal's bubbles. The contiguous sets of bubbles were getting closer to each other, meaning that Pascal was breathing faster.

That's to be expected, in any case. Ascending from such depths is like fighting to get out of quicksand, sucking you back down the more you move. You are going against gravity, and adding air to the buoyancy compensator device doesn't help much. The pressure below one hundred meters is too much for the air to expand and provide you with enough buoyancy. So going down is easy. Surfacing, in contrast, entails an escalating effort.

When Wiky reached my depth, seemingly excited, he presented his hand up with a *Nazi* salute.

"What the . . ." I recall thinking.

Perhaps affected with certain level of nitrogen narcosis, it took me a couple of seconds to realize that he only wanted a high-five. He was happy. Wiky had been exceptionally concerned for Audrey's safety and with this dive in particular.

Audrey completed the dive in two minutes and fifty-five seconds. According to her simulated dives on land—a type of training consisting of holding her breath while exercising—anything under three and a half minutes was safe before reaching the inherently risky point of suffering a blackout.

Back at the surface, we were all celebrating in ecstasy. The dive was so fast that I was required to do a short decompression. Pipin, however, omitted his deco-stop and came all the way up. He was as cheerful as everyone else. I congratulated Audrey by shaking hands in the air and joking,

"This little girl has bigger cojones than me!" To which Pipin replied with a big smile and a surprising acknowledgement,

"She has bigger cojones than me, too."

Credit: Angelo Cordero

Pipin observes with happiness as I hold hands with Audrey, *"She has bigger cojones than me!"* I said, to which Pipin acknowledged, *"She has bigger cojones than me, too."*

Then he looked at her with fondness and pride reflected on his face and so did she, and that made me hopeful of a better frame of mind between them and among all of us.

But concerned about the rigidity of Audrey's body during the ascent, and as soon as I had a chance, I quietly asked Matt. He's a coach for the U.S. Freediving team for the world championship and trainer for world-record holders. So I trusted his judgment on determining if Audrey was on the edge of a blackout when she surfaced.

"She was conscious, but she wasn't perfect," he said.

"Was she cyanotic?"

"Her lips and fingernails were kind of bluish, yes."

"So she was suffering towards the end?"

With the confidence that only years of experience can provide, he concluded, *"No doubt!"*

At certain point, while we were all in the boat waiting for Pascal to complete his long decompression, we received the visit of an expected guest, Kim McCoy, a physical oceanographer from *Ocean Sensors*, who had finally arrived after a thirty-two hour trip.

Kim didn't arrive the day before as it was planned due to a heavy fog at his home's airport in San Diego, California. The reduced visibility kept the airport closed for many hours. When he got to us it was too late, Audrey had already done her dive, but amazingly, instead of getting to his room and rest, Kim took a boat to reach us.

His boat ride wasn't a total waste of time, though. He seized the opportunity to check the calibration of his *Ocean Sensors* computer, a highly sophisticated and multifunctional device that would be used mostly to determine Audrey's depth the day of the record attempt.

While preparing his computer for calibration, and after finding out that Audrey had just done 170 meters, Kim joked with her,

"Sorry, Audrey, but this has been calibrated to only two hundred meters." She smiled, but not for long. Her smile stopped once she saw the wicked look in Pipin's eyes.

"Hey, are you going to send me to the other side of the planet?" she immediately said in a somber tone.

"With that physical shape of yours, you can do two hundred meters tomorrow," Pipin replied.

Initially, I thought he was just kidding, but I would later realize how serious he was. He really wanted to keep pushing the limits for Audrey.

Once Kim finished hooking the device to the end of a line with Tata's help, Kim lowered the computer to an estimated ninety-five meters, along with a standard diving computer attached next to his device to compare readings afterward.

The computer was quite simplistic in appearance, a just about two-feet long piece of transparent acrylic tube and about four inches in diameter. But inside were enough electronic components to build a laptop computer from scratch.

In the top end there was a piece of rubber that looked like an oversized cell phone antenna. The simplicity of its appearance, however, concealed the intricacy of its internal computing capabilities. The device could provide in-depth analysis of the entire dive once the data was downloaded into a laptop Kim carried with him. Rate of descent and ascent with the precision of seconds and millimeters, were among its incredible features.

When Tata pulled back the ninety-five plus meters of line, he took the standard dive computer next to Kim's device, and with eyes wide-open, he exclaimed,

"It went to nine hundred and sixty-five meters!"

Angelo and Wiky also looked at it, and with surprise reflected in their expressions, they both confirmed Tata's reading. Kim, Audrey, Pipin and I looked at each other in absolute disbelief, so I took the computer and checked it out,

"Tata, it reads ninety six 'point' five meters (96.5) . . . not nine hundred and sixty-five."

At this point I was unable to keep a straight face and we all laughed continuously.

"Coño, Tata, tu si que eres bruto," said Pipin in plain Spanish, who apart from of his rude remark, was also laughing.

Then I translated the hilarious situation to Matt and Bill. Unable to understand a word of Spanish, they kept asking what was going on. Kim on the other hand, although he is American-born, he speaks few other languages, fluently; including Spanish.

While waiting for Pascal to finish his decompression, we all received an unhealthy amount of sunlight for which we surely would pay the consequences the next day. We waited for Pascal's for almost two hours, and the boat offered no shade. With the depth Pascal had reached, there was no alternative; it was an anticipated long deco.

But in spite of the long wait, the mood was unusually good, especially after another entertaining situation occurred once Pascal was on board. Tata, Wiky and Angelo were pulling the heavy decompression line when one of them inadvertently dropped, I hope, strident flatulence. It was so loud that I even joked with the captain,

"Did you just start the engine?"

"No, they did," the captain said while pointing toward the *Cartoon Network.*

Audrey couldn't contain her laughter; neither could Kim nor the captain. Pipin, however, bawled them out, while Tata, Wiky and Angelo, ignoring Pipin, continued to blame each other for the anal burp, originating further jokes.

"Wiky, you've been breathing too much compressed air," said Tata barely containing his laughter.

"Hey, papito, you've been living in Mexico too long, you're eating too many burritos with refried beans," replied Wiky.

"Hey, guys," I interrupted, *"denying a gas is like denying your own child because it comes from your own innards. Be brave and accept paternity."*

"Oye, Tata," teased Wiky, *"based on the stench I think your little one was born dead."*

While they kept, lightheartedly, blaming each other for the thunder, I did notice how the stress level we all had the day before was traded for a sense of relief and even ecstasy. Audrey's proven capabilities conveyed a sense of confidence upon us. And in the end, I don't know whose flatulence produced the roaring noise since nobody claimed fatherhood, but I'm not sure that kind of knowledge would be enlightening in any way.

THE LAST ATTEMPT

As Pipin had kept pushing Audrey to go deeper and deeper, I openly expressed my sentiments in that regard on the report. But at least now, with Audrey having achieved 170 meters, he should stop pushing . . . or so I thought. Pipin had, however, a different plan in mind.

Chapter 7

The Divorce Request

OCTOBER 9, 2002
EARLY AFTERNOON

Back on shore we all went to our respective rooms to shower. I had just finished bathing when Pipin knocked on my door to go for lunch, but curiously, Audrey was not with him. He insisted on going to a different restaurant from the usual; this one was located by the center pool at the *Dominicus*, not the *Palace*.

The rest of the staff met for lunch at the usual place, so we wouldn't eat with them. I guessed that Pipin just wanted to stay away from the staff after the flatulence of mysterious origin.

Once there and not too talkative, Pipin gathered his food at the buffet and went to a table away from most people. While getting food on my plate, I saw Audrey. She had just arrived by herself and walked straight to the buffet. I approached her and noticed right away her long face and glassy, reddish eyes. It was the day of a remarkable endeavor, the day she reached the deepest mark ever with a single breath, and she was cheerless.

"Audrey, are you okay?"

"No, Carlos, I'm not okay. I've just asked Pipin for a divorce. I can't stand him anymore!"

Her tone was somber, yet sturdy. Then she walked away carrying her food while evidently fighting to contain her tears.

"Oh, God, this is not good."

Asking him for divorce was an act of insurrection, especially since he had said many times, proudly, that no woman ever leaves him; he leaves them. Now Audrey had placed Pipin in a peculiar and unfamiliar position.

THE LAST ATTEMPT

When I got to the table they were seated with an empty chair in between. That was surprising, but after what she said, it kind of made sense.

Her consternation was evident but I also noticed something perhaps inconspicuous for someone who didn't know Audrey, but I knew her well. There was a subtle rebellion against Pipin's control. She had served in her plate the kind and quantity of food Pipin had denied her before.

For two full weeks we had all seen how Pipin decided Audrey's menu. Although she was the one who served the food, it was under Pipin's supervision. But for the first time she was, quietly but solidly, challenging Pipin.

To make matters even worse, Audrey stood up before finishing her meal or waiting for him; she just got up and left. Pretending not knowing what was troubling her, I asked Pipin,

"What's wrong with Audrey?"

After a brief pause, "*She's just under a lot of stress, you know, with the record and all,*" he said while looking disconcerted as Audrey marched away from the restaurant.

"*That's odd. She should be relaxed now that she made it to one hundred and seventy meters,*" I said in an attempt to get Pipin into talking about the divorce request, but Pipin did not respond. Instead, he buried his face in the plate. So I let it rest and didn't push the issue anymore; after all, they were a couple and the issue in question was very personal.

After lunch, Pipin and I went to Bayahibe Bay again to ultimate details on the boat for Saturday, the nice and ample catamaran named *Energy* that we had seen before. The plan was for the staff to assemble the entire paraphernalia on the vessel and have it ready for a preliminary test on Friday.

LATE AFTERNOON

Falling behind the western horizon, the sun layered the water surface with a golden mantle as sparkles of crimsons in the heavens faded away. We were enjoying one of God's most spectacular masterpieces, using the sky and the ocean as a canvas.

The entire staff plus some additional guests had congregated by the east-side pool wearing a smile in their faces. Most of the guys were in a good mood. In the morning, Audrey had completed an historical dive and they were all happy for being part of it. It was just a practice dive, but it was the deepest ever made, male or female, with a single breath.

Like Knights of King Arthur's court, we assembled around one of the round pool tables. The aristocracy of freediving on this side of the Atlantic was in session. Joining our regular staff were two Italians and one French reporter. With the bar next to us, and by being in a celebrating mind-frame, some people took advantage and ordered some drinks.

But to ruin the fun for everyone, Pipin made a comment that left most of us flabbergasted. Looking straight at me, he said in plain and loud Spanish,

"¡Oye, Carlos, si ella puede hacer esa mierda, yo puedo hacer doscientos cincuenta metros!" ("Listen, Carlos, if she can do that shit, I can do two hundred and fifty meters!")

Suddenly, a dull calm invaded the previously strident table. The group was comprised of mostly Spanish speaking people and they all understood perfectly what Pipin had just said. The English, Italian and French speaking group remained silent just wondering what Pipin had muttered that hushed everyone.

Audrey was seated over Pipin's right hand side. Next to her was Pascal; they were both speaking in their native language along with a French reporter seated to Pascal's right. They had also interrupted their chat. Audrey looked at me across the table and silently buried her face with a tear running down her cheek. Her long and straight hair covered her heartbreaking expression, but only to the sides.

It must have been excruciating to hear such words from the person that she, despite her intention to break up with, loved the most. But Pipin's words reflected, precisely, why she wanted to split.

Troubled by what I heard, and responding to days of frustration with Pipin's uncontrolled egotistical foolishness, I reacted almost immediately,

"I can't believe what you've just said. That shit, as you just call it, nobody else has done it before; not even you," I said irritably while pointing an index finger at him.

Unwillingly, I had just become part of the *crowd* that kept rubbing in his face that he was second to Audrey. I had just poked the monster that lives within. Even so, someone had to come forward; nobody else would have done it, not even Audrey. She was the target of such a disgraceful statement, but she just kept quiet. As for the rest of the team, they were normally passive to Pipin's outburst. Any confrontation would place the daring staff member in Pipin's target list to give the impertinent a hard time.

I don't reproach the docility of the group towards Pipin; I was as guilty as any of them for tolerating his barmy rule. He's a big guy who can be quite intimidating, even savage-like in his altercations, but periodically, he needed a reality check, only that I was the one constantly providing it.

Perhaps my position as a partner and close friend made me almost an equal before his eyes, because for him, the rest of the guys were just inferior beings, servants of his legend and protectors of his myth. Most of them were payless workers, a workforce of volunteers serving Pipin; the greatest freediver of all times. That's enough pay, he probably thought.

Few minutes later and with a much somber atmosphere, we departed to *"La Scala"* Restaurant, a fancier *a-la-carte* eatery than the usual buffet. The Mediterranean style decoration and superb food minimized the hassle of having to make reservations. Besides, Chiara, an Italian lady in charge of group coordination for the Resort, helped us with the reservations.

During dinner, the main topic of conversation was, for a change, freediving; particularly Pipin's previous records. Audrey and I had already commented on previous nights about the lack of a different subject, so I asked her,

"Audrey, if you have a gun, please show mercy and shoot me, because I can't stand this freediving talk, anymore."

With her face semi-buried in her plate, only her eyes rolled up to give me the piercing but introverted *Lady Diana's* glance. She smiled back timidly but didn't say a word. Her expression reflected the sadness of a very complicated existence. The physical separation between her chair and Pipin's, also reflected the emotional detachment. Like Pipin, she had ordered *Rotelle Pasta Al Pesto with Asparagus*, which she barely touched. Pipin, however, kept on talking with Bill, who was seated to his right side.

Credit: Carlos Serra

Due to her dimmed expression, I avoided taking a picture of her face, but Audrey's arm is visible as she barely touched her pasta. The separation with Pipin's chair is also evident.

Despite her achievements, Audrey had more reasons to be discontent than joyful. She had come to the Dominican Republic with a goal in mind, but after two weeks of intense work, and on the verge of completing her goal, she was miserable. Pipin was as careless about his marriage as an elephant inside a crystal shop, and like a shattered glass, her love for Pipin was irremediably broken.

My attempt to make her forget Pipin's most recent statement was fruitless. For the rest of the group, however, enjoyment was up again thanks to Bill Stromberg. Bill, finally changing the topic, commented that he had recently competed in the Scandinavian version of the TV Show called, *Fear Factor.*

In that show you have to do some awful and grotesque stuff to prevail over other competitors and get a cash prize. To win Bill had to, among other equally grotesque things, eat raw goat eyes straight from the animal's eye sockets. The optical nerves were hanging out, the capillary veins visible all around and the gooey ocular mass with a gelatinous bloody fluid still dripping from it, according to Bill's description.

Paul Kotik, a reporter from DeeperBlue.net, was stunned to hear that the equivalent to US$5,000 was the prize.

"Bill, I would have paid five thousand dollars for not having to eat those nauseating eyeballs," said Paul making everybody laugh.

Walking right outside of the diner with a general better mood, we all gathered by the restaurant's front plaza, ornamented with a complementing Mediterranean style. Eventually, one by one, the staff members and other guests retired to their rooms for a placid sleep. But for me, another disagreement would arrive before having that opportunity.

"Carlos, I will replace Pascal as the safety diver at the bottom," stated Pipin. *"I'll take his place."*

"What! Are you, out of your mind? That's not going to happen, no way!"

Pipin's abilities as scuba-diver are inversely proportional to his freediving skills. With a tank in his back he's simply appalling. In addition, I had seen him doing some rather fast bounce-diving during training, descending from the surface to sixty meters and surfacing at vertiginous speed for no apparent reason.

"Going to one hundred and seventy meters would be a total disaster," I insisted. *"You have neither the training nor the common sense for such dive. You would kill yourself."*

Audrey, who would normally keep quiet, this time openly sided with me and refused Pipin's proposition,

"We have the best one down there with Pascal; you cannot do that," she said with uncommon resolution.

"I will not support your dementia any longer," I said firmly. *"If you do that, I'm out of here and I really mean it!"*

"I've done deeper dives than that," Pipin claimed.

"Oh, my God," I jumped. *"You truly are a tireless creator of magic tales, ah? Tell me, when did you do that?"*

"I did some deep dives for the Italian Navy, years ago."

"Aha, and did you do that before or after you trained Jacques Cousteau as an entry-level diver?"

"I'm not kidding, Carlos."

"Neither am I, Pipin, because you're not going to replace Pascal, and that's final."

THE LAST ATTEMPT

Pipin caressed his shaved head in frustration, looked down, made his habitual grimace and reluctantly accepted not to be the safety diver at the end of the line. That was an incredibly stupid proposition, anyway, and I would have not accepted it in a hundred years. He doesn't realize it, but he is to technical diving, what the *Wright Brothers* would be to a *Boeing-747*.

Something in his gaze, however, made me wonder; it was the kind of expression he makes when he doesn't intend to comply, or when he has an alternative plan.

THURSDAY, OCTOBER 10, 2002
6:30 A.M.

I had just walked out to the room's balcony when I looked to the east to see the sun just timidly showing over the water, but it was hot and humid, already. The resort looked abandoned, everyone was asleep and so was I. Without my usual morning coffee I'm just a sleepwalker, numbed by the sedating arms of *Morpheus*.

It was an early start as I was one of the two only members of the team scheduled to work this day. I had to teach a freediving course while everyone was enjoying a well-deserved day off. Wiky was the other one with pending duties. His task was to find a solution for the housing's leaking problem.

The course was organized to gather money and compensate for the expenses of the event. Pipin had pushed the event by two months earlier than planned because he didn't want Tanya Streeter to enjoy the female world-record she had taken from Audrey, for too long. Due to the rush, however, we couldn't find sponsors in time to cover all of the expenses.

The group of students was comprised of multiple nationalities, but most of them had come from the United States, Puerto Rico and Mexico. In the morning, we had the academic session, which in the beginning was spent mostly talking about the event. They were extraordinarily excited for the opportunity to interact with their freediving heroes; Pipin and Audrey, and getting to see the assemblage of a world record attempt.

"Most people only get to see this type of event through the Discovery Channel. Oh, man, this is cool," said one of the students, a guy in his mid-twenties with the facial expression of a seven year old kid unwrapping Christmas presents.

Having finished the academic segment, we had the first pool session at 2:30 p.m. Matt joined me to help with the practical part of the course. He's quite prolific and knowledgeable. He had become an instructor with Pipin and me when we visited Hawaii on the first of two occasions. Matt was also a coach to his wife Annabel Briseno, at the time a senior world record-holder in few different freediving categories, and member of the USA Freediving Team to the World Cup. With Matt's tutelage, the students were in excellent hands.

The pool session was uneventful for the most part. I didn't see Audrey that day but once, when she walked by the pool . . . alone. She shyly waved at me, but surprisingly, she didn't stop to salute the students as she normally would. With her face still reflecting anguish, I felt once again useless to help her or comfort her in any way.

Only minutes later Pipin appeared to join Matt and me in the water. He gave some demonstrations to the students as for which they were pleased. They wanted, logically, to see the world champion in action, and Pipin is quite prolific in terms of underwater performance.

Then Matt took over the class while Pipin and I tested and evaluated a mono-fin prototype just developed by *Mares*, the diving gear manufacturer sponsoring Pipin and Audrey.

A mono-fin is a single blade swimming apparatus which, unlike the standard double fins, forces the swimmer to kick with both legs simultaneously, just like a dolphin. Although they are not common in a pool filled with kids or in any local beach, they are the propulsion of choice for most top freedivers in the world. Pipin, on the contrary, is not too fond of the mono-fins.

"This piece of shit doesn't work," said Pipin while removing the mono-fin from his feet after a short try.

"Why would you say that, Pipin?" I asked curiously.

"They just don't work," he said obstinately.

"Pipin, I'm six-foot one and weight over two hundred pounds, meaning that I displace plenty of water. These fins moved me well, with minimum effort on my legs. It doesn't over-bend, run without creating turbulence in the water and the kickback is smooth. So, I'm just asking, why don't you like them?"

"You can send those pieces of shit back to Mares, they don't work," he concluded.

"Well, thank you for enlightening me with your professional evaluation," I said sarcastically.

It's been always intriguing for me to see Pipin judging and dismissing something without a reasoned testimony to validate his point. At first, it was very annoying but in time, I learned to deal with it and even made jokes impersonating his *"Piece of shit"* cliché. It always amused the team, and particularly Audrey. Even Pipin would take my impersonation lightheartedly, most of the time. But by now, he was really getting on my nerves with his attitude.

Later that day Pipin came to my room with a much nicer approach. His charismatic side was back. Once again, *Mr. Hide* was concealed within the labyrinths of his mind. We had made plans to visit Bayahibe Bay one more time for the final coordination on the catamaran.

To go to Bayahibe, we normally took one of the hotel boats used for Audrey's training dives. It was the fastest way to get there. While on the way, I decided to ask him,

"Where is Audrey?"

"In the hotel room, reading some book about Egypt."

"Oh, I guess she got hooked after her visit to the pyramids, ah?"

"¿Coño, chico, you're going to continue to mock with that?"

THE LAST ATTEMPT

"*Pipin, don't you see a pattern going on here; you never let Audrey get out of the room, for God's sake.*"

"*I don't want her to get distracted. She needs to remain focused.*"

"*What are you talking about? When it comes to a freediving record, she's one of the most focused people I've ever met.*"

"*Yeah, but those sapingos from the press are going to be asking all kinds of shit. I want her to stay away from them.*"

"*Ah, the press . . . so you don't let her out of the room because of the press?*"

"*Yeah.*"

"*I thought it was something else.*"

"*Like what?*"

I was in comfort with *Dr. Jekyll*, so I only added, "*I don't know, hmm, something else; never mind.*"

Besides, I didn't want to place Audrey in an awkward position. She had already pleaded me not mention the issue and I had just asked him about it. If I would have said what I had in mind, he most likely would had gone to their room and take it on her. Interestingly enough, the members of the press had been around the hotel for the last couple of days. Audrey had been secluded for week and a half by now, when no members of the press were around. Therefore Pipin's excuse was not too convincing.

Once we arrived to the catamaran, Pipin took over the coordination by telling the captain at what time he needed to be in front of the Resort's beach.

"*I rather stay at distance from the beach,*" responded the captain. "*Due to the size of this boat I prefer to avoid any inconvenience with the hotel.*"

"*And how the fuck you plan to board the people?*" asked Pipin.

The captain became visibly apprehensive with Pipin's tone. Unlike our team, he wasn't used to it.

"*We can ferry everyone from the beach,*" I interrupted while patting the captain on his back. "*We'll use the dive boats for that.*"

"*That'll do it. That'll work just fine,*" replied Pipin.

Chapter 8

Countdown To A Tragedy— Minus One Day

FRIDAY, OCTOBER 11, 2002
8:00 A.M.

Comprised by the Dominican Republic to the east and Haiti occupying the western third of the territory, the island of Hispaniola is the second-largest in the Caribbean after Cuba.

As all of the islands in the Caribbean, the Dominican Republic offers a hot and steamy weather distinctive of its tropical location. The tropics are the geographic area of the planet located above of the equator line and limited by the Tropic of Cancer to the north, and below the equator line limited by the Tropic of Capricorn to the south. It is in this region where the sun reaches its pinnacle at a 90° or directly above the head, and in no other part of Earth the sun reaches such peak.

The word "Tropics" comes from the Greek "tropos" meaning "turn", because the sun oscillates between the two Tropics (Cancer and Capricorn) during a calendar year. But the moment I walked out the cool freshness of air-conditioning of my room and headed to the restaurant, I wondered if the word "tropos" really meant another type of turning, because I felt like a roasted chicken spinning inside a flaming oven.

The sky was customarily clear; not a cloud was present to shield us from the whipping, burning flames being thrown by the sun.

As I sweated my way to the restaurant, I wondered if the heated situation between Audrey and Pipin had cooled off a bit, but it didn't take long to find out. They were both seated at the table, alone, and the long faces said it all. The rest of the staff arrived within minutes.

THE LAST ATTEMPT

During the mostly hushed breakfast, I did notice Wiky more restless than usual, so I called him apart after we all have finished.

"What is it, Wiky? You were uncharacteristically silent in the table this morning."

"Carlos, I don't like this record. Things between Pipin and Audrey are not good at all."

"Yeah, I know, but there is nothing we can do about it. They are a couple and couples need to resolve their own issues. Third parties' involvement is a bad idea."

"But look at her, she is on the edge . . . and let me tell you this . . ."

"Wiky, Wiky," I interrupted, "Leave everything the way it is. If you try to get involve, you know how Pipin is going to take it with you and with Audrey, as well."

Although Wiky was aware of their private conflict, I didn't think he was aware of Audrey's divorce. To avoid getting Wiky more concerned than he already was, I decided not to share that piece of information with him.

"Oye, we may not be able to do much about their private matters, but you must do something about the record," he said agitatedly.

"What do you mean?"

"Papito, he wants to send Audrey to one hundred and eighty meters on Saturday."

"Don't worry, Wiky. That's not going to happen."

"Oye, don't let him do it. You know he's crazy!"

"Wiky, I'm telling you. Audrey will not dive to one hundred and eighty meters."

"Okay," Wiky concurred alleviated, "I'm counting of you to stop him. Oye, Pipin esta loco!"

From the restaurant, Pipin and the team headed to the catamaran. Audrey and I remained behind. Later, we would take a boat to transport us to the bigger vessel. The plan was to rig the sled onboard ever since it was the first and only day to practice from this boat before the attempt.

Audrey and I headed towards the beach to wait and spent some time talking under the protective shade of a palm tree.

"One more day, Audrey; it's almost over."

"Yes, it's over," she said facing the sand.

"Hey, once we get back to Miami everything will get back to normal."

"No, Carlos, nothing is the same anymore."

"C'mon, Audrey; we all go through some harsh times in our marriages. It doesn't mean it has to end."

"Have you been on the edge of a divorce with Adriana?"

"Only once . . . a month. Especially when she has her period," and that made Audrey chuckle.

"No, seriously," she insisted.

"Actually, Adriana and I separated once."

"What happened?"

"She couldn't adapt to life in the United States. Besides, my dive shop was quite demanding. She barely got to see me on weekends because that's when I worked the most."

"But you don't mistreat her, do you?"

"Are you crazy? She'd kill me."

"And you never cheat on her; do you?"

"No way; especially since Adriana lights up candles everyday in front of a poster of Lorena Bobbitt."

"Who's that?"

"That's the woman who cut her husband's penis with a serrated kitchen knife and tossed it out the window."

While still laughing, Audrey added, *"Oh, yeah, I remember. That sounds like a good idea."*

"Hey, take it easy. No guy deserves such punishment."

"I can think of one who does."

"Let's go. There is Wiky coming for us. Besides, this conversation is making a part of my body hide in fear."

"Oh, yeah . . . hide where?" she inquired smilingly.

"Behind my balls."

"Oye!" she recriminated while hitting me on the shoulder with an open hand, but the smirk remained on her face.

"Well, stop asking, then."

Now she was in a happier mood and that's exactly what I was looking for. Then Audrey, Wiky and I headed to the catamaran. The boat giving us the ride was the same one used before for training, but the sled wasn't onboard anymore.

Besides been a safety diver, my job was to take underwater pictures for the press and posterity as if they were taken the day of the record. On Saturday I would be in the surface acting as a judge, leaving no one to take the underwater memories. Angelo was doing an excellent job on the surface but lacked of diving skills to replace me beneath it. So by the moment the record would have occurred, we already had the pictures taken the day before for worldwide distribution.

As always, Pipin assembled the sled with Matt, Tata and Wiky supporting him. Meanwhile, Audrey was getting interviewed by the local TV and the Mexican network, *Televisa*. Nothing was out of the ordinary, including Pipin's bad humor and Audrey's melancholy. The tension between the two was getting noticeably stronger everyday, but only for those close to them. In public, Pipin tried to hide it and presented the image of a happy couple, as he always did. Even so, he kept certain distance from her. Audrey, on the contrary, was not making any effort to continue the farce.

When the sled was finally rigged, the divers geared up and Audrey got in the water. I waited for her right below to protect her entrance. She was wearing a beautiful and quite dazzling neoprene wetsuit. At Pipin's request, the suits must be made with bright and contrasting colors and in this particular case, bright yellow and black.

Mares had sent a twin wetsuit for Pipin, as well. It was a 5m.m. thick wetsuit adorned with the names of the event's sponsors. It also included a hood for extra thermal protection.

With body-fat levels close to none, Audrey would normally get chilled rather easily, even in tropical waters. So although a hooded 5m.m. wetsuit in warm water is too much for most people, for Audrey was perfect. Besides, to the depth she was going the water is chilly no matter what.

It got my attention, though, that Pipin wasn't wearing his custom-made wetsuit, and that was odd. He was dressed with the same black and blue *Mares* wetsuit we were all wearing.

Something else caught my attention, too. Pipin didn't fill the pony-tank while the sled was onboard. Instead, he waited for the sled to be in the water to get it filled. The process was done by transferring air from a standard 80 cubic-feet aluminum tank to the pony-tank. The air got transferred via a hose interconnecting both cylinders.

Bill helped Pipin in the process by holding the bigger tank, while Pipin connected the yokes and opened the valves allowing the transfer of air. The importance of having the pony-tank appropriately filled resides on a single fact; that's the air to be used by Audrey to inflate the lift bag and propel safely to the surface. With an empty tank, Audrey would be stuck in the bottom of the ocean and her only chances of survival would depend on Pascal.

Credit: Carlos Serra

Assisted by Bill, Pipin fills the pony-tank. This would be the last time the tank received the crucial air.

The process of filling the pony-tank is simple but Pipin never allowed anyone else to do it. Sometimes he would be assisted by someone, but it was always him filling that tank, regardless. Actually, anything to do with the sled was always performed directly by Pipin.

"Every time I let anyone lay a hand on the sled they do a shitty job," he always said.

Even though we were out in the ocean, it wasn't a training day for Audrey, per se. After her 170-meter training dive last Wednesday, she was ready for the event. Instead, she did two shallow dives to 50 meters for the pictures. So the day was an easy one; assemble the sled and take the underwater pictures for the press.

Even though the assembling and photo session was trouble-free, I did notice Pipin exceptionally stressed out; even nervous. In the water surface he kept on rubbing his head and biting the tip of his tongue and not even before, when he had sent Audrey to abyssal depths, he was so tense.

Credit: Angelo Cordero

Pipin is seemingly restless. The frown and the rubbing of his head are trademark signs of a high stress level, but the dives were only to 50 meters.

2:30 P.M.

Back on shore and after lunch, another confrontation with Pipin brought me to the edge, again. We were in the hotel's lobby when Pipin insisted on Audrey to attempt 180 meters on Saturday. One more time I had to stand against Pipin and his endless supply of nonsense.

"What do you want; to dig a hole in the seafloor and send Audrey to China?" I protested.

Audrey remained silent, and I couldn't believe it. She had become, again, the submissive wife, accepting whatever her controlling husband would ask her to do. That's when I turned to her,

"Audrey, are you in agreement with this madness? Do you know that there is a limit for No-Limits? Do you want to be the one to find out where the limit is?"

"She can do it," insisted Pipin.

Timidly, she looked at me and then looked at Pipin, accepting passively his authority. No answer came out of her lips; she looked defeated. It was her own flesh being put at risk but it wouldn't be her decision. That disturbed me even more. Right then I knew how useless Audrey would be, so I kept disputing with Pipin.

"Even if she could do it, why keep pushing it?"

"Carlos, she's in excellent shape. She can do one hundred and eighty meters tomorrow."

"Well, if Audrey attempts one hundred and eighty meters, I'm taking the first airplane back home, because if you want to kill her, and it's obvious she doesn't care, be my guest, but I won't be part of it!"

Pipin started rubbing his shaved head and making his customary grimace, looking down and biting the tip of his tongue, just as he always does when something is not going the way he wants it. But I insisted,

"It's been two weeks of never-ending nonsense from your part. And now, twenty-four hours before the attempt, you want to increase twenty more meters to her last dive. Are you ever going to stop, damn it?"

"It's only ten more meters."

"Twenty, Pipin, twenty, or have you forgotten that she has to go back? She has to hold her breath for twenty more meters."

"She can do it."

"It's that your professional assessment? She can do it . . . she can do it . . . she can do it . . . That's all you can say? How do you know she can do it when no one has done it before?"

"The simulated dives on land . . ."

"Pipin, stop it. I've flown seven-forty-sevens from Miami to Honolulu in my computer thanks to Bill Gates and his Flight Simulator program. But the day I'll try to take-off from Miami on a real airliner, more like likely it'll end up in pieces all over Hialeah and the distance between my head and my feet, instead of six foot will be six miles."

"But that's only a computer game."

"And so is your simulated dives invention, because I think you are playing with Audrey's life."

"The simulated dives really work. I designed it."

"I don't care if it was designed by Albert Einstein himself. If Audrey does one-eighty, then I'm doing three things right now."

"What is it?" Pipin asked curiously.

"I'm going to La Romana and buy a shovel for you, Audrey, so you can dig a hole and bury yourself in the bottom of the ocean." She glimpsed at me and lowered her face again.

"Then I'll change my ticket to go back home tonight. And last, I'll buy a nice shirt for you, Pipin."

"You'll buy me a shirt?"

"Yeah, one of those with the extra long sleeves that you buckle on your back, because you are a lunatic!"

After few more minutes arguing, with Pipin giving me all kind of excuses based on Audrey's performances during the so-called simulated dives, we both agreed with adding only one more meter. Audrey would attempt 171 meters, and that's all the concession I was willing to give.

As much as Pipin tried to convince me, I would have never conceded. And the reasons were many. First, the simulated dives; although an ingenious concept that implemented breath-hold timing with exercising, it didn't account for water pressure, water temperature, currents, possible equalization problems and some other variables like stress. And Audrey had been undergoing a lot of it, lately.

Second, I had promised Wiky that I would not let Pipin send Audrey to such depth.

Third, I was already strained by the previously outrageous increases on depth and didn't want for that trend to continue; the time to stop it was long overdue.

Finally and most importantly, I was concerned about Audrey's wellbeing. In her last practice dive to one hundred and seventy meters, she surfaced with her body being visibly contracted, and that's a sign that her brain and body were suffering due to lack of oxygen. At one hundred and seventy meters she was reaching her limit.

7:00 P.M.

In the evening, while meeting by the usual east-side pool, Wiky called me apart and brought up something disturbing,

"Ay, papito, el loco is dressed in white."

"And so what, Wiky," I asked, although I knew what was coming next.

"He's doing his brujeria, chico," Wiky said agitatedly.

"He's doing witchcraft, you say?"

"Yes, that's what he's doing."

"Wiky, he is Santero and Santeros dress in white all the time. You know that."

"Pipin is more than Santero, he is Palero."

"And what the hell is that."

"You don't know?"

"No, man, what is Palero?"

THE LAST ATTEMPT

"Ay, papito, Paleros work with the dead."

"But Santeria is all about working with the Saints, isn't it? And saints are a whole bunch of dead people . . ."

"Nooo, muchacho, I'm talking about blood, dead bodies, sacrifices, and . . ."

"Okay, okay, Wiky," I interrupted. "That's a little too much information for me. Let's just focus on Audrey and her record attempt tomorrow, okay?"

"Alright, but I'm telling you, Pipin is cooking something and I don't like it."

With the presence of the regular staff, plus the addition of the resort's diving instructors lead by Laura, we now had a much broader scale meeting. They would be part of the safety divers to be placed in the water for Audrey's official record attempt the following day.

Also Eddie Matos and his crew of rescuers, assisted. They were all neatly dressed with dark shorts and navy blue polo-type knits with the logo of their Beach Patrol Team, a bunch of Baywatch-style rescuers but without the red bikinis or the girls to wear them.

"Hey, Eddie, when you and your guys are on the beach rescuing people like Baywatch, do you wear a red thong with hairy asses overflowing all over?" I jokingly asked Eddie.

"No, Carlos, ours are pink."

"Eddie, that's disgusting. Thank you for ruining my appetite."

"Well, you asked."

Also congregating by the swimming pool tables were the catamaran's crew, Kim McCoy and Sam, the person Pipin had introduced to everyone as Audrey's personal doctor.

In addition to the key people for the event, reporters from the US, Italy, France and the Dominican Republic were there, as well.

In the middle of a festive mood, Pipin interrupted to address everyone. It was time for Pipin's briefing about the record day; the final day.

Pipin performed the briefing as he always did; short, uninformative and threatening. That probably came as a surprise for the new bystanders, but it wasn't new for the staff. In the many years I had spent teaching diving instructors on how to perform a briefing and subsequent debrief, I had listened to thousands of them, literally. Pipin's briefings, however, are by far the worse I have ever heard, but somewhat amusing, I admit.

It reminded me of a wrestler's speech before a fight; the same tone of voice, facial expressions and body language. And yet, the most distinctive aspect was the shortness of it and the lack of information.

Actually, Pipin would normally spend between two to three minutes max, which for the tenor of his briefing is a good thing; it wasn't long enough to make people run away. But a good briefing for such complicated operation as a world-record attempt, should take enough time to cover specific and crucial details to ensure a smooth and well-coordinated operation.

A basic textbook-like briefing should always include the following, but not necessarily in that order: *Who—What—When—Where—Why and How.*

Although I'd tried many times to improve his briefings, Pipin could never harness the essence of it. Just to illustrate the point, this is—more or less—a condensed version of Pipin's briefings that night,

"Tomorrow, everything will be just the same as today. I don't want to see anyone screwing things up. If you do, you better take an airplane and go back to Miami. I don't want any stupid shit happening tomorrow. Is that clear? Do you have any question?"

Of course not; it would be unwise to ask a question. Besides, the veterans of the group like Tata, Wiky or Pascal already knew—for the most part—what to do. The others were just flabbergasted; they had been bawled-out for something they haven't done yet. Sometimes, and to ease everybody's nerves, and just when Pipin considered his briefing finished, I would ask him,

"What is it that we are going to do?"

He would know right away that I was just pulling his leg and would answer back with a Mona Lisa smile, because somehow, somewhere, hidden in the intricacy of Pipin's menacing personality, there is a hint of sense of humor, but to see it, he has to be away from the spotlight of a record attempt, the press and their cameras.

That Friday night, though, I didn't feel like joking with Pipin as there were no signs of good humor on him. The press was present and we were on the brink of a world-record attempt; for that reason, I avoided making any comment and kept taking pictures of the meeting.

But just before Pipin finished his briefing, a new unexpected shift in the pattern of the event was made,

"By the way, from now on Carlos will be responsible for everything," he said while pointing at me. *"Don't ask me, I know nothing. Whatever happens tomorrow, he's the boss, not me."*

"Wow, what the hell was that for?" I thought. I even got to take a picture of the moment. I was standing right behind Audrey when he raised his left arm over her head to point at me. That's when the camera clicked, but I believe I pressed the shutter out of surprise.

THE LAST ATTEMPT

Credit: Carlos Serra

The moment of the sudden delegation on me; a bewildering last-minute entrustment of responsibilities that at the time, made no sense.

A week before arriving to the Dominican Republic I was supposed to be the event coordinator, but it took me just one day—while still training in Miami—to realize that, as always, Pipin was taking over most aspects of the operation.

My job was relegated to finding the catamaran with him; coordinate with Laura the boats for the press, protect Audrey as a safety diver during her practice dives, take pictures, and write the Internet report. Not to mention my self-assigned duties as mediator between Pipin and anyone else. But the coordination of the most crucial aspects of the event, like the number of safety divers in the water, the medical team, the paraphernalia coordination, and the event's guidelines were all in Pipin's hands since day one.

In fact, I didn't have much trouble with that. After all, it was his wife doing the record and even though Pipin specializes in rushed and improvised events, he should know better than anyone how this type of event should be planned; he had been doing it for fourteen years. That's why this sudden change of heart was puzzling, it made no sense, whatsoever, and many questions immediately crossed my mind that moment.

Kim McCoy was also baffled, but he took it lightheartedly. He had known Pipin for few years but only within a record attempt organization, though. Nevertheless, he had seen Pipin's peculiar actions before.

CARLOS SERRA

"So, Carlos, you are now El Jefe," Kim said teasingly while I was requesting a Diet Coke at the bar.

"Hey, Kim, do you have any idea where that's coming from? Because, I'm clueless."

"Hey, that's Pipin, he's full of surprises, isn't he?" replied Kim obviously not giving too much thought to it. But I remained astonished. I couldn't help it. Something about that announcement was unbefitting, completely out of place.

To increase my perplexity, Pipin right after the briefing started to coordinate with the boat captain the time and location for the catamaran to be. He also spoke with Eddie Matos about safety measures to keep people away from Audrey, claiming that he wanted no distractions for her; that no one could get close to her. Then he spoke with Pascal about his gas mixture, and that was like seeing him telling Bill Gates how to design the *Flight Simulator* program.

Minutes later Pipin was arguing with Wiky. Pascal had offered the latest to do a *Trimix* breathing mixture for him to increase his safety margins, but Pipin refused vigorously. Pipin prohibited Wiky to use the much safer blend than regular compressed-air for the depth Pipin himself had assigned Wiky to be; ninety meters of depth.

Hence there was Pipin, with the meeting having finished just minutes before, in absolute control of his show. Thus, my perplexity only increased and the question remained; why the previous diversion? Why this last minute delegation?

Chapter 9

THE DAY WHEN TIME STOOD STILL

SATURDAY, OCTOBER 12, 2002
8:00 A.M.

Two weeks had passed; thirteen days to be exact. The day of Audrey's record attempt had finally arrived. But unlike the preceding twelve, lightning-laced clouds continuously discharged its high-voltage cargo all around us. A ferocious storm was pounding the, until now, paradisiacal complex.

With the wind blowing at rampant speed, rain drops became needles piercing the skin. Vivid memories of the hurricanes we have survived in Miami came to mind. The storm was part of a low pressure system recently formed near Puerto Rico and headed west; we just happened to be in its path.

Challenging the storm, the crew gathered around the dive center where Wiky, Tata, Angelo and Pascal were assembling the equipment. While the guys worked on the gear, Audrey and Pipin showed up at the breakfast buffet. We sat down together at one of the tables as we watched the tempest through the windows. The storm was awful-looking, but Pipin and Audrey didn't look any better. They had a storm of their own lasting few days by now. Audrey was quiet, much quieter than usual, so I attempted to break the iceberg by kidding around with her,

"Audrey, looks like Christopher Columbus doesn't want you as the central figure today."

It was October 12, the date when the famous navigator had set foot in the New World for the first time. Although Columbus first discovered the island he later baptized as San Salvador, in what is currently The Bahamas, he later explored the northern coast of

Hispaniola by December 5, during his first voyage to the Americas. Due to this historical fact, the date has an extraordinary significance in the island.

"Amazing," I added, *"how much credit is given to Columbus for discovering the new world when, first, he was lost, and second, he wasn't the first one to travel across the Atlantic."*

"Ah, no?" asked Pipin.

"Nope . . . Some other navigators had come before."

"Who?" he asked seemingly intrigued.

"I remember only one, a guy named Ericsson, I believe. He discovered what it's known today as North America and Canada about four hundred years before Columbus came to this neighborhood."

"So nobody remembers the dick-sucker with a telephone name," Pipin said, *"but everyone remembers Columbus. That means Columbus was smarter. That's the way it is."*

"Hmm, just like believing that Mammalian diving reflex was discovered because of you and not Mayol, right?"

Pipin gave me an icy gaze. So, changing the subject I turned to Audrey,

"In any case, Audrey, it seems like Columbus got pissed because you're taking attention away from him."

Even though I wasn't looking at Pipin, I felt the piercing gaze still coming my way. Only then I realized how my comment could have taken a dual meaning.

Audrey lifted her head from the plate of fruits and responded with a short glance and a shorter smile. Then, in what it had become a common gesture lately, she buried her face back in the plate. I got the message; circumstances were gloomy all around.

"Great, now we have two storms to deal with," I thought.

Breakfast continued without much talking until they finished, and with a simple but authoritative, *"Let's go,"* they stood up and left.

Before departing, Pipin, with a somber face, asked me how everything was going with the guys and the equipment.

"Everything is taken care of. You make sure she's alright," I replied.

"Let me know when the storm passes. We'll be in the room."

Under the heavy rain, I headed back to the dive shop to meet with the crew and look for a weather report. Once there I found Laura, who didn't have good news,

"The storm is going to take a while before it's gone," she said with a solemn expression; then she added,

"Do you think the event will take place? There are reporters waiting to get an update."

"Let them wait," I said. *"They can look up to the sky and get an update directly from the one in command,"* I responded while pointing up to the sinister-looking clouds above. Then, I proceeded to see if the guys had everything ready, and indeed, all the gear was organized. At that point I realized that not much could be done. So I decided to give Pipin and Audrey an update and see if I could help to alleviate the tension between the two.

THE LAST ATTEMPT

Stepping up the stairs towards their room I heard two people exchanging blows and the closer I got, the louder the yelling would be. There was an obvious fight between a woman and a man coming from one of the rooms. As I stood in front of their door, I hesitated to knock. Pipin and Audrey were having a fight. My immediate consideration was Pipin's impeccable timing to put that kind of pressure on her before the dive; particularly a plunge to 171 meters never before attempted.

While debating my options I tried to elucidate what the screaming was all about. It wasn't easy since one voice was screaming on top of the other, but to my surprise, Audrey was screaming almost as loud as Pipin.

After few seconds I decided not to knock and leave. It wasn't appropriate for me to be there in the first place. In the end a simple fact remained, they were a couple and third parties are better left out. But in any case, the subject was clear; she wanted out. That made me particularly concerned about Audrey's mental state to attempt the dive.

Back at the dive shop, Laura exasperatingly insisted that I had to give the press an update. I understood her concerns but she wasn't aware of mine. The tense situation between Audrey and Pipin was a lot more disquieting than having the press informed of what it was obvious, the storm was on and the event was off. Since Laura had no idea of what was going on and to avoid any more pressure from her, I headed with her towards the Resort's Customer Service lobby.

With buckets of water being poured relentlessly over us, we ran through the walking path between the buildings to reach the Customer Service lobby. Once there I realized what the press really wanted; a free lunch at the resort's expense, and if they had the time, they wouldn't miss the opportunity. It took me just a glimpse to the sky to see that we had time. I told them to go ahead and eat but to expedite the "feast" just in case the weather should clear soon. In the tropics, storms normally go as fast as they come.

12:15 P.M.

With the reporters heading to the restaurant, I went straight to the resort's center pool. There I found the majority of the crew, under a shack used as a bar during the evening hours. They were chatting about different topics, some related to the day's activities and others not related to the event, at all.

Not long after, Pipin appeared, seemingly impatient and determined. He wanted for the event to start right away. I tried to convince him to wait a little bit longer, it was about noon and the reporters had just started lunch. I also added that although the intensity of the storm was subsiding, the blustery weather was still going on. But he insisted that everything was ready and to start right away.

Customarily on him, he gave no specific reason for the sudden rush. Reluctantly, I complied; it was his event after all. That's when I asked Laura if she could notify the press that the event would soon start.

Meanwhile, Pipin wanted to depart immediately to the catamaran to rig the sled. He approached Eddie Matos to request one radio for him and one for me. Eddie asked one of his assistants to give his radio to Pipin while Eddie gave me his.

"*That's your radio Eddie, what are you going to use?*" I said while refusing to take the radio, but Eddie insisted,

"*Hey, the boss,*" pointing at Pipin, "*wants me to give you a radio; so take it,*" and so I did; I knew I wouldn't win.

I didn't see the need for taking Eddie's radios since we had our own. I had acquired two handheld radios in Miami just before the event. They had the capacity to communicate from five miles away and the distance from the beach to the catamaran was not only closer than that, but free of obstacles. However, something I had learned throughout the years is that everything Pipin does is for a reason; a veiled, peculiar or bizarre reason, perhaps, but there is always one.

Couple of minutes later, and before reaching the boat, Pipin used the radio to call me. He asked me to remain back at the hotel and wait for his call. Then I would go to his room to get Audrey and bring her to the catamaran. I responded affirmatively, but when we broke contact, Bill Stromberg, who was seating right in front of me and had listened to the just finished conversation, inquired about,

"*Why's Pipin using the radio when he could have just talked to you? He's right there!*"

With his right-index finger Bill pointed in Pipin's direction, right behind me. I turned around and noticed that Pipin was, indeed, no more than ten meters away. I was giving him my back, so I kept responding through the radio not knowing how close he was.

Surrounding Pipin were reporters different from the ones having lunch; some were filming and some others were taking pictures. Pretending not to, he was all-out striking poses for the press and the crowd encircling him.

That's when I got it. Pipin wanted Eddie's radios for the *Show*. *Professional Handheld Police Scanners* looked much cooler in front of the press than the two *Cobra* radios I had obtained at *Best Buy* for $120 a pair. After all, the radios I had bought are popular among shoppers at the mall or families visiting *Disneyworld*, but Pipin probably thought they looked *Mickey Mouse*. For him, appearance is always more important than practicality, because it was impractical for Eddie, as the person responsible for safety and head of the rescue team, not to have a radio. Then I turned back to Bill,

"*That's Pipin's Show and it's now officially open.*"

Pipin headed then to the boat transporting him to the catamaran. The double-hull vessel was anchored about a thousand meters away from shore. I waited for Laura and the reporters, while the rest of the staff waited patiently for Pipin's call.

About one hour later he finally called, asking me to bring Audrey. He claimed having everything ready for her. But as I went to Audrey's room to get her, Audrey was already coming. Her distressed gaze conveyed upon me a sad feeling, but I decided not to say a word. I already knew what had happened to her moments ago. But something rather peculiar got my attention. She was already semi-suited with the one-piece black and yellow wetsuit. It was unzipped and folded down to her waist. On top she wore a navy blue t-shirt with the acronym *IAFD* screened in yellow letters.

That was unusual because Audrey, proud carrier of a great figure, would normally wear her bikini all the way out to the training spot and put on her wetsuit while on board. With the rainfall, however, and the wind still blowing, for Audrey to be completely covered it kind of made sense.

Audrey and I continued walking towards the beach where the guests and the press were congregating a small crowd. At their request, she stopped for a moment to pose. Pascal met her right there and anchored himself next to Audrey to pose for the pictures, too.

I took the opportunity to take some photographs, as well. After taking a couple of shots, I noticed one name and two initials written down with black marker in Audrey's wetsuit. The name *"Cedric"* was written over the wetsuit's right shoulder and the initials *"J.J."* over the left shoulder.

The first one was Pascal's former diving partner while the second one was Audrey's cousin. Two things they both had in common, though; they were French and they were dead.

Cedric had died on December 2001 while diving with Pascal in some deep-water cave, whereas *J.J.* had also died few months back, but in a car accident, I believe. A moment later I noticed Wiky seemingly perturbed.

Credit: Angelo Cordero

The initials of two dead people, along with the red bandana wrapped around her wrist, got Wiky concerned about a ritual or ceremony of some sort happening.

"Is everything okay, Wiky?" I asked intrigued.

"Muchacho," he exclaimed. *"What is Audrey doing with those dead people over her shoulders?"* He asked rhetorically because he already knew the answer. *"That's Santeria, Chico . . . that's Pipin's witchcraft, I told you!"*

"And what's the meaning of that?" I asked intrigued.

"Hmm, you don't want to know, but imagine, she's going to the bottom of the ocean carrying two dead people over her shoulders . . . I don't like this; I don't like it, at all!"

Wiky's concern was based on his knowledge over Pipin's so-called religion; Santeria. Happens that Wiky is also a devotee of the cult but he practices only the white side of it. Just like the *Force* from George Lucas' *Star Wars*, there is a dark side to this creed. And that's Pipin's liking, according to Wiky.

Personally, I'm more inclined to believe that *Darth Vader* and *Luke Skywalker* are fighting with light-sabers in a galaxy far, far away, than in beheading a goat in exchange for favors from the Saints. But Wiky with his statement rubbed an ice-cube on my back. Audrey was to be escorted to the bottom of the ocean by the esoteric presence of two dead people.

We waited at the beach for the remaining members of the press; they were still eating lunch, but as soon as they arrived, about 20 minutes later, and after coordinating with Laura their distribution aboard the small boats, we departed towards the catamaran.

Credit: Angelo Cordero

Waiting for the boat in front of a small crowd, from left to right, Bill Stromberg, Carlos Serra, Audrey and Eddie Matos.

THE LAST ATTEMPT

Audrey and I boarded one of the small diving boats with other six people on board. As we sat next to each other, I immediately perceived the downward spiral in her mood. Only minutes ago she was smiling and posing for the cameras, but now she seemed lost, absent minded, just as if her thoughts were wandering another planet. The shadowy long rings under her eyes gave her a gloomy and lifeless expression.

With the boat now running towards the Cat, I got closer to her, placed my hand over hers and whispered to her ear,

"Audrey, I know you are not feeling too well today, but hang in there, it's almost over."

Without hesitation she reacted back,

"I'm sick and tired of this, Carlos . . . I'm tired of these records . . . I'm tired of Pipin and his temper . . ." she paused and the sighed.

"Yeah, I don't know what's gotten into him, recently. He's been a lot more irrational than usual."

Audrey remained silent and contemplative for few seconds, and then added,

"I still love him, Carlos . . . but it's so painful."

"Audrey, love doesn't cause pain, people do and no matter what, you must love yourself above anyone."

"That's why I'm going to leave him, this time for ever. He has gone too far," she affirmed with tears ready to burst.

While trying to maintain my own composure, I said,

"I know you two are not getting along too well, lately; but maybe it's just the stress the event is laying down in all of us, and you know he's better without these events."

"No, Carlos, there is a lot more than just this event," she said emotively. "But this is my last one, anyway. I don't want to continue with these records. I don't want to continue with Pipin; none of this makes sense, anymore."

"How do you think he's going to react?"

"I don't know, I'm scared, but I can't be with him any longer. I feel asphyxiated."

"Knowing him, he's not going to let you go just like that . . . he's quite possessive, as you know."

She kept silent while glancing towards the catamaran; we were getting closer. Then she continued,

"Carlos, I've loved Pipin with all my heart, I can't control that, but nothing I do ever pleases him, and I have done certain things for him that you know and some others that you would never believe—ever."

"Things like what?"

"It's too embarrassing. That's why I've never told you anything about it, but I had enough of his . . ." she sighed again. Then she held back. Whatever she was going to say she kept it with her. She looked ready to burst out crying. At that point I felt compelled not to ask any further.

"It's okay, Audrey. You must do what is best for you. And for what it's worth, you have my unconditional support. But right now, just hang in there, focus on your record today, and tomorrow will be another day."

Audrey and I had had many heart-to-heart conversations before about personal issues. I would talk about my son Alexander, and how proud I felt as a father. She would listen carefully to my whining about having lost my dive-center in Key Largo, Florida, to an unethical guy from Holland and my struggle to collect the tens of thousands of dollars the Dutch owed me.

We would also talk about my enthusiasm for oil-painting as she was also fascinated with art. Even though we talked about a variety of subjects like freediving, the office, and plans for the future, our conversations for the most part spun around her most intimate issues; particularly her parents and her at times tremulous relationship with Pipin.

It was during one of our after-meal conversations at the *Boston Market* restaurant nearby the office, right on the corner of Biscayne Boulevard and 125th Street, in Miami, when Audrey told me about her most painful moments in life; particularly when she attempted to commit suicide twice by slicing her wrist open.

I was familiar with Pipin's extra curricular adventures and Audrey knew all about it, but there was something else, something that must have been so awful that she preferred to keep to herself, something *"embarrassing,"* as she said.

One way or another, I didn't want to dig out any more. I was afraid of the possible consequences on her psyche if she kept on talking about depressing affairs. For the moment, she needed to carry on and focus on the attempt, not in her troubled marital life.

Nevertheless, I had made plans to meet with her privately after the record to offer a shoulder to cry on. I had never seen her so frustrated, so depressed, so fed-up, but conversely, so firm about ending her marriage. That kind of determination to overcome Pipin's overpowering control was not natural on her; she must have had enough, but I still had my reservations. All marriages have their ups and downs.

When we finally reached the catamaran, Pipin had everything ready to go. From our boat, and while still approaching the vessel, I saw Pipin walking away from the starboard side of the boat; the side where we would be tying our little boat. Once there, Audrey was not received by Pipin, but by a crew member. His task was to shield her away from everyone.

Audrey was escorted to a solitary place right by the center of the boat, an elongated slim platform where no one could get to her. Only one person at the time could walk the raised area, and one person stood between her and anyone else.

Audrey seated herself half-way the platform, but Pipin came, leaned over her and extended his left arm telling her to move farther away. Without even looking up to him, she complied immediately.

For some mysterious reason, Pipin wanted her isolated. It was heartbreaking to see the sadness her eyes reflected, seated lonely and visibly depressed. By now the turbulent situation between the two was becoming evident, even for those usually oblivious to it.

"Is Audrey okay?" Tata asked me, almost whispering.

As I kept looking at her from the distance, I sighed and got to answer, *"No, I don't think she's okay, Tata."*

"What's happening?"

That's when I turned to see Tata straight to his eyes, harshly. It was hard for me to believe that he had to ask. Seemingly clueless, Tata kept waiting for an answer that never came. I just turned back to see Audrey, once again.

She reclined against the bulk formed by the folding of one of the ship's sails, contracted her chest, pulled her shoulders forward, retrieved her legs and supported both elbows over her knees. Her hands entwined ahead with a red bandanna wrapped around her right wrist. I found out later that it was another one of Pipin's "magical charms". The bandanna had some lugubrious meaning in his witchcraft devotion.

As she remained motionless, her pale face became languid and her eyelids dropped halfway. Those once vivacious and flirtatious eyes now lacked of expression; they were looking inward, into her thoughts. The corners of her mouth were drawn downwards. Physically she was there, though her spirit had long departed. She looked like a virgin in the offering altar ready to be sacrificed.

Credit: Angelo Cordero

This picture better describes how she looked.

Soon after, the sled was placed in the water. And to ensure that Pipin wouldn't try to increase Audrey's depth beyond what we had agreed, I helped him out with the setting of the line in the water. Then Pipin put on his wetsuit, entered the water, and got positioned next to the sled.

The storm had gone away, so the conditions were becoming favorable. The sea was relatively calm. The waves were fluctuating between one and two feet, and that's less than Miami's average. The wind was dying down to mere gusts and the current was mild. But the sky remained overcast, just as if Audrey's gloomy state had influenced the surroundings; not a direct ray of sunlight could make it through. Other than that, conditions were good enough.

While positioning myself on the port side of the Cat, I saw Wiky bringing a scuba tank and the transfer-whip to the same side of the boat. The transfer-whip is a high pressure hose with a valve or yoke at each end, which allows transferring compressed air from a scuba tank into the sled's pony-tank.

"Pipin, here are the tank and the whip to fill the pony-tank," while stretching his left index finger towards the sled.

Pipin's response from the water surface was an infuriated,

"Go away with the other divers, go, go, GO!"

"Pipin, here is the tank to fill the pony in the sled," persisted Wiky, but Pipin overlapped his voice over Wiky's and repeated his command, insisting for Wiky to go away and to join the rest of the divers in the other boat. Wiky complied, but while looking straight at Pipin, he pointed at the sled one last time.

The rest of the diving team was, indeed, in another boat tied to the catamaran's starboard side, just next to the one in which Audrey and I had arrived. Minutes later, Tata, who apparently hadn't seen the previous dispute between Pipin and Wiky, stood about a couple of meters in front of me, and while pointing at the sled, he asked,

"Pipin, is the pony-tank full?"

Pipin reacted immediately by crossing his right hand once, vigorously, from left to right and just above his head,

"Yeah, it's taken care of!" he yelled perceptibly annoyed.

He seemed aggravated, as if the inquiry about the tank was insulting. And maybe it was, because filling-up the pony-tank was something so basic that he probably had done it before we arrived. He had spent over an hour in the big boat rigging the sled, and that's plenty of time.

Normally, I would have asked that very same question, just like I did many times before. But after watching Pipin's irritated reaction, not once, but twice, I didn't find it necessary to ask.

"He had plenty of time to fill the tank before most of us arrived," I recall thinking. *"Of course he should have done it long ago."*

Then, moments before getting in the water, Audrey approached me,

"Carlos, do you know what this is for?"

She was asking about the meaning of the red bandanna wrapped around her right wrist. She mentioned that Pipin had asked her to place the garment there and told her not to remove it. Knowing Pipin's beliefs I responded,

"Maybe it has something to do with those little Voodoo-dolls he has in his closet."

I referred to a closet in their house transformed into a ceremonial shrine. The closet was occupied with wooden statues of Pipin's revered "saints", candles, sea shells, ritualistic stones and some other bizarre and arcane charms. I even saw once what it seemed like a glass of dry blood, but I'm not certain and never tried to find out. Then I added,

"Or maybe, we shouldn't even ask, Audrey. Let's just hope is a Lucky Charm, a Santeria version of a rabbit foot."

As if the red bandana wasn't enough, Audrey also opened her bag to show me a banana and asked me about it. According to her, she was told by Pipin to take the banana with her from the restaurant's breakfast buffet. At the time I had no idea about the meaning of it, but Audrey mentioned Pipin's instructions; something about peeling the fruit and tossing the skin in the water.

"Audrey, you know what I think about Pipin's beliefs and how little I want to know about it. However, maybe he just wants to increase your potassium levels before the dive, and that would be an excellent idea," I said jokingly. She smiled back, and that smile was comforting; she seemed to be in a slightly better mood.

Credit: Angelo Cordero

Audrey is asking me for the meaning of the Santeria icons Pipin had commanded Audrey to wear, but I was as puzzled as she was.

As a not-too-devoted Catholic and non believer of odd rituals, voodoo or else, the so-called "religion" Pipin observes is filled with ceremonies that place such creed more in the witchcraft category; in my opinion, that is. The invocation of some African saints, with animal sacrifices and the occasional manipulation of human remains, it's not what most people would accept as an orthodox religion and most certainly, I'm among those.

In one occasion one of Pipin's co-practitioners; therefore, a defendant of the cult argued with me that Catholics eat the flesh of Jesus and drink his blood.

"Yeah, sure, like to eating a paper-thin waffle with a glass of Cabernet Sauvignon compares to biting a white dove's neck and drinking goat's blood," I replied.

Unable to obtain a straight answer from me, Audrey proceeded then to the edge of the catamaran with Pipin rushing her, as usual. I took the megaphone and positioned myself over the port side hull. But before entering the water, Audrey tossed the banana peel.

Credit: Angelo Cordero

This is the moment just before Audrey pulls the banana peel from the fin's foot pocket and tosses it in the water.

2:10 P.M.

Audrey started her warm-up routine, consisting of a series of ventilations followed by submersions along the line. That was the standard routine to activate her mammalian diving reflex and increase her apnea capacity.

Meanwhile, I was getting ready to perform my duties as a judge. Executing the countdown was among those duties. This countdown helped Audrey to regulate the pace of her breathing pattern and gave the divers enough time to get ready and eventually plunge to their pre-assigned depths.

The diver who needed greater anticipation, as always, was Pascal. He carried enough equipment for three divers as he was going to the maximum depth; 171 meters.

The catamaran was surrounded by boats of all sizes and styles. Fishing boats, sport boats, cruise boats, and even other catamarans were part of the escort. They had formed a semicircle around the catamaran's port side from which Audrey would attempt the record.

AUDREY'S DIVE

From this point on I can recall every aspect of Audrey's ordeal as if it would be happening right now, in the present time. It's as if a piece of time gets entrenched into the brain, only to be relived many times over. Past and present coexist within the same frame, and more likely, these enduring memories will continue to haunt me for the rest of my life.

2:25 P.M.

Once Audrey finishes her warm-up routine, she climbs on the sled. After nodding her head as a signal, I initiate the five-minute countdown. The event officially starts the moment the judge declares in loud voice,

"MINUS 5 MINUTES!"

At that precise moment silence takes over; divers are on alert to descend. Boat captains turn their engines off, and Audrey initiates her final ventilation pattern. The quietness should only be interrupted every minute.

"MINUS FOUR MINUTES!"

This is Pascal's cue to initiate his fall. He descends earlier since he is the deepest diver. His plan is to locate himself 10 meters above the exact depth of the record to bang his tank, warning Audrey of her approach to the end of the line. Then Pascal shall continue his descent and watch over her.

"MINUS THREE MINUTES!"

Now Wiky leaves the surface. This is the diver for whom I'm especially concerned. His planned depth is between 80 and 90 meters on compressed air, instead of the much safer gas mixture, *Trimix*. Wiky wanted to use *Trimix* as Pascal had offered to prepare the mixture for him, but Pipin refused. Many things in this event are too strange as I see Pipin, already in the water, not wearing the matching wetsuit.

"MINUS TWO MINUTES!"

Now the rest of the safety divers sink. Two of them carry video-cameras enclosed in housings. One is to position himself in about 60 meters and the other one in 30 meters. That's another odd situation; the two cameramen were assigned by Pipin in contradiction with the original plan. The dives made by Audrey the day before were filmed and photographed to avoid having to do so the day of the event. The divers should be focusing on Audrey's welfare instead of shooting video. And to increase my concerns, we were already short in safety divers.

Then, Pipin starts to manipulate the sled's video housing. *"He must be trying to turn it on,"* I presume.

"MINUS ONE MINUTE!"

Pipin continues to manipulate the sled's video housing. Apparently, he's having troubles with it. Wiky had made some repairs on the On/Off switch two days ago. Next, Audrey intensifies her ventilation rhythm, making it deeper and faster to increase the oxygen level in her blood stream. This last minute is crucial; most of the divers must be already at their designated depths while the freedivers are on alert.

Pascal should be close to the end of his abyssal descent. The reporters intensify the clicks of their cameras while pushing each other sideways with their elbows and shoulders for a better position.

Tension is in the air. Almost total silence takes over. Few individuals located in one small boat continue to mumble. They are drinking and having a small party. I ask them in vain to keep silence. Another boat remains with its engine running and gets dangerously close. With a harsh tone, I instruct them to run off. The noise, however, doesn't seem to disturb Audrey; she's much focused.

Credit: Angelo Cordero

With the megaphone and right above Audrey, I try to keep the boats away from her.

"MINUS 30 SECONDS—MENOS 30 SEGUNDOS"

THE LAST ATTEMPT

I shout in both; English and Spanish. Audrey stretches her left arm upward to reach with her hand the pony-tank's valve. The valve is at arms length over her head, sticking out from the lift bag. The pony-bottle is located inside the bag strapped to the vertical aluminum tube. By releasing small bursts of air inside the lift bag she can slow down the descent to ease equalization.

It is a rudimentary and yet efficient braking mechanism. The expansion of air inside the lift bag reduces her negative buoyancy. If she goes down too fast she may rip her eardrums, producing an incontrollable vertigo when the cold water gets in contact with the membrane that separates the middle-ear from the inner-ear. That's where the sense of balance in all humans is located.

That's also why both hands of the diver are placed in direct relationship with the elements that control equalization; left hand on the valve, right hand pinching the nose to block the air from escaping and redirecting this air inside the middle ear through the Eustachian tube. The pressure inside the ear must be equal to the pressure outside.

"MINUS 15 SECONDS—MENOS 15 SEGUNDOS!"

The countdown is coming to an end. Audrey's descent is seconds away.

"MINUS 10 . . . MINUS 5 . . . ANYTIME NOW!"

Pipin kisses Audrey; the one kiss that she welcomed with tenderness when they were happy, but the one she would hate when given right after she had been bawled out. She told me so during one of the practice dives few days back, and ever since I associated it with the most insincere kiss in history; the one Jesus received from Judas. But with the cameras around the show must go on; for him the kiss is business as usual. Although Audrey receives the kiss, she keeps her eyes closed.

Credit: Angelo Cordero

Audrey receives the trademark kiss, but she's either too focused or not too happy. Her eyes remains shut. Subtle but quite remarkable at the same time, is to see that Pipin is not wearing the wetsuit Mares has sent for him; the one identical to Audrey's wetsuit.

At this point in the count, Audrey is free to decide the moment to give the signal to Pipin; he's the one releasing the sled. She must do it quickly, though, to preserve the integrity of the safety divers below. The longer they stay down there, the greater the risk of getting in a low or out-of-air situation. A scuba tank may last one hour at ten meters, but at ninety meters only five or six minutes. Additionally, the more bottom-time the divers spend exponentially increases their chances to suffer decompression illness.

With her lungs filled with air, now Audrey closes her mouth and nods. That's a signal for Pipin, who while floating on the water next to her, grabs a short rope with a clip at the end. By pulling it, he will disconnect the sled from the mechanism holding it on the surface.

He pulls once—nothing happens. He pulls twice—and she remains on the surface. It's as if her guardian angel is tampering the mechanism to stop Audrey from plunging; a heavenly sign, perhaps?

"What's wrong?" I ask myself. *"He never fails to free the sled after the first pull. He's wasting time!"*

Audrey is already holding her breath at this point, consuming oxygen and wasting precious seconds that can make the difference between doing the record and suffering a shallow-water blackout. As per international rules, fainting at the surface would invalidate the attempt.

He pulls a third time and finally, the sled is free; Audrey is on her way to conquer glory by beating her husband's own world record. Only once before, thirteen years ago when it happened, a woman has broken a man's record. After only three minutes Audrey should be back and we'll be all celebrating.

The moment her nose hits the water I clicked on two chronometers, just like the ones used to time Track and Field competitions. One is to document the descent time only, while the other is for the overall time.

Credit: Angelo Cordero

After two failed attempts, Pipin finally disconnects the mechanism. Audrey is now plummeting towards destiny, along with the IAFD's name and reputation.

THE LAST ATTEMPT

With both timers running, I take both with my right hand, allowing me to place my left hand on the line from which the sled is riding down. I wanted to *feel* Audrey's dive. I'm accustomed to perceive the vibrations coming along the line and determine at what point in the dive she is.

Almost immediately upon her descent, Pipin, who for the same reason was also holding the cable, starts to curse,

"*Fuck, Fuck, Fuck!* It was very strange but he was cursing in plain English instead of Spanish.

Floating in the water while holding the line, he just raised his face to cuss repeatedly, and then place it back in the water to keep looking down.

"*What is it Pipin?*" I ask preoccupied.

He raises his head and looks straight at me with a knife-like gaze. I could see his eyes through his diving mask. But without giving me an answer, he looks back down.

"*¿Pipin, que pasa?*" I insist.

Obviously, he's alarmed but I can't see why. Then he finally says something other than cursing,

"*Why is she going so slowly?*" But there is no way for me to know. Tata, however, had gone down after Audrey to push the sled and compensate for the air that usually remained trapped inside the lift bag. That air would only slow down the descent during the first few meters, because once pressure starts to increase, the air volume diminishes rapidly, thus increasing the sled's speed.

"*I don't know, Pipin . . . maybe there's air still trapped inside the bag.*"

"*Fuck, Fuck, Fuck,*" Pipin continues to curse.

I check the chronometers knowing that if she is going slowly, I would be the first one to know. The moment the sled reaches the end of the line, a pull in the cable is felt.

1 MINUTE AND 34 SECONDS INTO THE DIVE

Pipin and I feel a soft pull on the line. We both say simultaneously that she had reached the end of the cable, but we also wonder why so softly. The *pull* didn't have the strength of previous occasions but it is possible. If Audrey had put too much air inside the lift bag, she could have descended softly over the safeguard tied-up at the end of the cable.

1 MINUTE AND 42 SECONDS

Now we feel a stronger *pull* and this one is typical; now Audrey had reached the bottom for real. Pipin and I look at each other wondering what caused the previous "thump".

"Maybe she hit one of the divers," I say, and based on the time passed, it has to be Pascal.

At this point Pipin starts cursing once again. I check the clocks and realize that Audrey's descent was actually better than expected.

CARLOS SERRA

"Pipin, she's alright; she has made the descent seven seconds faster than when she did one hundred and seventy meters," I say attempting to lessen his stress level.

He stares at me, but continues cussing anyway. Now I wonder why he would continue to be so troubled after finding out that Audrey had descended faster than expected.

But in just few seconds my perception changes. Pipin is moving nervously in the water. He senses something wrong; now I sense it, too. Few seconds after feeling the last and stronger *pull*, Audrey should have been in her way back. The sled should be brushing itself against the cable sending a constant and strong vibration all the way up to the two people holding the line, Pipin and me. But there is no vibration, whatsoever. The cable is dead still.

My heart starts to pound harder. Something out of the ordinary is happening and I don't know what it is. I feel incapable of doing anything other than watch the clocks.

Then Pipin asks for the scuba gear he had set apart already assembled. The equipment consists of a Buoyancy Compensator Device, a tank and a regulator system. He already had his mask, wetsuit, fins and weight belt on. He approaches the catamaran to grab the gear that is being handled down to him. But someone makes a mistake and grabs the supply-tank with the transfer-whip that Wiky had placed minutes before on the port side. Pipin refuses it and the right equipment is given to him within seconds. Then he gears up in the water and plunges looking for Audrey.

Earlier, I wondered why Pipin had asked for a scuba gear to be ready before hand. That was another strange situation. Pipin had never asked for scuba gear to be ready in advance, at least not in the record attempts I had witnessed prior to this one. He was one of the safety freedivers, and they are far more vital than *scubies*. The more likely situation to occur near the surface is a shallow-water blackout, where the speed and mobility of an apneista are, by a long shot, more critical.

4 MINUTES AND 30 SECONDS INTO THE DIVE

Tata lifts his face out of the water to yell, *"The balloon is coming up,"* just before he plunges himself to assist. Now a crushing force hits my chest and overwhelms my breath. My blood becomes as cold as the water beneath my feet the moment I see the lift bag, breaking the water surface, with Tata next to it . . . but no Audrey.

"Oh, God," I exclaim while my heart tries to burst out of my chest. I want to do something to help Audrey but there is nothing I can do, except wait and pray.

Something in the balloon itself already showed me that something is wrong. The balloon didn't erupt out of the water as it normally would. Even by carrying Audrey, the balloon could have jumped few feet up in the air, but without Audrey's weight, it should have burst out of the water like a rocket in takeoff. The amount of air inside the balloon was not even near the amount it should have had.

THE LAST ATTEMPT

8 MINUTES AND 38 SECONDS

I'm on the port side still holding the cable trying to feel something; anything that would tell me what's going on down there. Only this time the line is inert, it feel dead. I check the watches and over eight minutes have passed, but it feels like hours. Time has stood still. The feeling is quite unnerving. It's as if the brain stops perceiving time in a normal way.

"They are coming," yells Tata before plunging himself once more to assist.

Suddenly, a yellow color becomes distinguishable through the water, it is Audrey's wetsuit. After 8 minutes and 38 seconds exactly, Audrey breaks the surface without receiving oxygen. That's an impossible time for any human brain to survive.

But what I see shocks me to the core. Pipin is behind Audrey holding her from the throat and keeping her face up, but no regulator had been placed in her mouth.

"Oh, my God, what are you doing, Pipin?"

Because if that's the way he brought her all the way up, Audrey was being drowned. A simple but decisive rule when rescuing an unconscious apneist is to protect the airway; the rescuer must, at all cost, avoid for water to come in.

I'd hoped to see Audrey breathing from a regulator, but she wasn't. That's when a bombshell explodes in my mind; Audrey's motionless body presents no signs of life.

Pipin is attempting to provide mouth to mouth, yet ineffectively. Now, when it is required, he isn't opening Audrey's airway and fails to pinch her nose. Any attempt to supply air to her lungs would be futile. The air would escape through the nose. Besides, she is spurting a steady flow of bloody foam indicating that water had entered her lungs.

For few seconds I'm speechless. Like anyone else I'm mute. I can't hear a sound, or maybe it's me, in such state of shock that my brain isn't processing. But swiftly, reality strikes me, harshly. The vision of Pipin attempting an ineffective mouth to mouth brings me back to reality. Suddenly I realize the strident sound of Pipin's regulator bursting air away. If left in the water with the mouthpiece up it'll free-flow.

"Bring her here," I yell. *"Bring Audrey to the boat!"*

He approaches the catamaran bringing Audrey with him. Matt, Bill and Tata are helping him. Then I see Pipin pushing Audrey's neck up. With them pushing her up from the water, and the boat captain and Eddie Matos pulling Audrey from the boat, her body is brought up and laid down, facing up, on the port-side hull of the vessel. Meanwhile, I keep yelling for the doctor. Audrey's personal doctor is supposed to be here but . . . he isn't.

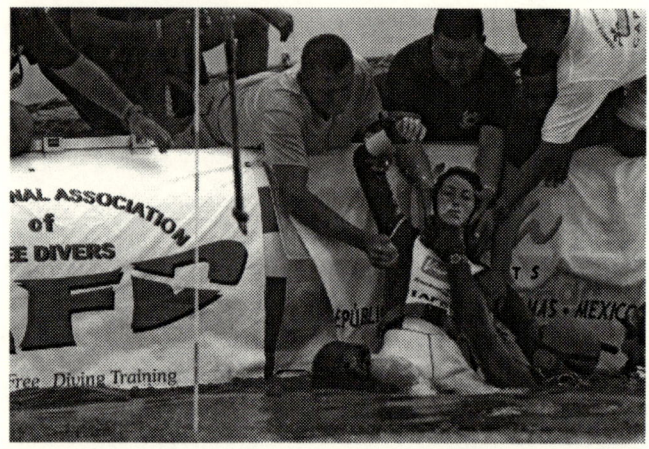

Credit: Angelo Cordero

Audrey's unresponsive body is brought on board. Her eyes are still open.

"¿Donde carajo esta el medico?" I ask frustrated. I had seen him before on the beach boarding one of the boats ferrying people, but he is not aboard the catamaran.

Audrey's body is placed along the narrow hull. I immediately grabbed her to immobilize her head and open the airway. Eddie cuts with scissors her black-and-yellow wetsuit from the neck, down to the waist. The zipper is on her back, so what Eddie does is faster. She's wearing a hood, five-millimeters in thickness just like the wetsuit. I start removing the hood from her head but Eddie cuts it, allowing me to check her carotidal pulse.

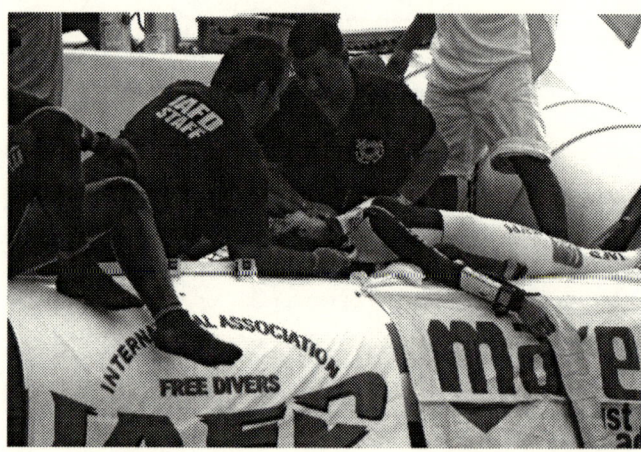

Credit: Angelo Cordero

At this point Audrey's pulse still strong and she's trying to breath, but her situation is hopeless.

THE LAST ATTEMPT

While holding Audrey's head from behind, her glassy eyes are staring straight at me. Those dreadful eyes are semi-open, telling a story of terror; the story of pain and misery she had endured lately, and now, this synopsis of despair and suffering she had to bear before finding peace and freedom. I almost succumb. Her pupils are dilated; a sign indicating no brain activity, but that's not for me to diagnose.

Then something eerie happens; her eyes close almost completely, as if the last person she wanted to see is me. As if there is something she's going to tell me, but she can't. That's an image I already know it will live embedded in my mind until my time comes.

Her whole face, once pretty, became grotesque with the aura of dead embedded on her expression. But she's not dead yet. With my right hand I feel her pulse while holding her head slightly leaned to her left side. I'm providing her a chance for the spurt of bloody foam to come out. The pink colored froth runs over my left hand.

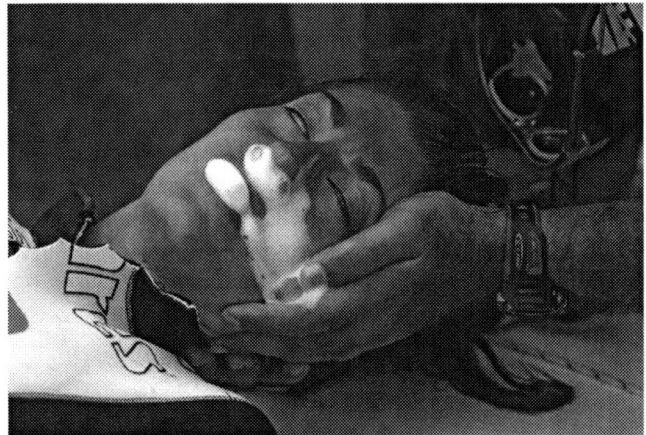

Credit: Angelo Cordero

For a moment I wonder if I should take my hand off; a large amount of her body fluids is in direct contact with my skin and that's an absolute no-no among rescuers, paramedics and doctors, but it's too late.

"*How come she has so much water in her lungs?*" I ask myself. "*This is not normal.*"

The panorama is surreal. Voices are around me, babbling and making no-sense. I try to recompose myself and maintain Audrey's airway open while evaluating the whole situation. Then I see Pipin, he seems shocked, in dismay, so I attempt to comfort him,

"*Pipin, she has a strong pulse and she's trying to breathe.*"

He stares at me, but no response, I don't like what I see. I don't know what to make of it. I only tried to give him hope. He had boarded the vessel and located himself at Audrey's feet.

Then Eddie, Laura and I turn Audrey to her left side to maximize the expelling of foam. Now blood with some kind of mucus comes out. Laura brings a green towel to clean her up. Meanwhile, Eddie Matos is providing oxygen, or at least trying to. It's difficult; while she's gasping for air, Audrey continues to spurt a great deal of the bloody foam, and with each inhalation, she inhales part of the foam back in.

"Where the fuck is the doctor, damn it," I yell in anger, once again. But the doctor is a no show.

One of the small dive boats from the Resort's dive center approaches the catamaran. The boat had been previously assigned as transportation in case of an emergency; I think it was Laura who had called the boat. We were trying to stabilize Audrey before attempting to move her. That plan, however, changes rapidly.

"We are loosing her," I yell, *"her pulse is fading. We must transport her to shore immediately."*

Pipin jumps into the other boat while few of us transfer Audrey to the small vessel. In the bewilderment, and acting impulsively, Pipin commands the boat captain to go,

"¡Vamos, dale, dale, dale!"

But I'm still trying to climb on board right at the moment when the captain pushes the throttle. I almost fall in the water, right behind the boat, with the boat's propeller only inches away from my feet.

Eddie Matos, who was right behind, grabs me by the t-shirt and helps me to get back into the catamaran. We are both left behind. We request another boat which comes in seconds, board it and hurry to shore. At least two well-trained people were there with Audrey; Matt and Amaury, a member of Eddie's Rescue Team. Between the two they initiated CPR immediately, because at this point, Audrey's pulse had faded away completely.

Chapter 10

The Aftermath

STILL SATURDAY 12

 Even before stopping, Eddie and I jumped off the boat into the sandy beach and ran directly inside the Resort's infirmary were Audrey was being attended. There were two people working on her, Rosa (not her real name), the lady in charge of the infirmary and a guy who, at first sight, didn't look like a doctor.

 Audrey had been laid down on a stretcher located by the wall just to the right of the door. Another surreal panorama was now in front of us; the air inside the small room was infused with an incisive paint odor. A metallic old-fashion grey desk, located just few steps ahead from the door, was occupying about a third of the space.

 The small room was packed with people, mostly curious who had no business whatsoever in what was happening. The man attending Audrey, who didn't looked like a physician, was wearing a *Speedo*-type swimsuit instead of the doctor's gown one may normally expect. I found out later that he was an Italian doctor on vacation, a tourist who either forced by Hippocratic Oath or out of a good heart, had come inside the infirmary to help. He was sunbathing at the beach when Audrey was being carried in front of him toward the resort's sickbay.

 But now a real shocker was to observe the Italian doctor, unsuccessfully, performing an intubation on Audrey while no CPR was being performed; at this point Audrey was becoming visibly cyanotic. Meanwhile, Rosa was attempting to make the defibrillator work; it was malfunctioning. After observing this frightening panorama for few seconds, I couldn't hold myself any longer and yelled,

 "What the hell are you doing? You cannot stop performing CPR!"

Rosa stopped her efforts to make the defibrillator function and attempted a mouth to mouth, but it wasn't doing any good, either. The stretcher where Audrey was placed had a protuberance, sort of embedded pillow that kept Audrey's head leaned forward; therefore, Audrey's lungs were not receiving the air. Her airway was not appropriately open.

Rosa had to raise Audrey's chin up to open the airway, but she failed to do so. She was, understandably, very nervous. I was trying to tip-off Rosa of the mistake when the Italian doctor interrupted the ventilation to keep forcing the tubing into Audrey's mouth, but it didn't fit. The doctor turned around in search of another tube and that's when I had enough. I literally pushed some people away, asked them to leave the room, and went to Audrey. Standing in front of her, I pointed to Amaury and asked,

"Do you know how to perform CPR?"

"Yes, of course!" he said as if I had asked the stupidest of questions. He was a rescuer, so he should know, but after what I had seen for the last few minutes,

"I just wanted to make sure," I replied. *"You take care of the chest compressions while I do the ventilations. We'll do fifteen to two. Got it?"*

"Let's do it," he responded decisively.

With a ratio of fifteen compressions for every two ventilations we both initiated CPR. Audrey's mouth still had residue of bloody froth sticking around her lips and cheeks, but it was dry by now. I peeked around searching a barrier or a clean cloth to clean it up, but nothing was in sight. Wanting to waste no more time, I raised her chin up to hyperextend the airway open and pressed my mouth against hers.

Finally, Audrey's chest was visibly expanding; she was getting air through her lungs. After few minutes, we only stopped CPR to allow the doctor, once again, to intubate Audrey and for Rosa to attempt defibrillating her, as well.

The intubation was finally a success, allowing now the addition of oxygen to the ventilations. The defibrillator, however, still didn't work. After few unsuccessful attempts, they stopped. Amaury and I continued the CPR procedure, but due to Amaury's exhaustion, we switched positions. He was now providing the ventilations while I took care of the chest compressions.

Then, I observed some subtle bruises on Audrey's chest, localized between the sternum and her breasts. I contemplated the possibility of rough handling when the CPR was initiated in the boat; perhaps, a hard-hitting fist in an attempt to stimulate the heart. It's incorrect to do so but some people still following what they have learned on TV. In any case, those contusions were not supposed to be there.

After few agonizing minutes, someone entered the room announcing that the ambulance was waiting outside. Audrey was translated to it with Pipin, Amaury and another team member from Eddie Matos' rescue group. Also Rosa and Laura boarded the vehicle through the back door. With so many people boarding the ambulance, I remained outside. That's when Pipin, opening the by-now closed back door, showed his head out and yelled,

"Where is Carlos?"

THE LAST ATTEMPT

Unable to distinguish me among the pack of curious circling the ambulance and all around me, I raised my hand,

"I'm here!"

"Come," he said. *"Come with me!"*

Pushing my way inside the crowded vehicle, I noticed the lack of essential items needed to provide assistance. There was no oxygen, no defibrillator or a bottle of rubbing alcohol. Even the oxygen from the infirmary had to be brought onboard.

The stretcher wasn't secure to the ambulance's floor, making CPR a difficult task. Amaury and I, however, continued with it. We both switched back and forth taking turns to rest while the other continued with the chest compressions. We were exhausted, but refused to stop. Audrey's cyanotic condition had turned to a pink coloration. The CPR procedure was providing an adequate amount of oxygen to her body, renewing our optimism but giving us false hope.

The ambulance was going quite fast for the country road in which we were. We were going to La Romana, a 20-minute ride due west from the resort. The road was a two-lane road; one eastbound and one westbound, and both exceptionally narrow. I was performing the chest compressions on Audrey when the speed of the ambulance forced me to look forward to the cabin, and through the windshield I saw a road sign indicating the shape of the curve ahead; a hard-left.

Going too fast to make the curve safely, I attempted to warn the driver but it was too late. The driver pushed the brakes hard trying to turn with the curve. The ambulance, however, didn't respond and slid sideways, propelled forward, straight as an arrow, and leaned sharply to its right.

For a moment I expected the ambulance to roll over, but it didn't. A tree was right ahead and that's the last thing I saw through the windshield before I fell down on Laura, who was between the back of the passenger-seat and me.

Amaury, who was resting next to my left, also fell along with Pipin on top of me. Audrey's inert body slid forward over the stretcher. She was held from falling down to the floor by the other rescuer and Rosa. They both fell down, too, but were stopped by a panel; a metal division behind the driver's seat.

On my way to the floor, while hearing the rumbling of the tires sliding over the gravel, I expected for a crash that never came. Either the hand of God or plain good luck, stopped the ambulance inches away from the tree.

As we all got up, someone asked if we were okay. It was the driver, I believe.

"It would do no good to Audrey if we all die," I yelled, *Coño, slow down a bit!"*

"He's a new driver," Rosa said with a shaken voice. *"He doesn't know this road too well."*

"Oh, great," I replied, *"that's very comforting."*

Then, Amaury, Pipin and I accommodated Audrey back over the stretcher to continue the CPR process. As the ambulance made it back on the road and continued the trip to La Romana, I kept compressing Audrey's chest while Rosa kept providing oxygen.

"*Come on, Audrey,*" I recall telling her. "*Respond . . . I'm exhausted. You are making us work too hard . . . come back . . . please, come back . . .*"

Amaury and I were, indeed, exhausted and barely had any strength left in our arms, and sweat from my forehead kept dripping over Audrey with every thrust, but the pinkness in Audrey's skin gave us the motivation to keep fighting.

Pipin was seated, keeping a hand over Audrey's left tight, but said nothing. He just seemed to be shocked.

When we finally arrived Pipin was the first one to step out of the ambulance, then Amaury and I followed right behind. The first thing I did was to look for the emergency staff. It took few seconds for them to appear. The staff was comprised of four women, nurses all of them. So I gave them a quick overview of what had happened.

"*She's a drowning patient; no vital signs, please, hurry.*"

Audrey was rushed inside over the stretcher still wearing the black and yellow wetsuit open at the chest. The nurses didn't seem to care much at this point; they have learned that she had being unresponsive for over an hour. They were much more lucid about Audrey's current condition than any of us. They had no emotional attachment to her as they weren't the ones loosing a beloved one. Their objectivity, however, came across as a bit cold. Almost a minute had passed before any of them would even attempt to check her pulse.

Then two of the nurses started to argue because one was trying to open a locked medicine cabinet.

"*You are not authorized to open that cabinet,*" one of the nurses said, to whom the other one responded with a sarcastic tone of voice, "*Uh-hmm, then you open it, I'm just trying to get the adrenaline for the woman,*" she said while pointing at Audrey, who was lifeless in the stretcher between the two arguing nurses. That's when I blew some more steam,

"*Would you two stop skirmishing like couple of fighting roosters? She needs attention!*"

Pipin, who had remained silently behind me, screamed to the nurses, as well, echoed my words and demanded care for Audrey. Surprisingly, that was Pipin's first reaction since he had left the catamaran.

Taking over the situation another nurse appeared, a bit older than the rest, and at first glance much more experienced. She calmed everyone down and proceeded to make a phone call. She called the doctor, and after a brief explanation, followed by a pause, she hung up.

"*Who's the closest relative to the girl?*" she asked.

I looked at Pipin. He was seated on a chair with its back against the wall. He went, once again, into an unresponsive state. I turned back to the chief nurse and while pointing at him I said,

"*He's her husband.*"

THE LAST ATTEMPT

Then she broke the news, Audrey was officially gone.

We had lost the long battle to save her; a fight that was lost even before she was brought to the surface about two hours ago by now. The ones who shared such a painful duty did it out of affection, just pure desperation to reverse the irreversible. There was nothing the nurses could have done at that point.

As the nurse shook the floor I was standing on, I collapsed over a chair and held my head down.

"Remove her jewelry, señor," I heard one of the nurses directing Pipin, *"we are going to take her inside."*

Pipin knelt down to Audrey's left side and removed the silver Mexican necklace she always wore; also the four earrings she had in her right ear and the golden dolphin-shaped earring from her left.

The sight was heartbreaking. With the exception of alternating the dolphin-shaped earring for another one shaped as a manta ray, she never removed them. And yet, while holding myself from crying right there, I couldn't avoid noticing Pipin's emotionless reaction.

When he finished, the chief-nurse gave him additional instructions. He needed to bring clothes for Audrey, make arrangements with the funeral home and bring her identification and insurance policy, if she had any. He looked back at the nurse, but no response came out. Then the nurse looked at me and added,

"Make sure you bring those items and hurry up with the funerary arrangements, we have no refrigeration here. The closest refrigerator is in Santo Domingo and that's about two hours away from here."

With a knot on my throat and my heart pounding hard, I nodded and walked away from the emergency room out to the street. I couldn't bear seeing Audrey's inert body and knowing that she was gone. I felt week and my body was trembling.

While dragging my feet out, a van stopped right in front of the entrance to the emergency area. Few people had come from the hotel, but I look for the friendliest face I could find. That was Matt's, who right after jumping off the van, asked me for Audrey. I shook my head and kept walking towards him. When I got closer, he extended his arms forward as we embraced each other in a hug. We both cried . . .

From the moment Audrey didn't surface when she was supposed to, until the moment the chief-nurse announced the shocking reality, emotions kept building up. With every second that Audrey wouldn't respond, our anguish grew inversely proportional to hope. Some inner strength, however, contained our painful emotions for a while, to help Audrey; to care for her. But those emotions had finally cracked. A beautiful human being had just died, inexplicably.

Then I look around to see that all, but one, were weeping. The one not shedding a tear was Pipin. He was now seated in a chair located by the entrance of the emergency room. He was leaning forward and supporting himself with his elbows over his knees, staring at Matt and me with icy eyes, giving me an uncomfortable feeling.

CARLOS SERRA

Having known him for years; knowing that stare; knowing his *macho-like* ways; and after the grimace he was making, I sensed some distorted rejection for what he had just seen. Matt and I had just embraced each other under the most pure expression of sadness and sorrow, consoling each other for the deep heartache we were feeling. Pipin, however, was most likely thinking in some other terms.

Chapter 11

THE WORST NEWS A PARENT CAN GET

SOMETIME BETWEEN 6:00 AND 6:30 P.M.

Not long after, we departed to the hotel. The van in which Matt had arrived was now offered to take us back for a silent ride. Once at the resort, Matt and I headed to Pipin's room with him. We searched for Audrey's DAN (Divers Alert Network) insurance card to begin the process of repatriating her body. While searching through Audrey's personal belongings; her purse, her luggage and inside the closet, the telephone rang.

Suddenly, I felt icicles running through my veins. My heart jumped off my chest as I felt my blood-pressure mounting. It had to be Audrey's mom calling. Pipin had already told me just moments before that she had planned to call Audrey late in the afternoon to congratulate her. But the real shocker was Pipin's unexpected request, *"If Anne-Marie calls, you talk to her; I don't want to speak with her."*

Now in the room, with the telephone ringing, he reiterated his request. *"That's Anne-Marie, you talk to her."*

Matt answered the phone and after few seconds, he covered the auricular to say in low voice,

"There is a lady on the line speaking in Spanish; I believe is Audrey's mom."

While seated on the edge of the bed I turned to my left to find Pipin resting over his left side. He immediately pointed at me, vigorously and whispered,

"You answer the call. You talk to her!" Matt, with the auricular still covered with his hand, extended it to me. Hesitantly, I took it,

"Hello," I said nervously.

"Hi, this is Audrey's mom, Anne-Marie. Who's this?"

"Hi, Anne-Marie, this is Carlos," I said with a trembling voice.

"Oh, hello, Carlos; how is Audrey, how did she do?" she asked cheerfully, obviously expecting good news.

I took a deep breath . . . sighed . . . and after a brief pause,

"Not too well, Anne-Marie . . . there was an accident . . ."

A gasp came through the line. I was trying to break the news in a sensitive way, but how is that possible?

"Is she alright?" Anne-Marie asked with a palpable fretfulness. I paused at that point, I didn't want to be abrupt, but I had no other choice,

"No, I'm afraid she's not," and without giving me opportunity to find a tactful answer, she asked in an alarming tone of voice,

"Is she alive?" she asked as I started to weep trying in vain to contain myself. My answer took few seconds, I was on the brink of breaking the hardest news a mother can get, and the only answer I could think of, is the one I gave her,

"No . . . I'm afraid she's not . . ."

That's when a nerve wrecking scream came from the other side of the line, piercing my ear and my heart. She shrieked as she would over and over every time I recall that moment.

While still screaming she hung up. I gave the phone back to Matt, looked down to the floor and cried my heart out. How will I ever erase that cry from my memory? No therapy would ever do that. Being a father of a toddler at the time, I could not imagine loosing my kid; I would rather die first. I felt even worse when I tried to visualize Anne-Marie's pain as a mother who has lost her only child.

"What did she said," Pipin kept asking, curiously. I couldn't answer right away; even if I could, I didn't want to. Looking back, I know I was feeling profoundly sad but also angry with him.

Matt remained in the room, probably not understanding much of whatever Pipin was saying in Spanish. Even so, Matt remained next to us, definitely waiting for any opportunity to provide his help and support. I knew he was a first-class guy, but his support throughout these painful times validated my discernment for ever.

About fifteen or twenty minutes had passed when the telephone rang; it was Anne-Marie once again. Matt answered for a second time, and probably realizing that Pipin wouldn't respond, he handled it back to me. And indeed, Pipin, again, refused to speak with her.

"Yes, Anne-Marie . . ." I responded while still trying to recompose myself.

"Carlos, I beg you," she implored while crying. *"Do not let anyone touch my daughter. Jean-Pierre is flying from France tomorrow to pick me up in Mexico City and continue to Santo Domingo. We will be there to see Audrey . . . We want to see our daughter one last time,"* and then she cried.

I responded affirmatively, but suddenly realizing the terrifying extent of her request. Audrey was in a morgue with no refrigeration and wearing a damped wetsuit. In addition, the temperature was averaging the ninety-plus degrees Fahrenheit. Decomposition was most certainly happening already and rather fast. I immediately wondered on what kind of condition Audrey's parents would get to see her.

I didn't, of course, tell Anne-Marie about the awful situation we had down there. It wasn't for her to know that, but it was up to me, now, to do whatever I could to preserve Audrey's remains.

Once we hung up with Anne-Marie, I rushed Pipin,

"Get up, we have to move quickly."

While Pipin gathered some clothes for Audrey, I briefly explained what Anne-Marie had told me. He placed the garments inside a plastic bag and we left the room within a minute.

Parked in front of the resort's lobby was the van. The driver and Carmen, the Resort's security assistance, were both waiting to take us back to the clinic. The Resort's management had offered full assistance with any logistics we might need, including transportation.

BACK TO LA ROMANA

It was already dark when we finally arrived at the clinic. The sun had set about an hour ago. Lit only by the street lights, four nurses were seating in the footsteps by the entrance of the emergency room. I couldn't recognize if they were the same ones, but evidently, they had no emergencies to deal with.

Stepping down from the Van I felt a tremendous discomfort. I didn't like the place; it was quite depressing, and on top of that the thought of having Audrey, laying lifeless inside that old-looking building, was overwhelming. Additionally, it was extremely hot and humid and my clothes were damped with sweat from the day's ordeal.

My navy blue t-shirt with the *IAFD* letters printed in yellow, just like the ones Audrey and the staff wore, was stained with paint from the Resort's infirmary. I must have brushed myself against the freshly painted wall while we were dealing with Audrey.

The dampness of my clothes actually elevated my anxiety; Audrey's damped wetsuit needed to be immediately replaced with dry clothes. So I expressed to the nurses the need to dress Audrey's body, and that Pipin needed to be guided to where she was. But another astonishing surprise came from him.

"I'm not going to change her," he said firmly.

He simply refused, supported his lower back against a vehicle parked in front of the clinic, and said nothing else. He just looked down while rubbing his shaved head with his right hand and the customary grimace adorning his face.

Stunned, I asked the nurses if they could change Audrey, but they looked dazed by the request. They kept glancing at each other as waiting for *the other one* to take over the unpleasant task. Finally one of them, I guess the bravest one, simply said,

"That's not our job, señor, we don't do that."

Disconcerted, I took a deep breath, grabbed the plastic bag containing Audrey's dry clothes and asked to be guided to where she was.

CARLOS SERRA

"I'll take you inside," said one of the nurses.

I wasn't eager about it. I didn't want to change Audrey's clothes, but I was willing to do it without delay. The damped wetsuit, the high temperature and over five hours that had passed since she left the water, had probably done enough damage by now. Not to mention how Anne-Marie's plead kept repeating over and over inside my head. But after having walked only a couple of steps, Carmen, the Resort's security assistant, stopped me by the arm.

"Don't you worry, Señor Carlos, I'll do it."

I looked straight at Carmen while giving her the plastic bag, held her hand and thank this kind woman from the bottom of my heart. She was like an Angel sent by heaven.

This Dominican native lady, probably in her late 20's or early 30's, had something I realized it was common among most Dominican people; they have a big and caring heart.

She took the plastic bag away from me and asked the nurse to show the way. I couldn't be more grateful, especially after finding out that she had her little daughter sick, back home, with Hepatitis, and that she was doing overtime, voluntarily, because of our tribulation.

After observing Carmen entering the clinic, I glanced back at the three remaining nurses with a recriminatory grimace on my face, but they just ignored me. With the same disdainful attitude I had seen earlier, they remained seated in the same steps. We were the *"show of the day"* and they had the best seats in the house.

Just then, I looked up to notice the name of the place, *Clinica Canela.*

"Who the hell would name a clinic, Cinnamon?" I whispered . . . and then sighed. But as I found out later, *"Canela"* is the founder's last name, Dr. Canela.

With Audrey being changed, we had another situation to take care of; paperwork. Audrey's body would not be released until the Death Certificate was signed. Also required was some sort of police discharge document.

In addition, we needed to make arrangements with the funeral home which would transport Audrey to Santo Domingo, but only after the required documentation had been delivered. To get the police release, however, a preliminary interview with all the key witnesses was needed.

A detective from La Romana Police Department was already in the clinic. He asked for the husband but Pipin refused to speak with him. I intervened begging for the detective's forgiveness claiming that Pipin was in no condition to talk right now. I told him that I would be glad to offer all the information he might need if he would be so kind and leave Pipin alone. Pipin at this point, had made some concerning remarks.

"I should be the one dead. I should not be alive." But despite the graveness of such statement, I didn't sense honesty in his words. It sounded like a badly performed melodrama, I must admit. Maybe I was wrong. Perhaps he really meant what he said and I was too disappointed with his dull reaction to the tragedy so far, but I didn't sense sincerity, at all.

To attempt committing the ultimate sin, your emotions and sense of self must be overwhelmed, just as it had happened to Audrey twice before. But Pipin, unlike Audrey, is extremely self-centered and not an emotional person. I had even played occasional jokes with him by saying that he was responsible for sinking *Titanic* after rubbing himself against the ship.

But Wiky, who had already showed up after a very long decompression, remained next to Pipin along with Eddie Matos. They didn't want to risk leaving Pipin alone.

Leaving them behind, I followed the detective to the local police precinct, located about two blocks away. It was another depressive place; like any other police precinct, I guess. The police headquarter was crowded and the atmosphere rather tense. All the cops seemed to be particularly agitated, but there was a reason. A cop from that same precinct had just been killed during a raid into a drug dealer's home in a nearby *barrio*.

The detective guided me through the intricate labyrinth of halls and tiny rooms filled with the lowest of the Dominican society. Some rough-looking guys were being interviewed by cops who didn't look any better. He led me into a room, no greater than six by ten feet, to question me. Being adapted to the ampleness of infrastructure in the U.S., the confined structures of the Dominican Republic felt claustrophobic.

After filling out the necessary documentation in an old-fashion *Olivetti* typewriter, we went back to the clinic. At arrival I saw Pipin wandering back and forth by the entrance of the emergency area. Next to him was Wiky. Eddie Matos, who had also shown his very helpful and sympathetic side, got ahead of me and went to take care of the funerary arrangements.

Now with the police report at hand, the detective and I looked for the doctor to have him sign the Death Certificate. But the doctor was not around, and that's when my contained frustration exploded.

"What the fuck is going on with these doctors who never appear when you need them!"

When the detective asked the nurses, they seemed to diverge from giving a straight answer. The detective, using coercion as a tool, found out that the doctor was in his house. I had conveyed to the detective, back in the precinct, of the urgency to transport Audrey's body as soon as possible to Santo Domingo.

Now moving fast, the driver, the detective, Carmen—who had just finished dressing Audrey—and I, got inside the van and rushed to the doctor's house. Once there, I was stepping out of the vehicle in rage when Carmen stopped me again,

"Don't worry, Señor Carlos, I'll get him," she said.

Few minutes later, Carmen walked out of the townhouse-style home with a man wearing shorts, a t-shirt and sandals, just as if the guy was headed for a beach party or to mown the lawn. To my surprise, that sporty-dressed fellow was the doctor. He boarded the van and sat next to me as we headed back to the clinic. Suppressing my anger and holding an innermost desire to hit him, I ignored the doctor and kept looking out the window to the crowded and narrow street.

Back in the clinic, the hearse was already waiting by the emergency entrance; some sort of Station Wagon from the 70's. The interior had been severely modified to accommodate the bodies, and neither the inside nor the outside were well maintained.

The flatbed in the back was made of plain plywood with no carpeting or even a hand of painting. It was set horizontally over the opening where the rear seats used to be. The shock absorbers were evidently expired since the backside of the vehicle was only a couple of inches away from scratching the pavement. The more I got to observe out of the confines of the resort's complex, the more I missed the state-of-the-art infrastructure of the United States.

The vehicle went around the building while Pipin stayed behind, by the emergency entry and accompanied by Wiky. He wouldn't let his friend of fourteen years, alone; not after what he had said not long before.

Meanwhile, Eddie Matos and I walked behind the hearse. Audrey's body would be delivered through a lateral service access, but the body had to be identified first to comply with the law. While walking towards the entrance, Eddie Matos stopped me by placing a hand over my chest. Then he said firmly but kindly,

"I'll do it, Carlos. You stay here." I wanted to thank him, but I couldn't. With a knot on my throat, I only gasped.

Eddie went inside and minutes later, a stretcher carrying Audrey's remains, completely covered with a blanket, came out. Right at that moment, unable to contain them any longer, more tears escaped. The rigor mortis was noticeable, even through the white cover.

In the van just minutes before, I was silently hoping for an absurd miracle; to get back to the clinic and see Audrey standing there. Maybe everything that had happened was an awful delusion; a well plotted scheme; a practical joke; Audrey's way to revenge the years of silly jokes she took from me.

Many absurd ideas crossed my mind that moment, clear evidence on how the brain searches for a way out looking for nonsense pretexts for a situation that made no sense. But the surrealism of the day's events collided with reality that moment when I saw her covered; she wasn't coming back.

With Audrey inside the hearse, I was ready to follow it to Santo Domingo, but Eddie stopped me, once more.

"Carlos, you've done enough. Go and get Pipin, go to the hotel, eat something and get some rest. It's been a long day."

"But, I need to make sure Audrey gets . . ."

"I'll go to Santo Domingo," Eddie interrupted. *"I live there anyway. And I'll make sure she makes it to the morgue to be placed in refrigeration immediately. Don't worry. You need to rest."*

"Alright, Eddie, thank you," I replied back, *"I'll see you tomorrow. We'll be going to Santo Domingo first thing in the morning."*

When the hearse left, I saw sparks blistering from underneath the vehicle. The exhaust pipe was scratching the pavement as the aged vehicle drove away. I tilted my head down, placed both hands over my face and whispered,

"This day can't get any worse," but I was wrong.

Chapter 12

WATCHING THE VIDEO

SUNDAY, OCTOBER 13, 2002
12:25 A.M.

B ack at the hotel, Pipin and I went directly to the restaurant. We hadn't eaten since breakfast, so we could only hope to find it open since it was well over their closing time. Only that now, eating at the resort's buffet wouldn't be a lavish culinary gratification but a vital necessity.

My body was shivering and my hands were shaky. At this point my blood-sugar levels were probably being dragged along with my feet. And yet we were lucky; since members of our staff were still eating, the restaurant was kept open a bit longer as a courtesy. The staff had waited for Pascal who decompressed well into the evening hours.

Being a key witness for what went wrong with Audrey at depth, I wanted to speak with him at once. Up until this point I had no clue on what exactly had happened. He was headed to the buffet, holding a plate, and ready to serve another portion of food when I approached him.

"Pascal, what happened down there?"

"Carlos, the tank was empty . . . Audrey opened it and very little air came out . . ."

"What? The pony-tank was empty?"

"That's what happened," he concluded.

Until that moment, I thought that Audrey suffered what I had feared the most; a physiological trauma due to the crushing pressure, but with an empty tank, the panorama changed drastically.

"Where is Pipin?" asked Pascal.

"He's in the lobby talking with Tata," I said in shock.

Pascal left the plate and headed out to speak with Pipin. Oddly, he seemed anxious to speak with him. They talked in the lobby, privately, for about twenty minutes.

After a quick dinner comprised of few leftover items from the buffet, we departed to the rooms. But before getting there, Angelo approached me to say that someone had to spend the night with Pipin. Wiky had shared with Angelo Pipin's suicidal remarks. I wasn't too concerned about it, but why risk it. I agreed with Angelo; Pipin needed some improvised suicide watch.

Angelo prepared *Tylenol PM* dissolved in water, and after drinking the concoction, Pipin went to bed followed by Wiky and Angelo. Tata and I remained downstairs in Angelo's room, located just below Pipin's. After Pascal's shocking revelation, I wanted to see the video from the sled.

While waiting for Wiky and Angelo; Tata and I exchanged some comments. Tata and the rest of the group had spoken earlier about the situation with Pascal and they confirmed what Pascal had told me in the dining room; the tank was near empty. Except that Tata also added that Pascal had offered a regulator to Audrey and she refused it. That's when Pascal started to put air in the lift bag with Audrey hanging from it.

1:30 A.M.

With Pipin now asleep, Angelo and Wiky came back downstairs. Angelo had the housing with the camera hidden inside a closet with the tape still inside. Then he hooked the camera to a small monitor and Tata, Wiky, Angelo and I watched the sled video for the first time, with all four faces only inches away from the little screen.

WHAT THE SLED'S TAPE SHOWS

The descent is normal; no signs of trouble or distress. Audrey even takes the time to break the seal of the hood on her face by pulling it, letting the water in. She does it to fill any possible air pockets with water to avoid an ear squeeze. Air can be compressed; water can't.

"Why was Pipin cussing so much?" I asked. *"Audrey wasn't going slowly."*

"Actually," replied Wiky, *"she seems to be going faster than normal. Look at the particles in the water—she's going fast."*

Amazingly, and despite being a very tight shot, Wiky appears just behind Audrey to the right of the screen. As planned, he's banging his tank to announce Audrey her current depth, around ninety meters. Then Pascal also appears moments later but behind her and slightly to the left.

Pascal is only ten meters above the record-mark of 171 meters. The plan was for Pascal to bang his tank notifying Audrey that she was only ten meters away; that it was time for her to apply the "brakes".

THE LAST ATTEMPT

That's exactly what happens. Pascal's banging can be heard on the tape, and Audrey, reacting immediately, opens the valve allowing air to enter the lift bag. This action would slow down the sled to avoid a harsh impact at the end of the line, and also save precious seconds by having the bag inflating before rocketing to the surface.

When Audrey finally reaches the bottom, she disconnects the clip holding the upper part (lift bag) of the sled. Then proceeds to open the valve completely, but instead of an immediate ascent, she moves upward few inches and comes back down. She opens her eyes momentarily, realizing the serious problem she has; glimpses at the sled and then closes her eyes once more. Aware of the emptiness of the pony-tank, she seems to be giving up. She grabs herself to the sled's upper section and remains motionless.

That's when Pascal rapidly intervenes; he had descended from above and recognized the problem. Then he pushes the sled's upper section up with Audrey hanging on to it. The lower portion of the sled remains down there, with the video running as Pascal and Audrey move upward to disappear in the upper part of the screen.

Wiky was the first one to verbalize his reaction,

"*Coño, Chico, the damned tank was empty. Pipin didn't fill the tank!*" he exclaimed with a thunderous tone.

"*Did he forget?*" Asked Angelo with his eyes wide open, but no answer came from any of us.

"*Maybe the tank emptied before she went down,*" Angelo insisted.

"*That's very unlikely,*" I replied. "*It takes a while for a full tank to get empty. Besides, someone in the boat would have heard the hissing sound of the air coming out.*"

"*Then what happened?*" Angelo asked impatiently.

"*That's the question, isn't it?*" I said. Angelo stared at me with his mouth semi-open.

Meanwhile Tata, Wiky and I looked at each other. All three of us were shedding tears. Angelo, who came only as a photographer, was the least experienced of the group. This was his first time in a world record attempt, while Tata, Wiky and I, altogether, had been in quite a few. We already knew that something had gone terribly wrong and it all pointed directly to the person who rigged the sled that tragic day; Pipin himself.

We all sat down in shock. The evidence leaned toward one option; Audrey's tank wasn't filled. But, although unlikely, there is the possibility of a mechanical problem. We kept silence for few seconds, or few minutes; I can't tell. It was as if time had stopped once again.

"*We need to know what happened,*" I said. "*Whatever it takes, the truth must be found.*"

Wiky seemed to be perturbed the most. While for me it could be a severe case of negligence from Pipin's part, for Wiky, there was something else.

"*He didn't want Audrey to take the record from him,*" he said irritably. "*And I know why!*"

I thought that Wiky, in his consternation, was overstating the issue.

"What are you saying, Wiky?" asked Tata.

"That I know why the tank was empty."

"Hold it, Wiky," I said. *"You are not suggesting that Pipin left it empty on purpose, are you?"*

"Listen; there are things about your partner that you don't know."

"Wiky, I believe it's too premature to come up with conclusions. We have to investigate the equipment first."

"Papito, you can investigate anything you want, but I know the truth."

"What truth, Wiky?" I asked.

"Carlos, in the catamaran today I brought the tank and the whip. I told Pipin to fill the pony and what did he do? He yelled at me and sent me away!"

"Yeah, I saw it."

"Then, why would he send me away in anger? He could have filled the pony right there if he had forgotten, right?"

"Wiky, he should've had it filled long before that."

"But he hadn't and I knew it. That's why I insisted."

"I can't believe it, man," interrupted Tata. *"If it wasn't for that tank, Audrey would be the deepest freediver in the world; even deeper than Pipin."*

"Hmm, she still is, Tata," I reflected. *"She still is."*

Then we all concurred that I should make a public statement as President of the *IAFD* to declare Audrey's last practice dive to 170-meters an official world record. She would be the second female freediver in history to surpass the dominant males.

"Oye, I agree, but you know Pipin is not going to like it if you declare Audrey deeper than him," Wiky stated.

"That's true," confirmed Tata.

"I don't care. As soon as I get to Miami, it's a done deal. Audrey will be officially pronounced as the deepest freediver in the world."

My resolution increased even more after remembering how I met Pipin and an awful remark he made back then.

"Did I ever tell you what Pipin said the first time I met him?"

Tata, Wiky and Angelo looked at each other, probably wondering how, whatever Pipin have said so long ago, could be related to declaring Audrey's practice dive an official record.

"What did he say?" Angelo adventured to ask.

"He said, 'No bitch is going to take my record away.'"

"Yeah, that sounds like him," said Wiky. *"He always calls women, putas."*

"But that's common among Cubans," defended Tata.

"That's common among balseros with no education," replied Wiky. *"Rafters use bitch as a synonym for woman; not well-educated Cubans."*

"Okay, guys," I interrupted. *"Let me tell you the story because I think it's pertinent. It'll tell you why I will declare Audrey's last practice dive an official world record, even if Pipin doesn't like it."*

THE LAST ATTEMPT

CARACAS, VENEZUELA—OCTOBER 1989
SAME MONTH—THIRTEEN YEARS AGO

Caracas is a modern metropolis of striking contrasts; a city where nature and technology blend in a harmonious disarray of peace and chaos. The metropolitan area is settled beneath the silent vigilance of a huge greenly mountain located to the north and running all the way from east to west. There, nature still pure and serene; butterflies in their erratic pattern fly along with hikers and nature lovers, who in a desperate attempt to detoxify their lungs, must also watch for criminals hiding in the bushes.

Combustion of leaded gasoline charges the air of the urban area with its residue, and eventually finding its way into the blood stream of the city's residents. Even though the leaded air has become a vital component of the Caraqueños' respiratory system, the occasional addition of oxygen continues to be a necessity.

Besides the mountain to the north, Caracas is surrounded by hills. That makes it hard for the air to move, so contamination remains overhead. Not even the vigorous wind of the Caribbean Sea, only few miles away to the north, can make it through. The marine breeze finds a gigantic wall that according to urban legend is a dormant volcano. For the skeptic it's just a mountain, filled with butterflies and cougars; hikers and criminals. The contrast of nature and humanity all combined in one place. Similar contrast I would find years later in Audrey and Pipin.

It was a clear and sunny afternoon in the city. I was on my way to meet an extreme sport-celebrity making his name in the freediving circles. As my friend Gianmarco drove through the rainbow of vehicles congesting the streets, the traffic was customarily heavy. Riding along on the passenger seat, I had the window down to inhale my daily dosage of freshly leaded breeze, infused with the relaxing aroma of carbon monoxide.

The prospect of sharing another day with the budding celebrity was an exciting one. He was waiting for us at his hotel for a second-day seminar in which he was the main attraction.

In a sport amply dominated by Europeans, the silly-sounding nickname of this Cuban athlete was gaining fast notoriety in South America.

"Pipin; what kind of stupid nickname is that?" asked Gianmarco.

"Yeap, it sounds medio-maricón."

But our cheerful mood would be rapidly spoiled. A moment after arrival, Pipin was standing at the hotel entrance but not to come with us. A taxi driver was placing his luggage in the trunk when Pipin, who was standing next to the cab, said seemingly upset:

"No bitch is going to take my record away, so I'm going back to Italy, today!"

"What are you talking about? Gianmarco asked puzzled. *"We have a conference room full of people waiting to see you in just few minutes. What am I going to say to them?"*

"Gianmarco, I got to go," Pipin said firmly as he boarded the cab waiting to take him to the airport. He slammed the door ignoring us and never looked back.

CARLOS SERRA

As the taxi bulldozed its way through the chaotic traffic, Gianmarco and I stood perplexed on the sidewalk. We were baffled. Pipin was leaving Venezuela and about three hundred people waiting for him in a conference room.

Coincidentally, the conference room was located at the *"Petroleos de Venezuela"* headquarters; the same oil-refining company responsible for the Caraqueños' daily intake of lead.

In that room, Pipin was expected to fulfill a promise made the day before, when a huge crowd showed up to see and hear the newest freediving hero. But the room was already filled beyond capacity. All chairs were occupied and there was no standing room left. Many people couldn't get in. In consequence, Pipin promised another seminar the following day to address the fans that had been excluded.

The first seminar was alright. It became obvious that Pipin's abilities as an orator were in direct contrast with his capacity as a freediver, but with the exception of his at-times vulgar speech, he was a hit. Nobody seemed to care and neither did we.

Besides a commanding presence, six feet tall, his curly peroxide-blondish hair and rudimentary facial features protruded as his most prominent distinctiveness. His large mouth, bulky lips and outgrown teeth evidenced some unclear ancestry in spite of his light skin. His accent was purely Cuban, but based on his vocabulary, a lack of formal education was immediately evident. Gianmarco even mentioned that Pipin needed some coaching to set his career in the right direction.

"If you remove the word 'shit' from his vocabulary, he'd be speechless," Gianmarco stated while laughing quietly.

Gianmarco Assandria chuckles often. This good-humored Venezuelan of Italian heritage owns *Sesto Continente*, a dive operation located in an upper-class neighborhood. Well-mannered and soft spoken, Gianmarco is the consummated entrepreneur, ever-concerned with his business' success.

As a way to increase exposure for his company, he brought Pipin to Venezuela for this seminar. Gianmarco, however, did not anticipate the crowd that Pipin's increasing popularity would bring; nobody would have, really. The conference room was simply too small.

At the time, Pipin had been a professional freediver for just about a year, but his accomplishments had made it to the ears of Venezuelan freediving fans. He had just matched a five-year old record set by freediving legend Jacques Mayol, who despite his retirement, continued to be popular.

Actually, Mayol's popularity reached new and unprecedented heights after the premiere of *"The Big Blue"* in 1988, a feature film directed by Luc Besson (*The Professional, La Femme Nikita, The Fifth Element* and *The Transporter* among others). Mayol's athletic achievements, along with a rivalry with his Italian counterpart, Enzo Maiorca, were the basis of the film's plot. Now Pipin, who had unofficially matched Mayol's last record, was benefiting from the popularity of the French icon.

To celebrate the first seminar's success, and after reiterating his promise to repeat it the following day, we went out for dinner with Pipin. Everyone was happy; starting with

THE LAST ATTEMPT

Gianmarco and his always-cheerful brother, Vittorio. Some of the diving instructors who worked at *Sesto Continente* were there as well, all in a festive mood.

The meal was excellent and the conversation was entertaining. The main topic of conversation was freediving, and of course, Pipin, who went over his latest record of 105-meters matching Mayol's very last mark.

Pipin was noticeably proud, perhaps even haughty about having matched Mayol's record. He also talked about how he had left Cuba thanks to his new citizenship acquired after marrying an Italian lady he met on his native land. But halfway through the *sobremesa* chitchat, Alfredo, a senior instructor working for Gianmarco and my diving tutor, as well, dropped a bomb,

"*Pipin, what do you think about Angela Bandini? I just heard today that she broke your record.*"

"*What?*" astonished, Pipin asked. "*Say that again!*"

"*Yeah, she did one hundred and seven meters in Italy,*" Alfredo confirmed.

Pipin's face went from an attentive frown to an enraged expression in less than a second.

"*She's Mayol's bitch. She's a cheater; she breaths air through a hidden hose*" and then again, "*That's not a record, I'm the record holder, she's just a bitch!*" he continued engulfed in rage.

For that record, Bandini was trained by her mentor, Jacques Mayol himself. To prepare someone to break his own record was a gallant act from Mayol's part, especially since his record was official—Pipin's mark wasn't.

It was in the wind that, despite their substantial difference in age, Mayol and Bandini shared a close relationship. But whether that was true or not, is irrelevant; she accomplished a tremendous feat by being the first athlete, male or female, to break Mayol's official record and Pipin's unofficial record, on top. Bandini set the record in the island of Elba, Italy, in October 4, 1989.

But we were all shocked. Pipin not only verbally shattered another competitor's performance, but also insulted her in the most degrading way. After leaving Pipin at his hotel, we all departed for some well-deserved sleep. We went home with high hopes for the next day, only that Pipin would receive Gianmarco the following day with his reprehensible statement, "*No bitch is going to take my record away.*"

After finishing the story on how I had met Pipin, Wiky was the first one to react, "*Carlos, you must declare Audrey the absolute world-record holder. I'll support you.*" Tata and Angelo just nodded and we all called it a day.

SUNDAY, OCTOBER 13, 2002
7:00 A.M.

By sunrise, Pipin and I departed to Santo Domingo. After a short but deep *Tylenol PM*-induced sleep, he seemed recovered. I wasn't. I couldn't sleep all night long. The fresh and vivid memories of Audrey's drama, especially after watching the video, unfolded time and time again in my head, making sleep an unachievable objective.

The van and the driver were waiting for us by the main lobby. I was glad to see that Carmen wasn't there. She was home taking care of her ill, little daughter. It was a silent trip for a while until Pipin broke the stillness to ask,

"Carlos, what are we going to tell the press now?"

Stumbling for a moment, I sighed, and then reacted, *"I don't know Pipin, and I don't care. We have some more important issues to deal with, first. Don't you think?"*

As disturbed and upset as I was, it troubled me even further how he seemed more concerned about the press and public relations than what had happened to Audrey. In addition, I knew now about the empty tank but I didn't mention the issue to him. I would wait for a better occasion.

After two hours on the road, we reached the morgue. At arrival, the van carrying the two of us entered a building encircled by a metallic fence. Eddie Matos was already there.

The building was an old-looking construction painted in light yellow. As I walked towards the entrance, the feeling I got was of a lugubrious place; a place with a sepulchral aura so intense that it could suck the life out of you.

A double-door allowed us to enter a wide lobby with a desk and two chairs in front of it. Against the walls were some more chairs for the living visitors. Quite depressing place, but it got even worse when one of the pathologists came out through a door directly connected to the autopsy room. I got to see Audrey laying face up and partially covered with a blanket. I gasped; my legs almost failed me and a shiver electrified my body. It was a sensation for which I could never get accustomed to, but that for the last eighteen hours or so, I had become familiar with.

After recovering my breath from the impact, I turned around to see if Pipin had seen the same, but he was looking for a chair and didn't see her. Then I wondered about the gross architectural flaw that allowed direct view into the autopsy room from the main hall. Having worked in architecture for many years before switching careers to diving, a designing flaw like that was just too evident.

The forensic staff had just completed the autopsy, making Pipin extremely upset, because he didn't want an autopsy to be performed. It took a lot of convincing from Eddie to make him understand that it was the law. No way around that one.

"I want her cremated right away!"

Eddie explained him that cremation was not available in the entire country. In any case, the autopsy was a done deal.

The pathologist, who just came out, and after identifying Pipin as the husband, asked him about the fact that Audrey had been pregnant within the last year.

"She wasn't pregnant!" Pipin said irritated.

But that wasn't true. I was aware of Audrey's abortion ordeal the previous year 2001. She had told my wife about it and later in time, she told me as well. She was afraid of loosing Pipin with the pregnancy as it happened to the mothers of Pipin's first two

THE LAST ATTEMPT

children. As he had said many times before, *"Women turn into shit (se vuelven mierda) with pregnancy; that's why I leave them"*.

An employee of the company had taken Audrey to a clinic in Kendall, coincidentally not far from my home, because Pipin, allegedly, refused to accompany her.

So the pathologist just confirmed a not publicly disclosed fact, but it got my attention, nevertheless, how Pipin would bluntly contradict science. Doctors know better. The pathologist even managed to give a time frame—within the last year—which happens to be correct. The doctor didn't seem to mind Pipin's reaction, though, as he continued to put some paperwork together.

Eddie Matos, who had stepped out of the building, came inside to warn us; reporters from the Dominican TV had just arrived. They wanted to interview Pipin, but as he looked at me, I knew what he wanted,

"I'll take care," I said, while escorted by Eddie, I headed to the front yard to meet the press.

I gave them a brief statement and pleaded them to provide some breathing space for a grieving husband. They seemed to respond affirmatively, but they had orders to follow. So instead of the interview with Pipin, they asked me some questions and went around the building to catch the images of Audrey's sarcophagus leaving the morgue in its way to the funeral home.

After signing some official documents, Pipin and I boarded the Resort's van. Eddie climbed on board his own vehicle. Only then I noticed a familiar face behind the wheel of Eddie's car; it was Amaury, who after the ordeal we had endured the day before trying to cheat death from taking Audrey, we greeted each other as old comrades.

Then, the van drove around the building to the point where the press was already waiting. The gasket containing Audrey's remains was placed in a far nicer hearse than the one that brought her from La Romana the night before. We followed the hearse to the funeral home.

Once there, we were greeted by the manager, who sympathetically, took us to a private office away from the reporters and their cameras' unrelenting clicking. The funeral home was very clean and modern, with open spaces that resembled more the lobby of a nice hotel than a place where the main trade is death.

Even so, the way the staff ran their business was definitively appropriate. They were courteous and caring to the minimum detail. It was an uplifting sight, especially after the morgue experience where the adjectives used to refer to Audrey were, *"The French woman,"* *"The girl,"* or just *"The cadaver"*.

Earlier, at the morgue, I even stood up to the chief-pathologist and requested her to change the adjectives used to address Audrey, for more thoughtful ones; particularly in front of Pipin. I expressed my annoyance after the chief-pathologist, a middle-age lady, shouted to one of her aids,

"¡Preparen el cadáver de la Francesa para la entrega!" which translates to, *"Prepare the cadaver of the French woman for delivery!"*

CARLOS SERRA

"She's not a French ham to be distributed to a Deli bistro, for God's sake. And her name is Audrey!" I recall saying to the pathologist with a harsh tone but a broken voice, as I continued to struggle with my own emotions. But unlike the morgue, the funeral home's staff was much more sensitive in their choice of words.

To *Blandino Funeral Home* arrived the representative of the Italian Consulate. They were notified about the tragic event and wanted to assist if Audrey's remains should be transported to Italy. That was just an assumption based on Pipin's nationality. He had obtained the Italian citizenship—and way out of Cuba—through his first marriage to Simona, a tourist agent working in Varadero at the time.

Actually, besides the Italian consulate, the diplomatic offices of France, Mexico and the USA were all notified. It was done that way since Pipin was unable to make a decision; he wanted to wait until Audrey's parents' arrival to find out where they wanted Audrey to be repatriated.

"Jesus, Pipin, she's your wife," I said in recriminatory tone. *"It's your decision, and the most logical choice would be Miami, where you both live."*

"No, no, no, let's wait. Maybe they want to take her to France."

The French Consulate was notified due to Audrey's nationality and most of her family still lives in France.

During her late teen years and early 20's, Audrey lived in Mexico with her parents. Although her parents were French, her dad had been transferred to Mexico by the company he worked for. Audrey lived there until she engaged with Pipin and moved to the U.S.; her place of residency the moment she passed away.

Eddie notified the four consulates to be a step ahead with the formalities. Despite Pipin's constant hesitation, the only aspect in which he was convinced and quite persistent was,

"I want her cremated right now!" But the manager at *Blandino* just confirmed to Pipin what Eddie had said before; there was no cremation available, neither legally nor practically. Pipin, however, senselessly insisted,

"I want her cremated; that's what Audrey wanted," except that cremation would have to wait until the return to Miami.

But on the other hand, it made me wonder if Pipin would have Audrey cremated even before Audrey's mom had arrived. She had pleaded to see her daughter one last time, and I'm sure she didn't mean to see her ashes.

Minutes after the cremation debate, the manager called me apart from Pipin. He notified me of some major work needed to correct the damage done by decomposition. To present Audrey in an open gasket, complying with her parent's wishes to see her, they had to embalm the body and apply some costly make-up. They needed Pipin's approval to do so but they preferred for somebody close to him to explain the process. Obviously, the manager was already aware on how difficult dealing with Pipin could be.

"Sir, go ahead and do it."

"But, aren't you going to ask mister Ferreras?"

THE LAST ATTEMPT

At this point I turned to see Pipin through the semi-opened door of an office. He was seated inside with his elbow supported over a small round table, looking down and both hands holding his head.

"*No need for; please go ahead and proceed, and the sooner the better.*"

"*Yes, Señor Serra,*" the manager acknowledged while bowing with respect, "*we'll start right away.*"

Having nothing else to do in Santo Domingo, we departed to the Resort, but before leaving, Eddie assured Pipin that he would maintain a line of communication open with the different consulates until Audrey's final resting place was determined. And yet, Pipin didn't seem to be listening. He just kept on walking and boarded the van. Looking at me, Eddie asked,

"*Is there anything else I can do?*"

"*You're doing great, Eddie,*" I said while patting him in the shoulder. "*Thank you for your help and support.*"

"*C'mon, man; don't mention it. You have my cell phone number; call me if you need me.*"

In an incredible display of resourcefulness and determination, Eddie got in touch with all four consulates although it was a Sunday. Even more remarkable is that because of *Columbus Day,* those diplomatic offices would also be close the next day, Monday 14. But Eddie, somehow, found the right person to deal with and habilitated all four diplomatic entities, regardless.

Now, with Audrey's body taken care of, particularly after her parent's wishes to see her, it was time to confront Pipin about the empty tank; it was time to start looking for answers.

Chapter 13

Facing Audrey's Parents

Back at the hotel, Pipin and I headed to my room to talk. I was surprised that he hadn't asked about what had happened to Audrey down there; why she didn't make it. I could only speculate that he had asked Pascal when they met the night before at the lobby. Or perhaps, he had recalled not having filled the tank.

Once in my room, he sat in one of the two double beds, reclining his back against the headboard. I sat in the stool where I would normally write the daily report for the website; I had written the last one on Friday. On top of the table behind me, was the laptop computer from which no report would be made this day, or the days to come. Then I took the courage to confront him with the awful fact; Audrey failed to ascend because the tank in the sled was empty.

"Pipin, did you fill the pony-tank?"

He shook his head and while looking down, avoiding direct eye contact and rubbing his shaved head, he replied,

"Yes, I did."

"Well, something happened then, because there was no air in that tank."

"I'm sure I did it," Pipin responded with poise. But he didn't respond any further. He kept rubbing his shaved head in a circular motion, like he always does when stressed.

Throughout the years, I've learned to identify the different signs that Pipin's personality emits; clear and distinctive messages that if interpreted correctly, it makes your interaction with him a lot easier. In this case, the scratching of the head, the evasive eye contact, the shaking of his head in denial and the lack of response, were clear and distinctive signs. He had just isolated himself with an invisible cocoon that would not be possible to break through; not without risking confrontation with his argumentative side. I didn't feel like arguing, so I let it rest . . . for now.

THE LAST ATTEMPT

The moment after Pipin departed from my room, I received a phone call from Miami. It was our assistant in the company calling from her house. Carolina is a short and slim Venezuelan girl, very sharp when it comes to the technicality of computers, but also exceptionally creative.

She was profoundly saddened by the news, and while giving her the account of what happened to Audrey, we both cried. Somehow, Carolina manage through the weeping to tell me that *CNN Headline News* had been airing the awful news of Audrey's passing; that's how she found out. I apologized for not calling her before and having to find out through a different source, but I didn't have her home phone number with me. Besides, I had been dreadfully busy.

Once we hung up, I turned the TV on, tuned to *CNN Headlines News* and minutes later, with my eyes clouded with tears, I saw the shocking images of Audrey being pulled out of the water.

MONDAY, OCTOBER 14, 2002
THE PARENTS ARRIVAL
9:00 A.M.

Audrey's parents were programmed to arrive. Eddie Matos met with us at the hotel; he had come from Santo Domingo with an update on his diligent duties contacting the consulates. And that's when Pipin, in front of Eddie, dropped another shocking request,

"Carlos, I'm not feeling well; you go to the airport to pick them up," he said in demanding tone. But not wasting a second, my determined replied came,

"No, Pipin, here's where I draw the line."

Now Pipin seemed in dismay with my answer. He was comfortably accustomed to having some else taking over the unpleasant responsibilities, but not anymore. While Eddie observed silently, I added,

"You go to the airport and you pick them up. That's your obligation, not mine. It's about time you do something."

The prospect of meeting with Anne-Marie and Jean-Pierre was not a thrilling one, but I would have done it if it was my responsibility. But it was about time for Pipin to act as a grownup and face his duties. So, he went to the airport, alone, since I even refused to accompany him. I wasn't avoiding a meeting that, eventually, would happen anyway. I just avoided that first encounter at the airport which I was sure it would be extremely emotional.

Few hours later, when Pipin, Anne-Marie and Jean-Pierre made it to the hotel, I was seated at the lobby waiting for them. It was a long wait. They had gone from the airport directly to see Audrey at the funeral home.

At their arrival, Jean-Pierre and I embraced each other in a painfully emotional hug; we cried inconsolably. I could not impede the flow of emotions and tears. Then I knew that not going to the airport didn't make much difference.

But a moment later, Jean-Pierre shook the floor where I was standing when he held me by the shoulders to ask,

"Why didn't you have more divers down there? Why wasn't another diver between Wiky and Pascal to help my daughter?"

The question stroke me like a sledge hammer hitting simultaneously my brain and heart. It wasn't me who had decided not to have any more divers; it was Pipin! He had refused to have any divers between 90 and 171 meters; an irrational and dreadful gap of 81 meters. And yet, this gap is a trademark for Pipin's record attempts, anyway; at least the latest ones.

Then I looked over Jean-Pierre's shoulder to see Pipin, who standing right behind Audrey's dad, locked his piercing eyes on me and shook his head. Silently, he was asking me to remain hushed.

Once again, I was in a very upsetting position, standing before a mournful father searching for answers while holding loyalty towards the person unquestionably responsible for the lack of divers, among many other things. In particular the tank issue, which was not brought up by Jean-Pierre and that's what, ultimately, sealed Audrey's faith.

Not waiting for an answer, Jean-Pierre walked away weeping and holding his face with his hands. Then Anne-Marie embraced me, too. She was crying, as well, but neither asked any question nor said a word. She only hugged me for a while and then walked away. She went straight to one of the seats at the entrance of the Lobby where Jean-Pierre was now seated, still holding his face down and crying. She joined him while some other family members, whom had come with them, surrounded Jean-Pierre in support.

That's when I had enough, and in a very inquisitive tone I whispered to Pipin,

"Why is he asking me for the lack of divers in the water? What kind of disparate story did you give then in the way here? Haven't I done enough for you to also take the blame for what happened to Audrey?"

"Carlos, brother . . . wait . . ." Pipin was clearly hesitant.

That's when I turned around and, enraged, departed to my room leaving Pipin behind. No more than five minutes had passed when someone knocked on my door. It was him, with a fretful expression in his face.

"Carlos, take it easy, I don't know why Jean-Pierre asked you those questions. I have no idea."

"Pipin, don't give me any of your famous bullshit, I know you too well," I said while thumping my right index-finger into his chest. *"How would Jean-Pierre know about the gap between Wiky and Pascal?"*

"I don't know, man. Maybe through the report you wrote on the internet."

"I've never wrote anything about the number of divers in the water, so cut the crap."

"Don't worry about it, Carlos."

"Of course I worry about it. I had argued with you back in Miami about the lack of divers. You even refused to have Mike, the FBI agent who helped us with Audrey's record in Fort Lauderdale last year, remember?"

THE LAST ATTEMPT

Pipin became elusive once again, rubbing his head and looking down. But this time I continued pounding on him.

"And why isn't he asking for what actually caused her death? Does Jean-Pierre know about the damned tank being empty? How come he didn't say a word about that?"

An uneasy Pipin kept negating having said anything to Audrey's parents about the tragedy, but that's illogical. The first question they probably asked is what happened.

TUESDAY, OCTOBER 15
AROUND 2:30 A.M.

On another sleepless night, I was wandering around the hotel when few newspapers in the lobby caught my attention. They all had Audrey's tragedy in the front page. But one of the headlines shocked me immensely as they described Audrey's melancholic state before the attempt.

"How could they possibly know?"

"Listin Diario", one of the largest Dominican newspapers, published on October 14, 2002, the following headline:

"Audrey Mestre was sad before entering the water."

Then the reporter, Florentino Duran, wrote in the article following the headline:

"Despite being one of the most important moments in her life, athlete Audrey Mestre, who died last Saturday in the vicinity of Bayahibe Bay, while trying to obtain a world record in freediving, was observed sad and contemplative moments before the attempt that cost her life."

Another newspaper, *"El Dia"*, published the same day—October 14—a large size picture of Audrey. It was the same picture that *Associated Press* had distributed around the world showing a contemplating Audrey seating lonely on the boat's center raised area. Impressive was the size of it; the picture alone covered almost half the page. It was obvious the intention to make the point clear, because underneath the picture, the following caption was written:

"French Audrey Mestre, who seems troubled, is seeing here meditating moments before submerging and attempting a new world record in freediving."

What really stunned me is that even the press had noticed Audrey's emotional state. I knew how depressed she was; I had spoken with her minutes before she died, and I knew the reason for her depressive condition. But even people who didn't know her, or had interacted with her, were able to perceive her profound sadness.

"I wonder if . . ." but before going any further with my thoughts, I concluded, *"No, that can't be."*

The idea that had just crossed my mind was too awful, so I shook my head and gathered the newspapers, placed them folded under my armpit and went to the beach to watch the stars, reflect on the ordeal and let the ocean caress my feet; the same water that only meters ahead had taken Audrey's life few hours ago.

With the intention of clearing my mind and search for answers, I remained on the edge of the water for a while. Embedded in my mind were the images I had seen in the video, when Audrey opened the valve of the tank to find it empty . . . a tank that perhaps Pipin had left unfilled.

Then the same possibility that crossed my mind at the lobby returned with bloodcurdling effect.

"Oh, no; that's not possible," I said to myself once again. *"That can't be . . ."*

I shook my head to swirl away the recurrent and alarming thought, but that's when the spine-tingling sensation intensified. I felt something unexplainable, like a blurry and ghostly presence nearby but no one was around. I turned the backlight of my wristwatch; it was 3:33 a.m.

"Hmm, time to rest. I'm not thinking straight and I'm starting to feel weird things."

Chapter 14

BACK TO MIAMI

WEDNESDAY, OCTOBER 16, 2002

 Matt Briseno and I flew back to Miami early in the morning. Matt, just like Wiky, was convinced about Pipin's responsibility in Audrey's death. He had told me before and confirmed it once again during the flight, that he attempted to fill the pony-tank but was stopped. That made three the number of people who had either asked Pipin or attempted to fill the tank before Audrey's descent.

 At arrival to *Miami International Airport*, my wife Adriana and our 22-months-old son, Alexander, were waiting outside at the curb. I immediately looked inside the vehicle searching for my kid, and when I finally saw him in the back seat I hugged him tightly; the recent experience of suddenly loosing a close friend made me realize the vulnerability of our transitory journey through this life. Yet, the stress caused by Audrey's tragedy became bearable, at least for a moment.

 My son was weeping and shivering with emotion. I trembled, too. I had spent over two weeks away from him. It must have been a long time for him, but for me, it was an eternity. I fought against my own feelings to avoid bursting to tears; although, one or two came out anyway. An upbringing listening to the old and false cliché, *"Tough guys don't cry,"* still affecting my notions of strength. I swept those tears rapidly before my wife would find out that I wasn't so tough, after all.

 After saying goodbye to Matt and Paul Kotik, the correspondent from *DeeperBlue.net* who had come to pick Matt, I climbed up my vehicle and went home. Paul had returned earlier in the week from the Dominican Republic, and Matt would spend couple of days in Paul's home before heading back to Hawaii.

Pipin, Anne-Marie, Jean-Pierre, the rest of the relatives and Audrey's remains returned later that same day. Therefore, I returned to the airport afterward with Wiky, who had flown back to Miami as originally planned, on Monday 14. Wiky waited in front of the *American Airlines* terminal with the vehicle's engine running, as I stepped inside the terminal looking for Pipin and Audrey's family. The Spanish TV Networks, *Telemundo* and *Univision*, were waiting at the airport, but no interviews were given despite their insistence.

SATURDAY, OCTOBER 19, 2002

Exactly one week after Audrey's death had passed. The last couple of days were spent making arrangements for cremation, as Pipin so desperately wanted. In the evening, there was a vigil at Pipin's house, which allowed for dozens of people to come and pay their respects. Among them was the press.

Entering the house, held by a tripod easel, was a poster size picture of a smiley Audrey. Next to the picture was a table containing dozens of flower-bouquets, and at the center of it, the urn with Audrey's ashes inside. It was a beautifully presented setting over the dining room table, but most people, after paying their respects, gathered in the back patio; it's by the water and has a magnificent view of Miami's skyline.

The back patio, incidentally, was the only place of the house I liked. The entrance of the residence has no windows, and the hall, with its claustrophobic walls, were made of dark wood. The lugubrious doorway and the steps ahead are an invitation for an accident, unless, you already knew where the steps were. Luckily, most people entering the house would stop first to allow for the pupils to dilate to the darkness, and even so, throughout the countless visits I had paid to the residence, I saw more than one person tripping over the dark-hidden steps.

Having survived the hallway, hanging on the walls of the living room, dozens of tinted wooden masks embedded with African features, greeted the guests with a smirk that would make a catholic priest hold on tight to his crucifix.

Over the floor, small wooden statuettes representing different African gods adorned the place, and they weren't any prettier than the masks on the walls. Without a doubt, the decoration is influenced by Pipin's devotion for Santeria and its African ancestry.

To the vigil I assisted with my wife, Adriana, who broke in tears the moment she saw the urn, perhaps remembering the times when the two of them were close friends. I hugged her in consolation, but I was barely holding myself.

Adriana and Audrey became friends in the summer of 1999 during a trip to Spain, where I had made arrangements for a freediving course to be taught by Pipin and Audrey. The course was set in the island of Mallorca, with the help of a friend, Juan Carlos Caraglia, a scuba-instructor I had trained. But before getting to Mallorca, we spent couple of days in Madrid.

THE LAST ATTEMPT

As I spent my time visiting *El Museo del Prado*, Adriana and Audrey shared a lot of time together shopping around, buying mainly Audrey's favorite items; body and facial creams.

The reason for our delayed transit in Madrid was Pipin. As soon as we landed in Spain's capital city, he immediately departed to Italy to sign his divorce papers. He was finally and legally disintegrating his marriage with Simona, the Italian lady he had wedded before leaving Cuba.

Despite many years of separation and having lived with Audrey for more than three years, he was still married to Simona. He expedited the divorce due to his plans to marry Audrey later in 1999.

Unable to keep herself together any longer, Adriana freed herself from my arm and went to the back patio. Just like anyone else, she couldn't bear seeing the urn and imagining Audrey, being reduced to ashes.

As she walked away, I remained standing in front of the urn, reflecting over Audrey's last moments and what could have possibly gone through her mind. In the cold and lonesome bottom of the ocean, her senses must have been overwhelmed the moment she opened the valve of that tank, just to find it empty.

Then I remembered the moment when, while standing on the beach of the resort, during the wee hours of Tuesday 15, at exactly 3:33 a.m. an awful thought crossed my mind.

"Audrey, what happened," I reflected while staring at her poster. *"What truly happened down there? I wish there was a way for you to tell me."*

And while contemplating Audrey's picture, a comforting arm fell from behind just over my shoulders; it was Audrey's dad, Jean-Pierre. Holding me tight, he accommodated himself to my left side as we both faced the picture and said,

"She was pretty, ah, Carlos?"

"Yes, indeed, Jean-Pierre, she was beautiful, externally and internally."

Despite the sadness, his face showed the grin of a proud dad. At least for a moment, sadness was not the prevailing sentiment in his heart. I felt glad for him. Unfortunately, it didn't last long. A momentary silent was abruptly broken moments later by his lament.

"I didn't want her to do this record, Carlos . . . too deep, too risky," he said with a broken voice.

What Jean-Pierre had just said is something that, before departing to the Dominican Republic, saddened Audrey greatly. When Audrey announced to her dad, over the phone, the intention to do another record, they argued.

"Yeah, sure, go ahead and kill yourself. What the heck; I only have one child." This quote is more or less what Audrey recalled, with tears running down her face.

It was the protecting love of a father attempting to bring some sense into her only kid, but for a passenger in a bullet-train called Pipin, bailing out is not that easy. And in the end, Jean-Pierre ended up supporting Audrey.

But probably remembering those same painful words, Jean-Pierre walked away, sat in a nearby chair and cried. Anne-Marie approached him, and while seating herself in the chair's armrest, she caressed his hair. They were both devastated, but she seemed to be holding better, much better than him. She was the stronger one, or perhaps, her emotional pain threshold was higher.

That's when a tear ran down my face; it was impossible to see such a touching sight and not shed one. No parent would ever accept, complacently, the idea of surviving a child.

At the distance I saw Angelo, so I decided to get away from Audrey's parents as a way to keep my composure and give them privacy at the same time. Approaching Angelo I congratulated him for the poster; I knew it had to be his doing. He went to the Dominican Republic as a photographer and the picture in the poster was taken by him.

Then, Wiky call me apart from Angelo; he seemed upset, unnerved, as if something was awfully wrong.

"Carlos, after tomorrow's ceremony you will never see me in this house or around Pipin . . . ever!" he said forcefully. The ceremony he was referring to was the spreading of the ashes in the ocean.

"Okay, Wiky, calm down. Tell me what's going on?"

While pointing an index finger right at my chest he said,

"You and I know what he did to her . . ."

"Hey, Wiky, hold it," I interrupted. "I don't know exactly what happened, not yet. But I promise I will find out."

"I don't need to investigate; I know Pipin too well and that tank was not empty by accident."

"Well, Wiky, I respect your position, but it's very hard for me to believe that Pipin could have done something like that on purpose."

I looked around searching for Pipin; I was hoping not to see him nearby listening to Wiky's statements. That could have created an unpleasant situation right there, but he was about ten yards away, near the water chatting with someone. Then Wiky started to talk about the one subject I always disliked the most, Pipin's fondness for bizarre rituals.

He stated that Audrey's death was intimately related to it; the dead people's names in Audrey's wetsuit, the red bandana wrapped on her wrist and the ceremony with the banana, offered vast proof that Audrey was an involuntary constituent of a major ritual, according to Wiky.

Actually, Wiky's speculation took a dramatic twist when later that evening, after most visitors had left the house, Pipin took the small urn containing Audrey's remains to his room. He said that he wanted to spend one last night with Audrey, but Wiky's face turned red and visibly shaken.

While watching Pipin taking the urn and closing the door behind, I kept wondering if what I had just seen was a bizarre act of love or just another melodramatic performance, the grossest ever this time from Pipin's part.

THE LAST ATTEMPT

When I turned back to Wiky, he was storming his way out of the house. I remained behind for few more minutes, but shortly after, I told Adriana that it was time to leave. One way or the other, seeing Pipin taking the urn with him, gave me unwanted and irrepressible chills.

SUNDAY, OCTOBER 20, 2002
8:00 A.M.

The day was just like the emotions around; gloomy. It was overcast and chilly, at least for South Florida standards. Surprisingly, reporters with their cameras, lights, microphones and the whole paraphernalia were present at Pipin's house. He had made arrangements with them the night before but not to report the weather. The plan for the day was the spreading of Audrey's ashes into the ocean and Pipin had invited the press to cover the occasion.

Few other boats would accompany the main vessel, the *Olokún*, a 32-feet long converted-craft with open cabin. It was Pipin and Audrey's training boat and it was docked right behind their home. The name of the boat honors the mythical *God of the Sea* of the *Yoruba* people in the African nation of Nigeria.

Devoted practitioners of Santeria rituals, like Pipin, revere this underwater god and dedicate their rituals to him. It is said by believers that due to the large number of lives lost at sea, *Olokún* is closely connected to the dead. It's also said that to gain the favors of *Olokún*, a person should offer a sacrifice; for smaller favors a dove would do, but for bigger favors, the offering must also increase in significance. According to legend the offering of humans, alive or otherwise, shall bring incalculable fame and wealth to the devotee.

One of the last ones to arrive to the house was Wiky, and after what had occurred the night before, I decided to approach him, especially since he didn't seem to be in a better mood.

"Why are reporters here?" he asked without greeting.

"I believe Pipin invited them."

"Ah, of course . . . this is another show; Pipin's show."

Initially, I didn't like Wiky's connotation. We always referred to Pipin's display with the press and the cameras as, *"Pipin's Show"*, but to a certain degree I had to agree; there was no need for the press to be there. It was a time for bringing closure and to begin the grieving process in a private fashion, not for sharing images of people mourning the death of a family member or friend with the rest of the world, I thought.

But Pipin, nevertheless, has always loved having a camera around, and this time, despite the significance of the occasion, it would be no different. Perhaps the significance of the occasion is the very own reason he had to allow the press. It was free advertisement and an excellent opportunity to improve his deteriorated image within the freediving world. The press should give a more benevolent image of him mourning the death of his wife. It was a revolting thought, yes, but the signs were too obvious to be ignored.

What gave me the feeling that Wiky was in the right track, was the moment Pipin brought out to the dock the urn containing Audrey's ashes. First, he had given instructions for the press to be ready. Second, he walked with the urn from the house to the *Olokún*, with the press filming and shooting pictures, and handled it to Jean-Pierre, who brought it on board. Third, and possibly the most significant aspect of all was the wetsuit. Pipin was now wearing the duplicate of the wetsuit worn by Audrey, but oddly enough, he had refused to wear that very same wetsuit the day of Audrey's faithful event.

"What is he doing with a wetsuit and that wetsuit in particular?" I wondered. *"For spreading ashes from a boat there is no need for it."*

On board the *Olokún* were the family members and closest friends of Audrey, including Anne-Marie, Jean-Pierre, Audrey's cousins, Pipin, Carolina and her husband Chelique, Angelo, Tata, Wiky and me.

A caravan of boats followed the *Olokún* to a place previously marked in the boat's GPS as Audrey's training spot. By law, the spreading of the ashes could not take place within the 3-mile jurisdiction or marine platform. Consequently, the boat went further out until we were beyond the three nautical miles. Even a police boat was kindly dispatched by the city to escort the caravan.

Pipin, as always, took command of the entire operation. He drove the boat from the flying-bridge and had called me to seat next to him. He gave constant instructions to Tata and Angelo down below. He constantly checked for the other boat's location and speed, and kept looking for the boat carrying the press. I couldn't help it, but I noticed that he was striking his customary macho-like poses for the cameras, as he always does. The more I observed Pipin, the more the situation reminded me of another record. Wiky was right, it was a show, but the biggest surprise was still to come.

The moment we arrived at the destination, Pipin started to gear up. The always obedient and silent Tata had brought out Pipin's fins and mask. Tata assisted him to get in the water just like getting ready for another record attempt. That's when my suspicions became evident; Pipin would not spread the ashes from the boat along with Audrey's parents. He would get in the water and do it alone.

Then, the most grotesque display took place when Pipin entered the water, swam to a place between the circle of boats, opened the urn and the ashes were all around him. Standing next to the boat's platform, I witnessed in dismay the bizarre exhibition Pipin was putting on.

Then I felt someone standing next to me. It was Wiky, and visibly disturbed, he said,

"Do you see that? I told you, that's Pipin's show . . . do I know him or what? That's why the press is here."

"Yeah . . ." I replied back, baffled. *"I can see your point now; but it's still hard for me to believe it."*

THE LAST ATTEMPT

When I turned to see Wiky, his eyes were infused with red, glassy with tears ready to overflow. With a broken voice he added,

"Carlos, you know him well, too. Don't allow Pipin to fool you for a second. He has fooled many people before. He has fooled all these people here; he has fooled the world with his records, but don't let him fool you, as well. You know his records are nothing else but a show, but this is the greater show he has ever done."

With Pipin back on board, flowers were tossed into the ocean and everyone on board was weeping, except one person; Pipin. He looked wretched, but for whatever reason, he didn't drop a tear. I didn't see him crying in the Dominican Republic after Audrey's death. I didn't see him crying two or three days later, or even a week after.

People have their own personal way to grieve. Some cry openly while some others sob internally, from the deepest part of their soul. But I didn't see much pain or sorrow on Pipin, only piercing, inquisitive eyes and apprehension.

What really got me later, back at his house, was to see Pipin giving an interview to the press. And with him seated on the couch of his living room, he asked me to be seated next to him to respond some of the questions.

Pipin's eyes, for the first time, became glassy in front of the camera. It was a touching sight; he was finally showing a human emotion. But a moment later and with the interview over, he became the same Pipin I knew, directing the orchestra without a hint of sadness. Wiky also noticed that,

"Look at him, Carlos. Is that the same guy who was just weeping for his dead wife in front of a camera minutes ago?"

"What are you trying to say, Wiky?"

"That it is all an act, a performance."

The press had already left, but few other people remained in the house and Pipin was, again, giving directions to Tata. Moments later Wiky told me the very last words I would hear from him for the next few months,

"Carlos, I respect you as the professional and tremendous diver you are, but from now on, I want nothing to do with Pipin, the IAFD, or anything related to him."

Next, he went straight to Pipin and to his face, he said,

"This is the last time you'll see me in this house. This is the last time you'll see me with you. You better don't call me again, ever. I know what you did and why, so the best you can do is to leave me alone. Erase my number from your cell phone. I don't even exist for you."

Then, he left the house leaving Pipin visibly bewildered.

After fourteen years of loyal support, that was the last time for Pipin to see Wiky next to him.

Besides Wiky's statement, something about Pipin and the whole tragedy was really getting on my nerves, especially after finding out about the empty tank. I also became concerned about the series of seemingly illogical situations before and after Audrey's passing.

"Pipin always behaves strangely," I reflected. *"He's not a normal person, I know. But I wonder why he behaved so extraordinarily abnormal this time. I wonder if there is a connection."*

Even so, I refused to give much credit to Wiky's allegations or to believe any wrongdoing from Pipin's part, at least not intentional. Nevertheless, and as I had promised to the press, on camera, moments before,

"I will investigate and find out what ultimately happened."

Chapter 15

THE INVESTIGATION BEGINS

EARLY NOVEMBER 2002
TWO WEEKS LATER

Overwhelmed by unbearable memories, I remained at home with my family to recompose my emotional state and bring it back to acceptable levels. But after two weeks off, it was time for me to go back to the office. The prospect of returning to the place where I used to share an average of ten hours a day with Audrey, five days a week, was not enticing.

The first day back, I stood by the building's access door with the key on my hand, hesitating. It was around 7:45 a.m. I wanted to go back to my car and run away. A feeling of anguish invaded my body, once more, and even though it was a familiar sensation by now, it remained unpleasant.

The small building in which the offices of the *IAFD* were located, was in a block of mostly residential homes. More likely, people inside those houses were waking up, either having breakfast or skirmishing over the use of the bathroom. In all probability, they were getting ready to go to work or school; just moving on with their regular and uneventful life. For a moment, I envied them.

So early in the morning, none of our employees had arrived. Their schedule started at nine o'clock. With no one around and barely any traffic, the silence amplified the desolating feeling. It was as if I was ready to open a portal into another dimension, a place of nothingness; a place of emptiness.

The moment I turned the lock with the key and pushed the door open, the dreariness of the place sucked away any positive emotion I could have had. Gloominess was the one and only sentiment, but that wasn't new. The installations were gloomy even before

CARLOS SERRA

Audrey's tragedy, as I had conveyed before to Pipin, Audrey and the employees, the creepy feeling the building transpired.

"Yeah," affirmed Pipin on one occasion. *"I think this place was used for Santeria rituals before we bought it, and I'm sure there is a body buried in here."*

"And how would you know such thing," I asked then, incredulously and yet curiously.

"Because we restored this place after a fire. It was burned and I think it happen while the previous owners were performing a Santeria ritual with candles all over."

"That explains the fire, but what about the dead body?"

"I can feel it," he said with confidence.

Now, standing alone in the middle of the lounge by the main entry, I believed Pipin. There was something awful about that place and turning the lights on, didn't help. I locked the door behind, but before heading to my office on the second floor, I looked towards Audrey's office first. I couldn't help it; knowing that she would never be back in there, a wistful sadness made me realize how much I'd miss her.

As I walked towards the hallway, I did see the dozen of wetsuits that were hanging on the walls of the sitting area and the hall. With the exception of one, a white one, they were all Pipin's. Along with multiple poster-size pictures of him and none of Audrey, the whole place was an exhibit venerating his achievements.

Back in my office, I was bombarded with messages left by reporters who wanted more information. Sue Cocking from *The Miami Herald* and Adrian Sainz from *Associated Press* were the most persistent. But reporters from *United Press International*, *Time Magazine*, *Sun-Sentinel* from Miami, *Univision* and *Telemundo* had left messages, as well. Some of them even called me at home. I evaded them for days, but it was time to confront the unavoidable.

The next time they called I answered, and the response was what I knew so far. The tank was empty and as a result, Audrey didn't have enough lifting to make it to the surface.

"Who was responsible for the tank?" they all asked.

There was no way around that one. Pipin was the person responsible for the sled and the tank. The facts, however, were given off-the-record until more evidence could be gathered.

Some key elements remained to be analyzed. The computer that Audrey was wearing, provided by Kim McCoy, added another piece to the puzzle; during the ascent, the sled stopped for 30 seconds at 164 meters.

Also to be clarified was why Pascal didn't provide Audrey a regulator allowing her to breathe and possibly save her life. According to Pascal's testimony the very same night Audrey died, she had refused the regulator more than once. I needed to confirm that version, though, but he was back in France and I couldn't reach him. In addition, I had to wait for Kim McCoy's concluding report to sustain whatever final result would come out from the investigation. Kim was back in San Diego analyzing in-depth the computer data.

THE RISE AND FALL OF FREEDIVERPRO

Later that day Pipin came to the office and blew me away with an astonishing request. I had mentioned my intention to publish the next edition of our magazine, *FreediverPro*, as an especial edition posthumous tribute for Audrey when Pipin categorically refused,
"*I don't want any magazine.*"
"*Pipin, the publication would honor Audrey's life and achievements, and would be distributed for free.*"
"*That's going to cost money.*"
"*And so what? This is about Audrey and the cost will be recovered on the next issue with all the advertisement clients we already have.*"
"*I prefer for us to concentrate on the FreediverPro line of equipment. It's better to invest money on that,*" he insisted.
"*Pipin, thanks to the deal I came up with between Mares and you, the line of equipment is going to require zero investment from our part. You know that.*"
"*I don't want the magazine anymore, Carlos.*"
Knowing his hardheaded nature, I left the issue go and pursued it no more. But his lack of interest to honor Audrey through our publication saddened me, to say the least. On the other hand, I had an important issue in sight, anyway.

LATE NOVEMBER 2002

Less than a month after Audrey's death, I had analyzed the equipment involved in the tragedy. The sled, the pony-tank, the cable and the lift bag were the most important pieces of evidence. The multiple courses and clinics taken with manufacturers, and years of experience in the scuba industry, gave me plenty of credentials to scrutinize the gear. Despite Pipin's public request to cease any investigation, supported by Audrey's mom, I continued the search for facts.

I started with the tank, the determining factor in Audrey's faith. I had checked it looking for a potential leak but found no problems with the valve or its seal. I filled the tank with compressed air to its full working pressure: three thousand pounds per-square-inch (3000 psi), and left the valve open at different apertures. The objective was to determine the noise level the air would make. So I placed myself at different distances from the "hissing" sound to find out how far I needed to be before I couldn't hear the sound of the leaking air. In the end, and although through experience I already knew the answer, there is no way that anyone that day aboard the catamaran, couldn't have heard the noise produced by a leaking tank.

I also let the pony-tank drain the air completely with a minimum opening of the valve. I wanted to determine how long would it take for the tank to get empty. In conclusion, it took almost two hours for the tank to be totally drained. Assuming that Pipin would have filled the tank one hour before the attempt, it was not possible for the tank to be completely empty. The tank was in proper working condition. As a result, and by a basic process of elimination, the answer was simple; the tank wasn't filled that day.

Back in the Dominican Republic I had spoken with Kim McCoy, who accompanied Pipin to the catamaran early that fatidic day. He said that he did not see Pipin filling the tank. This fact alone doesn't say much; Pipin could have filled the tank while McCoy was busy setting up the computer for Audrey. However, nobody saw Pipin filling the tank; not even Tata, who was also on board with Pipin the whole time.

Really troubling is that later that day, Wiky brought up a scuba tank with the transfer-whip to fill the pony-bottle and Pipin bawled him away. Then I saw Tata only minutes after, asking Pipin if the tank had been filled; Pipin answered affirmatively. That could only mean that Tata did not see Pipin filling the tank in the over one hour they had spent on board the vessel before the rest of us arrived.

The question was not if Pipin filled the tank or not; I was positively and definitively sure he didn't. Now the question remaining was why he didn't? And if he had forgotten, why telling Tata that he had done it? Why send Wiky away?

By now, Ricardo Hernandez, a former employee of the *IAFD*, had started a campaign over the internet accusing Pipin and me of having killed Audrey. His accusations were so outrageous in nature that I joined Pipin in a lawsuit against him.

In combination with Ricardo, the former owner of the *IAFD* franchise for Spain, Juan Llantada, also started to write discrediting and accusatory remarks all over the Internet. Juan Llantada was already disgruntled and had dropped the franchise altogether due to conflicts with Pipin. Many of the promises he had received from my partner were never granted, and the way Pipin handled the monies was a bit strange, to say the least, and for which I was kept in the dark.

Actually, how much money, how or when Juan Llantada paid the *IAFD* is something I could never determine. There was no trace of paperwork in the office and Pipin either claimed that the money was owed or evaded the subject.

Additionally, Pipin received a large sum of money from Juan Llantada for a world record attempt that never occurred. The attempt was set up in La Palma, Spain, but once there, and after suffering a blackout during practice, Pipin decided to have Audrey perform the attempt, instead.

Since I still had my dive shop back then, I couldn't assist due to scheduling conflicts. At the time, I had a scuba instructor-training course to teach for divemasters coming from different parts of the world. Therefore, I only received one side of the story; Pipin's side, and according to him he got screwed by Juan Llantada and denied the blackout.

The sad part is that in spite of the troubles, I wanted to keep Juan Llantada associated with us. But just as it had happened with the owner of the *IAFD* franchise for Europe, Juan Carlos Caraglia, also from Spain, they both abandoned their respective franchises and ended up mad at me, as well.

What disturbed me the most is that I am who introduced Juan Carlos Caraglia to Pipin. Juan Carlos is a former student of mine with whom I had kept communicating after his intense week-long class was over. He professed candid admiration and respect for me after the help I provide him during his, at times, overwhelming course. He even sent me a letter once for which my wife stated, jokingly, that he was in love with me. Juan Carlos, however, was a straight as an arrow grown-up man with the heart and frankness of a kid.

Juan Llantada, on the other hand, was introduced to the *IAFD* by Juan Carlos. And even though their business relationship was occasionally challenging, they were both fully committed to promote the sport in their respective areas. In reality, the problem was in many times instigated by the pressure independently placed upon them by Pipin.

Many of Pipin's dealings with the two of them occurred without my knowledge, thus ignorant of what was going on, I kept supporting Pipin and eventually lost the friendship of the Spaniards; something that to these days I regret. They were hard-working people with a noble cause, and besides their dedication, they had a profound admiration for Pipin; at least until they discovered his other side. They both finished up disillusioned and losing tens of thousands of dollars.

But for Pipin, losing these two franchises was nothing new. Before my times with the *IAFD*, he had lost another licensee for Scandinavian countries and for the same reason; money given to him for promises never granted.

TWO MONTHS LATER

Meanwhile, Pipin stayed at home, or at least that's what he said, and for over three months he didn't show up for work. Every so often he would come in and leave right away, claiming the office stirred too many sad memories and preferring to stay home.

"And the house doesn't bring sad memories, Pipin?"

"No . . . well," he responded hesitantly, *"I'm not spending much time in the house."*

Now Pipin contradicted himself but I knew the truth; he was not in the house for the most part. The few occasions I had seen him, he was definitely suntanned. He was spending time crossing the Florida stretch in his boat going to the Bahamas to spearfish with some fine company.

Pipin was never too fond of going to the office, anyway. Many times he had left Audrey and me taking care of the business while he went for a spearfishing trip. Now he was doing what he always wanted to do; leave me in charge of the company while he would go hunting for fish.

But one day, when he finally came to the office for an update, the update became an argument. After mentioning that I was conducting an examination of the equipment, he immediately jumped, repeating what he had said before,

"I want no investigation, whatsoever. Leave everything the way it is."

"That's not going to happen," I said forcefully. *"People want an answer . . . I want an answer."*

"But whatever you do is not going to bring Audrey back. Just leave it that way. Let Audrey rest in peace."

"It is quite the contrary. She would be the first one searching for answers, don't you think?"

"But she's dead, what are you going to achieve with that? What's your goal? What do you want?"

"Pipin, there are some other athletes doing No-Limits, and whatever happened to Audrey we must share it, so that it never happens again."

"You are talking about those dick-suckers from AIDA. I don't give a fuck about what happens to them."

"Well, I do. They are freedivers like us and human beings like anyone else."

"Carlos, brother, what you have to do is, make a statement as President of the IAFD and tell everyone that it was an accident. And leave it at that."

"What? If you want such statement, you do it yourself. This matter is way too delicate to be playing with it. I still don't know exactly what happened, or why. I will not rule it out as an accident until I have the evidence that says so."

Pipin got up visibly upset and ready to leave my office, but not before stating his position once again,

"Audrey was my wife and I don't want any investigation. Anne-Marie is her mother and she doesn't want it, either. So leave it that way."

While he fast-paced out of the office, I only got to say, *"That won't happen."*

Two days later he published a statement in which he declared not wanting an investigation. He also shared the blame with Audrey for getting her into freediving and Audrey for wanting it. Pipin was obstinately avoiding an investigation or analysis of any kind, but I already had a different prompt on my *To-do* list; especially after his strange demand.

For the next few days the rest of the equipment was evaluated to determine some other factors. The sled had stopped for no apparent reason at 164 meters for exactly 30 seconds. I checked the line in that point, and with the exception of some scratch markings and a little twist, there was nothing that could indicate such abrupt stop.

The sled had a Teflon-made ring inserted on top of the vertical tube to minimize friction with the cable, and this ring was partially broken, presumably since the training day when the sled hit the bottom of the boat during the ascent.

The interaction of the sled and the line alone couldn't have caused the sled to stop. The lack of weight, however, at the end of the line as an adding factor, might have caused a twist on the line, stopping the sled.

The presumed "twist" could have been caused by a bungee effect due to the wave's action at the surface, but this part of the investigation remained inconclusive. Only the exact reenactment of all the factors involved could determine if the sled could have been stopped in such way. The only remaining factor is not mechanical, but human. Pascal could have stopped the sled, but that seemed improbable and for what reason, anyway.

THE LAST ATTEMPT

Another item was the lift bag. It presented a tiny tear in the upper part of it, but not enough to cause massive leakage of air. The bag, assuming that it would have been filled with air, should have brought Audrey to the surface, as always.

As the search for clues continued, especially clues that would explain why the sled stopped in the way up, one element became certain; equipment failure did not cause the pony-tank to empty. The pony-tank must have been unfilled. The conclusive evidence is that Pipin filled the pony-tank for the last time on Friday, the day before the event, as pictures I took that day clearly show him, assisted by Bill Stromberg, doing so. There are neither pictures nor videos showing Pipin filling the tank that fatidic Saturday, October 12.

Looking for more evidence, I painfully reviewed the video that was set in Audrey's sled, over and over again. The following is a more detailed description of the video showing Audrey's last moments:

THE DESCENT

The sled is at the surface partly submerged. Audrey is already on it and performing her final ventilations. The video housing is attached to the bottom of the sled and pointing upward to record Audrey's face. The video camera is running with Audrey's yellow wetsuit showing through the water movement. Her face is undistinguishable; the housing is submerged but Audrey's face is not. Pipin's hand is moving all over the lens. It is obvious that he's manipulating the housing for some reason. The camera is already running and pointing in the right angle, so there is no apparent reason for this manipulation. This situation last until just before Audrey's descent.

When Audrey's sled is released, her torso and face becomes clearly visible; she's is now submerged. Her left hand is up, holding the tank valve located in the upper part of the sled. Her right arm is around the vertical tube while her hand is pinching her nose to equalize.

Few seconds into the dive she adjusts her hood. At around 80 or 90 meters, Wiky appears in the right hand side of the screen and behind Audrey. He's banging his tank as planned to warn Audrey of her current depth. Wiky's banging can be heard in the tape's audio. The descent continues with no visible signs of distress. Moments after, another continuous banging can be heard; is Pascal banging his tank. Seconds later Pascal also appears in the screen, behind Audrey and slightly to the left (Audrey's right hand side). Pascal's banging is to warn Audrey that she's ten meters away from the bottom.

As planned, this is the moment when Audrey, with her left hand holding the tank valve, opens it. A hissing sound can be heard but it lasts about a second. The sound is generated by a residual amount of air that comes from inside the tank.

> Note: *Opening the valve 10 meters before touching bottom has a dual motive. The first reason is to allow air to get inside the lift bag to slow down the descent. The sled's impact at the end of the line could be harsh if this maneuver is not*

attempted. Second, to gain time; the moment Audrey hits the end of the line, she's been putting air inside the lift bag for the last ten meters. Physics takes few seconds to react; the air inside the lift bag takes a while to displace the water and make it buoyant. So when Audrey releases the sled's upper part, she would have a jump start to the surface. This way few precious seconds are gained.

THE BOTTOM

Audrey continues to open the valve until the sled reaches the end of the line. As expected, she leaves the valve open, releases the sled's upper part, but nothing happens. She spins the valve handle to ensure that it's open, but no results. At this point the lift bag, with Audrey holding the frame that contains it, should have left the bottom and go up at a dazzling speed. It doesn't. Instead, the lift bag, by means of a pushing action from Audrey, rises up few inches and falls back down. Audrey, who throughout the entire dive had her eyes close, opens them briefly to glance forward and then shuts them again. She stops handling the valve, places both hands on the lift bag's frame, and attempts nothing else.

THE ASCENT

Pascal, who had descended ten more meters after signaling Audrey, reacted rapidly and assisted her by pushing the lift bag upward. Audrey, without reacting, is still holding on to it. Then they disappear from the screen for a while; the video housing is attached to the lower portion of the sled; therefore, it remains down there. Few seconds later Pascal's fins become visible in the upper edge of the screen while he is attempting to put air inside the lift bag.

According to the dive profile provided by the *Ocean Sensors* computer (OS500-D) worn by Audrey, she came to a full stop at 164 meters for 30 seconds. The time frame provided by the computer matches the time in the video when Pascal's fins are visible. Audrey's fins are not visible.

After that, Audrey, now with some air added to the balloon by Pascal, continued her ascent but slower than normal; much slower. This data was provided by the *Ocean Sensors* computers she had on her back.

THE LAST ATTEMPT

GRAPHIC OF AUDREY'S DIVE PROVIDED BY THE OCEAN SENSORS COMPUTER

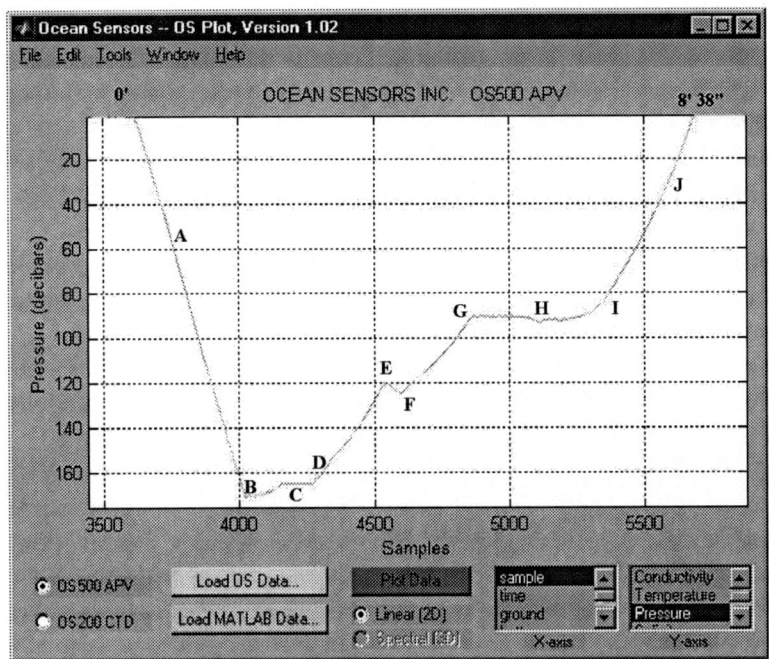

A- NORMAL DESCENT, ACTUALLY FASTER THAN PREVIOUS DIVE / B- AUDREY FINDS HERSELF WITH NO AIR INSIDE PONY-TANK / C- SLED GETS STUCK FOR 30 SECONDS D- PASCAL INFLATES LIFT BAG AND AUDREY ASCENDS / E- AUDREY LOSES CONSCIOUSNESS AND FALLS 4 METERS / F- PASCAL RETRIEVES AUDREY AND BRINGS HER UP / G- PASCAL STOPS AT 90 METERS / H- PIPIN TAKES AUDREY FROM PASCAL / I- AMPLE CURVE SHOWS SLOW INITIAL ASCENT / J- PIPIN IS NOW SURFACING FAST

But right at 120 meters, the computer registered a stop and an immediate slow descent. The fall continued for about 4 meters before she started to ascend, once again.

What the computer registered is Audrey losing consciousness exactly at 120 meters and free-falling for those 4 meters before Pascal, who had followed Audrey, catches her and continues up until 90 meters where he expected to find Wiky.

Wiky, however, had ascended about ten meters to preserve his by now precariously low amount of air. He kept waiting for Pascal to bring her up to him, but Pascal was unable to ascend any longer; not without hurting himself. Pascal's ascent had already exceeded all safety standards.

After examining the tape, interviewing witnesses, and inspecting the equipment, the following conclusions are definitive:

The chain of events that terminated Audrey's life was initiated by a near-empty tank. Equipment failure *did not* cause the tank to be near-empty. The ultimate conclusion is that the tank wasn't filled. However, what's still inconclusive so far is why.

That's when I found myself in a dead-end alley. How could I say that Pipin didn't fill the tank on purpose? He was my friend and partner. Besides, I had never been involved with anyone with a potential plot to murder his wife, assuming that was the case. That kind of situation only occurs in the movies or to somebody else, I thought. But something was truly wrong.

Meanwhile, Pipin was getting visibly anxious to announce something new about himself in the website. As always, the self-absorbed side of him was in control. The *IAFD's* site already had, back then, three times more pictures of Pipin than Audrey.

Pipin's presence on our website was overwhelmingly high as he kept Carolina, the office's assistant and webmaster, constantly updating and changing the site, ensuring this way his strong presence on it.

After Audrey's demise I advised him to maintain low key, at least for a while; that it was important to deal with the facts of Audrey's death before attempting any public image display.

Pipin, conversely, had already started to work on a book about Audrey and him, and getting contacts to make it happen. I attempted to discourage him from working on a book deal because of the timing. In my opinion, it was too early. I told him that people would not understand why he would be writing about Audrey right after her death. That it would look as if he was attempting to profit from the overwhelming amount of publicity her death generated.

"If I'm going to write about her anyway, what difference does it makes to write now or a year from now?" he asked.

"Let me explain it this way, Pipin. If you announce that you are getting married two years from now, people would support you. But if you announce that you are marrying another woman next week, people would despise you. It's a matter of timing."

The analogy was eloquent enough to hold Pipin from making a public statement about his plan to write the book, but it didn't deter him from searching for the way to obtain a book deal, and it didn't take long.

Chapter 16

PROFITING FROM AUDREY'S DEATH

REGAN BOOKS AND HARPER COLLINS

Days later Pipin came into my office uncharacteristically excited. Somehow a communication channel between *Regan Books* and him was opened, and now he had the support of a major publishing company to fulfill his most immediate plan.

After few weeks of negotiating, the deal was sealed. Pipin would sit down with a writer contracted by *Regan Books* to tell his story. Pipin wanted to be the writer but his capacity in this department is null. So to appear as the writer of the book, Pipin needed a *ghost writer*. After few interviews with different candidates, Pipin and *Regan Books* finally agreed on Linda Robertson, a reputable sports writer for *The Miami Herald*.

Regan Books would publish the manuscript through its affiliated *Harper Collins*, one of the largest publishing companies in the United States. This fact alone would guarantee widespread distribution for the book and translation to different languages, so Pipin's exhilaration couldn't be any greater; at least for him, grief was nowhere to be found.

But not long after Linda Robertson had started a series of interviews with Pipin and other key players in Audrey's event, she found herself debating between Pipin's version and everyone else's. Linda Robertson was under tremendous pressure and had a big dilemma at hand; meet the terms of the contract by writing Pipin's fairy-tale, or breaking the contract and walk away from the deal. After all, she had a reputation to preserve.

The problem with writing Pipin's biography is to discern between the fabricated fables and fact. For example, there is an old tale involving an alleged trip Pipin made to Tibet to study *yoga* in a monastery. He claims having learned to control his breathing thanks to the Buddhist's teachings.

He even told me once that while in Tibet, he had personally met with the *Dalai Lama* because the spiritual leader wanted to meet the famous Pipin. But anyone with a basic knowledge about Tibet and its culture would know that, even though yoga went over the Himalayas, from India to Tibet, about a thousand years ago, and merged into the Buddhists meditation routine, most people wouldn't consider going to Tibet to practice it. And their teachings take decades of daily and constant practice to achieve mastery; not just a couple of weeks with a tourist visa stamp.

At the time, the Dalai Lama had been living in exile in India since 1959, as he couldn't enter Tibet without risking being incarcerated by the ruling Chinese authorities.

What's more, the Buddhist monks schooling follows a complete assortment of sacred moral principles to which they adhere, vehemently. They pursue enlightening of the mind as part of their rituals and beliefs, which are in no way, incidentally, related to witchcraft. In fact, their lives are regulated by the eradication of five central immoral deeds:

1. Killing
2. Taking what is not given
3. Sexual Misconduct
4. Lying
5. Ingestion of Intoxicants

"Pipin," I joked with him in one occasion, *"if you went to Tibet to study with the Buddhist monks, you missed the school bus few times, buddy."*

The connection, however, between freediving and the Buddhist/yoga life-style do exist. It was first made popular by Jacques Mayol back in the 60's, when the French freediving icon—who was born in Shanghai, China—had indeed studied meditation with the Buddhist monks, learned their secrets to breath-hold control, and applied it to diving.

So when it comes to the spiritual side Pipin is attempting to project, he's just an astute copycat. Pipin just wanted to make his, the truly spiritual image strongly connected with Jacques Mayol.

The French apneist created a tendency in the apnea diving circles that everyone wanted to imitate—including Pipin—particularly after the big success, among divers, of the now cult-movie *The Big Blue,* in 1988. This is, coincidentally, the same year Pipin launched his career as a professional.

To illustrate this point even more, let's compare these historical facts about Mayol and Pipin, but keeping in mind that Mayol started his career in 1966, when he reached 66 meters in The Bahamas. That's over twenty years before Pipin even initiated his:

- Mayol was into Yoga and meditation; Pipin takes pictures of himself supposedly practicing both.
- Mayol went to Japan and Tibet to study meditation; Pipin alleges having visited Tibet and flooded the Internet with pictures of him in yoga-like positions.

THE LAST ATTEMPT

- Mayol was popular with women; Pipin is a womanizer.
- Mayol was allegedly involved with a much younger woman; so was Pipin.
- Mayol was French; Pipin married a French girl.
- Mayol coached his girlfriend to break records; so did Pipin.
- Mayol focused in No-Limits; so did Pipin.
- Mayol initiated his international career in The Bahamas; so did Pipin.
- Mayol had a legendary rivalry with Italian legend Enzo Maiorca; Pipin created one with Italian legend Umberto Pelizzari.
- Mayol was known for his affection for Dolphins; Pipin had photo sessions with trained Dolphins in Mexico and Belize and posted the pictures in the Internet. In many of the pictures, Pipin's posturing is basically identical to the ones publicly known with Mayol and Dolphins, taken at least 20 years before.
- Mayol's book, *Homo Delphinus*, suffered a severe case of plagiarism. Pipin's book, *Planeta Oceanus* carried full sentences and entire paragraphs copied from Mayol's book. This particular situation was brought to my attention by former employees of the company who participated in the making of Pipin's book. Then it was later confirmed by Maurizio Russo, Vice-President of *Idelson-Gnocchi,* and publisher of Mayol's book.
- Mayol's signature consists of his name with a downward extension of a straight line from the "y" representing a plunge into the abyss. Pipin's signature consists of his nickname with a downward extension of a straight line from the second "p" in Pipin representing a plunge into the abyss.

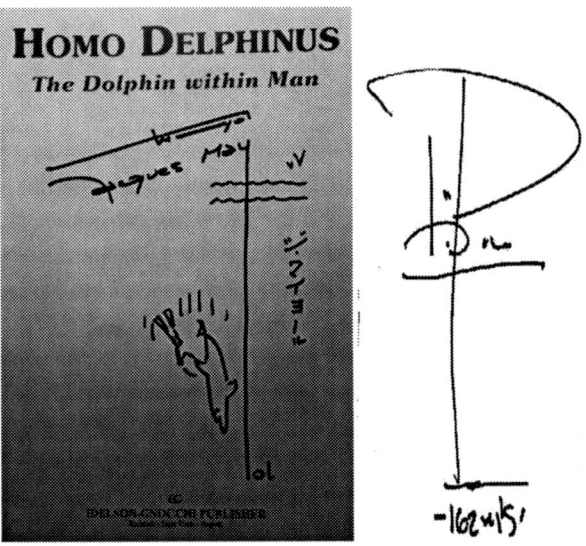

The resemblance between Mayol and Pipin includes the signature; only that Mayol had signed the same way for decades before Pipin would appear.

The points of concurrence are too many for just a coincidence, and none of the other top freediving athletes coincides with Mayol in more than one or two of the previous points.

But Mayol is not the only victim of this copycat inclination. Enzo Maiorca, the other freediving legend of Italian origin, fell victim of Pipin's bootlegging. Pipin has openly claimed that he came up with the idea of reversing the water plunge known as head-first, to the one he actually uses, the feet-first entry. The truth is that Maiorca is who introduced the feet-first plunge when Pipin was making a living selling fish in a local flea market in Matanzas, Cuba.

Whether Pipin's deception strategy is consciously plotted, or the result of unawareness when it comes to ethical issues and respect for other people's rights, his course of action has been so successful so far, that he went from the enclosure of freediving fans and into major corporation executives. That's the case of the Mexican Television Network, *Televisa*.

As part of the book deal negotiated after Audrey's death, Pipin was selling his life's rights to *Regan Books*. But it was discovered later that Pipin had signed a previous contract with *Televisa* for similar rights, and that Pipin was in breach of contract with the Mexican giant.

Furthermore, the rumor is that two other companies came out with similar claims over Pipin's video files, which were part of Pipin's contract with *Regan Books*.

Some of these different disputed contracts appeared at the same time, just when Pipin was certain that as a consequence of Audrey's death, he had made the deal of a lifetime. But Pipin not only was on the verge of making the book; he was also featured in the most reputable sport-magazine in the United States.

SPORTS ILLUSTRATED

In the spring of 2003, Gary Smith, Senior writer for *Sports Illustrated* came to Florida from his native Georgia. He came preceded by a big name as a writer for one of the most prestigious sport-magazines in the world. Gary Smith only writes about four articles a year, but each article is between ten to twelve pages long. He had done some excellent works on famous athletes; including the one Pipin admires the most, boxer, ear-eater and also role model on respectful treatment of women, Mike Tyson.

Gary Smith spent few days in Miami, interviewing most of the people involved in Audrey's ordeal. But the one person he could not interview was Wiky. As he had promised, he refused to answer any question related to Pipin, the *IAFD*, or Audrey.

After many days of constant interviews and having completed his job, Smith returned back home to Georgia. Meanwhile, I was getting convinced of Pipin's responsibility for Audrey's tragedy, but I wasn't sure about the reasons. Therefore, feeling trapped in a dead-end without the possibility to determine why he had failed to fill the tank, I left Pipin and the office with no intentions of coming back.

THE LAST ATTEMPT

Pipin, however, with constant phone calls and a much nicer attitude, tried to convince me to come back to set up his new world record.

"*Oye, hermano, I need you to help me with my next record. You know I can't do it alone, man,*" he pleaded over the phone.

"*I have no interest, Pipin. In those records you get out of control. Besides, after Audrey's death, I won't carry yours over my shoulders, because if you coordinate things again, that's what's going to happen.*"

"*No, brother, you'll be in charge of everything this time.*"

"*That's what you said last time. Should I remind you of what happened? I will not go through that again.*"

"*Hey, this record is to honor Audrey. I know she was like a sister to you, and she loved you like a brother, too. Do it for her, man.*"

After some smooth talking utilizing my known affection for Audrey, I came back. But immediately after my return—in June 16, 2003—Smith's eleven-page article came out.

In it, Smith involuntarily played Pipin's game by implying that Wiky wasn't down there in the water when Pascal brought Audrey up from 171 meters to 90 meters. That Wiky had left his post and had ascended because he was short on air. Pipin had, by then, started to place the blame over Wiky for Audrey's death. He claimed that when he descended to rescue Audrey, Wiky wasn't there; that Wiky had gone to the surface, and for that reason, abandoned Audrey.

Pascal had also joined Pipin in this allegation and declared to Smith that Wiky wasn't in sight when he ascended to 90 meters with Audrey's inert body. That above him was nothing but water.

Now Gary Smith, backed up by Pascal's statement, was involuntarily echoing Pipin's accusations, although I had personally warned Smith that Wiky was in the water at depth, unable to descend to Pascal, yes, but he was in sight.

In that regard, along with few other details, the article is inaccurate. The most accurate testimony is the video taken by the diver located at 60 meters the day Audrey died.

In this video Wiky appears clearly and Pipin, while descending to take Audrey from Pascal, literally bumped into Wiky. Wiky was, definitively and irrefutably, down there; not in the surface.

I had seen the video only once before, as I kept focused on the video from the sled. But it would take many months for me to observe the video again and discover something outrageously disquieting that would only appear on the ascent part of Pipin's rescue.

Not long after the article came out, Wiky called me for the first time ever since he parted from Pipin eight months ago, and he was in infuriated. He had just read the article that gave him the first dosage of blame.

"*Carlos, I've just read an article in Sports Illustrated saying that I was not in the water to save Audrey. What the fuck is this? I'm the one to be blamed, now?*"

"*Wiky, relax . . .*"

"How can I be relaxed? You guys are blaming me now for Audrey's death."

"I'm not blaming you, so don't include me."

"Then who's saying it?"

"Pipin is the one suggesting that you were not down there to help Audrey."

"That madman is lying!"

"I know, Wiky."

"Did you tell Smith I was there?"

"Yes, I did."

"Then why this guy, Smith, wrote this stupid thing?"

"Smith has to believe the two people who were at depth besides you. I wasn't at depth."

"Two people?" Wiky asked curiously, *"who's the other one?"*

"It's Pascal, of course. It's in the article."

"What? So Pascal is accusing me, too?"

"That seems to be the case, Wiky."

"Pipin left the tank empty and Pascal didn't give Audrey a regulator to save her, but they are both accusing me? That makes a lot of sense."

Pipin had initially blamed Pascal, privately, for not giving Audrey a regulator, but he suddenly stopped blaming Pascal and took it on Wiky. The switch happened soon after Wiky left Pipin, when the first accused the latest for what had happened to Audrey.

Right after Wiky's phone call, I confronted Pipin in my office regarding Gary Smith's article, and after telling him that the only person responsible for Audrey's death was the one who didn't fill the tank, Pipin said in rage,

"Pascal is more responsible than me. He failed to give a regulator to Audrey; that was lack of leadership from his part," he said. *"Then, Wiky; he wasn't there to help her. And finally Audrey . . . and you, because you both stopped me from being the safety diver in one hundred and seventy-one meters and Audrey supported you . . . If I would have been down there as I had planned, I would have forced her to breathe from a regulator."*

At this point my heart was pounding hard on my chest while a bulging pressure kept mounting up to the very edges of a heart attack . . .

"Should you have been the safety diver at one hundred and seventy-one meters we would have had two bodies to recover," I responded in rage while leaning forward, banging the top of my desk with my fist. Pipin was seated in the other side of the desk, taking a defensive posture on his chair. Then I added,

"So don't you ever dare to say that again. The only person responsible for Audrey's death is the one who didn't fill the tank, and that person is YOU!"

Now Pipin was rubbing his shaved head and grimacing while looking down. This is the signal that normally meant for me to stop arguing with him, but I wasn't about to stop; not this time. I wanted to bring everything out, no matter what.

"Don't you realize that you are a disgrace when it comes to scuba? Is your monstrous ego blinding you so much that you don't see that? And you, doing one hundred and seventy-one meters on scuba, you would have killed yourself."

THE LAST ATTEMPT

"You always say that I have an ego. I don't have an ego," he responded as he always did when I addressed his haughty ways; in denial. *"I could have done that dive easily."*

"Yeah, right, and I can fly a Space Shuttle and couple it with the International Space Station . . . blindfolded!"

"Carlos, I've done deeper dives for the Italian Navy."

"Oh, Pipin, spare me your crap with the Italian Navy. Leave it for the regular public who believe all of your fairy-tales. Besides, we had the best person in the world to cover the spot, that's Pascal, why would you want to be in one hundred and seventy-one meters? Were you expecting for something to go wrong? Did I screw up for you a plan of some sort by standing against that stupid proposal?"

That's when Pipin stood up and left my office visibly upset. But even though he was exiting my office, I insisted,

"Why are you leaving? Tell me, why did you leave the tank empty? Why didn't you fill it?"

And that's the moment when my uncertainties started to increase significantly. I had placed Pipin against the corner, but before incriminating himself any further, he just slid under and walked away.

The questions were quite valid, but his refusal to answer them left me with a profound fear and suspicions spinning around my head: Why would Pipin want to replace one of the most prolific deep-divers in the world and put himself in harm's way? Why after so many years, he wouldn't trust Pascal this time? Was it there an ultimate plan?

Chapter 17

HOLLYWOOD WANTS THE STORY

LATE JUNE, EARLY JULY OF 2003

After having read the *Sports Illustrated* article, James Cameron, the famous Hollywood director, became interested in taking Gary Smith's story to the big screen. It would be Cameron's first dramatic film since his blockbuster *Titanic*.

Cameron contacted our office and made arrangements to meet with Pipin, and that happened in July 10, 2003. The renowned director came to Miami from neighboring Fort Lauderdale, where he was working on the preliminary stages of a project to document thermal vents in the Atlantic, near the Azores islands. This latest project would be named, *Aliens of the Deep* and would be filmed in 3D-Imax format.

Since Cameron was only thirty minutes away from Pipin's house, the meeting was easy to set up. Pipin and I were together reviewing some video materials when Cameron arrived. It was an early afternoon and he was dressed quite casual with kaki shorts, a white t-shirt and *Nike* walking shoes. Since us both are taller than the average, Cameron's height, surprised us by having to see him up.

The first impression I received is of a person with an intellect well above average, but being one of the most successful directors in Hollywood, that's a given. The second impression I got is that he was condescending and agreeable with anything Pipin said or asked, and if that was the case, the strategy was reasonably smart. Cameron had probably done his homework investigating him before hand.

Pipin had already made a fool of himself during the shooting of the movie *OceanMen*, a film made by a German production company in *IMAX* format, with its plot being based on his well-known rivalry with Umberto Pelizzari.

THE LAST ATTEMPT

During the filming, Pipin had many heated arguments with director Bob Talbot, who is one of the most renowned underwater photographers in the world, and had worked as the director of wild marine-life photography in the now classic movie, *Free Willy*.

Pipin's arguments with Talbot were based in conflicting opinions regarding technical and creative aspects of the movie. Pipin even used some unkind epithets against the renowned photographer and movie maker claiming that Talbot *"doesn't know shit about photography"*.

Perhaps Cameron came to Miami with a clear picture of Pipin's conceited personality, which is not a secret for anyone in the diving world. And by feeding his ego, Pipin's charismatic side flourishes like flowers in springtime, making his personality blossom with kindness and humor.

After a brief conversation in Pipin's house about the plans for a new movie, the three of us departed for lunch to a Cuban Café located in the heart of South Beach; Pipin's favorite hang-out district.

At arrival, I looked around to determine if Cameron would be recognized by someone. After all, South Beach is the heart of hip-hop culture and celebrity-worship in South Florida. But no one seemed to recognize Cameron. I even recall thinking that if it was Leo DiCaprio walking through South Beach, a disturbance of disastrous proportions would have occurred.

But setting aside my personal disappointment with humanity for admiring looks before brains, lunch went fine for the most part. Interestingly enough, it didn't take long for Pipin to show signs of his controlling nature. He agreed to accept Cameron to make the movie, but there were few conditions. The most interesting ones were: A) Pipin would have a voice in the selection of the actors and, B) Pipin would be a cameraman for the underwater takes.

Both requests seemed logical. The first one sounds like a reasonable concern about who would portray Pipin and Audrey's role. The second request came across like a personal interest to appear in the credits as an underwater cameraman, and there is nothing wrong with that. But what Pipin had in mind was quite different.

Just before the meeting with Cameron, actress Salma Hayek had contacted our office showing her interest to portray Audrey. That's when Pipin set up a meeting with the Mexican actress. In an alleged first meeting they both had at his house, they ended up in bed.

She had arrived from London, according to Pipin, but before heading to California, she came straight to Miami just to meet with him. And, after a bottle of wine by the water in Pipin's patio, she became irresistibly seduced by his enchantment and ended up opening and exposing her feminine attributes to him. Well, all of this according to what Pipin told me, of course, and in crudest terms.

He couldn't wait to tell me about the alleged encounter, so he called me over the phone the following morning and asked me to meet with him at his house. He gave me unsolicited and explicit details on how she shared his sheets, among other things. That she ended up in his Jacuzzi lighting up some candles around the tub while he was sleeping, recovering from a first passionate session, and then how she made some noises to wake him up and surprise him.

Pipin told me that he found that romantic display *"ridiculous"*; that Audrey was the last person who had done that and he *"kicked"* her out of the Jacuzzi. Pipin even said, proudly, that it was the first and last time Audrey would attempt to light candles around the Jacuzzi.

"Oh, Pipin, I've always been delighted by your tender side," was my response when he told me so.

The way he allegedly treated Audrey didn't surprise me. Besides, Audrey had told me about the Jacuzzi affair. But regarding Salma Hayek, I didn't give Pipin much credibility then, and I still don't believe that such thing ever happened outside Pipin's undomesticated imagination.

Even so, Pipin insisted on repeated sexual encounters he had with *"Parking-Meter,"* (as he calls her due to her short stature) for the weeks to come. Therefore, the subject of Pipin's "romantic" nights with Salma Hayek eventually started to get on my nerves. I've never been interested in someone else's sexual life; celebrity or not, and the explicitness of Pipin's dialogue was embarrassing, to say the least. Subsequently, it didn't take long before I said,

"Pipin, Salma Hayek is one of the most desired women in Hollywood. If I ended up in bed with her, even my wife would congratulate me. So if you took her to bed, good for you, but if not, you need a mental evaluation."

He continued to brag, anyway. In the end, that's what it was all about, to brag about having taken the Mexican superstar to bed. But the point is that Pipin's interest to have a saying in the selection of the actors had nothing to do with being concerned about Audrey's image or his, and had everything to do with bringing Salma Hayek into the movie as a way to conquer her.

The sad part is that Audrey, in life, wanted for another actress to perform her role in *Ocean Women*, the movie Pipin, Audrey and I had envisioned to produce. The event in the Dominican Republic was, in fact, part of that project. The name of the actress is Natascha McElhone, who played the character of Rheya in *Solaris*, along with George Clooney. *Solaris* is, coincidentally, a movie produced by Cameron.

The resemblance between Audrey and Natascha McElhone is simply remarkable, and that's why Audrey wanted McElhone to portray her. Sadly, Pipin wasn't looking to honor Audrey's wishes; he wanted Salma Hayek as a sexual trophy.

Regarding Pipin's request to be an underwater cameraman, he told me that it was a way to control the quality of the submarine scenes and avoid the *"grotesque mistakes that dick-sucker made in OceanMen,"* as Pipin said in reference to Bob Talbot.

THE LAST ATTEMPT

JULY 18, 2003

Pipin and I met with Cameron again; this time in Nassau, Bahamas. Cameron invited us to further discuss the movie project. The famed director had moved with his ship to the islands, to test two mini-subs to be used in the film before crossing the Atlantic. The Bahamas would become his operational base for the next few days.

The day we arrived, Pipin and I remained in the hotel waiting for Cameron to contact us. He was out in the ocean testing the mini-subs and the filming gear. In the afternoon, we were picked by a van that Cameron had sent and met with him on the *Ares*, the ship being used by Cameron and his crew. The *Ares* was docked at Nassau's port between two gigantic cruise ships; the *Galaxy* from Celebrity Cruises and *Fascination* from Carnival.

After the formal introductions to the crew, Cameron gave us a tour throughout the ship that ended in the main deck. The mini-subs, along with the paraphernalia involved to make them work, was eye-catching.

While Cameron was giving Pipin an explanation of the operational details, I kept taking pictures, as Pipin wanted. He had made plans already to post the pictures on the Internet and announce Cameron's interest on making a movie about him. Although the deal wasn't sealed yet, Pipin, who is an expert in self-promotion, was ready to flood the Internet with the pictures.

"Those dick-suckers are going to die of envy," Pipin exclaimed.

"Who are you referring to," I asked curiously.

"Umberto Pelizzari, Tanya Streeter, Patrick Musimu, and all of those come-pingas from AIDA. Now they're going to know who the brave is!"

With celebrated director James Cameron aboard the Ares. I gave my camera to a crew member to take this photo, but Pipin, visibly upset, wanted me out of the picture, literally.

During the evening, the three of us went out for dinner to a restaurant located at the lavish *Atlantis Hotel,* where an enticing buffet of seafood was being served along with a wide variety of appetizing dishes.

But as the spiny-lobster tails and jumbo-shrimps were steaming up, so was the tone of conversation between Pipin and me. He refused to allow *AIDA* judges to oversee his next world record attempt planned for October 2002, in Cabo San Lucas, Mexico.

That came as a surprise since I had convinced him about the need to bring an institution, other than our *IAFD,* to certify his record. Before Cameron appeared, Pipin had agreed to *AIDA's* judging, and I had coordinated *AIDA's* assistance with its then president, Sebastien Nagel.

In spite of past heated disputes with *AIDA*, I had come to peaceful terms with them after Audrey's death. While some former supporters and members of the *IAFD* were attacking us without compassion, *AIDA* as a rival agency was supporting and understanding. Their attitude after the tragedy made me realize that I was fighting with the wrong people. So when I openly thank them for their support, a line of communication was cordially open. That's when I thought of bringing the two agencies together while pursuing three specific goals:

- For Pipin to perform a clean and true record, especially after some distressing information I had gathered regarding the way he executes his attempts.
- To bring the two discrepant entities together for a common cause to promote freediving. That's a dream that Audrey always wanted to see becoming reality.
- To force Pipin to have all the safety measures needed to protect his life and of those with him underwater.

Even though Pipin had reluctantly accepted *AIDA*, Cameron's presence rapidly changed his mind.

"Jim will be there," referring to Cameron. *"I'm not going to give AIDA that kind of publicity."*

"Pipin, after what happened to Audrey, the IAFD lacks of credibility to oversee a record attempt, even worse if you are the one to attempt it."

"We don't need AIDA or anyone else. Jim will be there with his cameras and that's the best witness for the record."

Knowing of Pipin's fondness for boxing and Mike Tyson, I attempted to open his mind with the following analogy,

"Hey, not because you have a fight between Hollyfield and Tyson through Pay-per-View, you can say that an official referee and judges are not needed."

Cameron observed the argument silently while Pipin continued inflexible in the issue; he would not have *AIDA* judges. He insisted on me to be the judge.

"Then we better call it a demonstration and not a world record," I replied, and that was the end of the argument.

THE LAST ATTEMPT

Cameron just added that his presence in Cabo San Lucas would in no way interfere with the event. It was clear that while Pipin wanted to use Cameron's presence as a form of "validation", Cameron would just do his job, and that was filming. Cameron was, after all, using plain common sense. He was neither a judge nor a freediving entity, while Pipin wanted to get away with another record without appropriate supervision or scrutiny.

Back at the hotel, Pipin followed me to my room and continued the debate. He asked me why I wanted to bring *AIDA* judges to Cabo.

"Because the IAFD died along with Audrey, and because your credibility is null. Everyone in the freediving circles says that you cheat on your records."

"Who says that?"

"Jacques Mayol said it, just to start with."

"He never said that."

"Oh, yes he did, and not only had he said it, he even wrote it in his book."

"He was jealous of me and that's why he hanged himself by the neck. That old dick-sucker could not resist my success. But who else?"

"In that old article in Outside Magazine, your friend Pierce Hoover referred to your records as 'stunt dives'."

"He's another dick-sucker!"

"In addition," I continued, "AIDA doesn't recognize your records and you know why?"

"That's because they are idiots and they don't know dick."

"No, Pipin, it's because you don't videotape your ascent. You never place divers between one hundred meters and Pascal at the bottom. You never take an anti-doping test. You have a loose hose coming from the tank that allows you to breathe, and you have proven that you can breathe at depth."

"I've never done that."

"Yes, you have. Or have you forgotten the Cayman Islands and the SpareAir record? You actually breathed compressed air underwater and really deep, didn't you?"

"But everyone says that you cannot breathe compressed air while freediving, right?" Pipin asked sardonically.

"Oh, I get it. You're counting on the fact that people believe it's dangerous or maybe not possible to breathe underwater, is that it?"

"That's what they say, which comes to prove those sapingos don't know dick."

"But you shot yourself in the foot because you have proven them wrong. You even declared to the Mexican magazine, Espacio Profundo, that you know how to exhale the air before it hurts your lungs. So you do breathe underwater in your record attempts, don't you?"

That's when Pipin's trademark grimace and look-down, head-rubbing motion started, and seconds after Pipin left the room, but not before emphasizing that he didn't want *AIDA* in his attempt.

"Well, then I will make sure that everything is in place to ensure a fair and valid record, and that all the requirements to protect your life and the divers' are in place, whether you like it or not."

JULY 19, 2003

The next day on board the *Ares,* I was impressed by Cameron's well-oiled human machinery. The staff left nothing to uncertainties or luck, and even last minute improvisations were thoroughly thought out and executed.

Credit: Carlos Serra

Cameron coordinated a carefully crafted operation for his movie/documentary, Aliens of the Deep.

Cameron seemed to be in absolute command of his entire operation; it was his money and reputation at stake, after all, but that's when Pipin referred to him as a *control freak* and anticipated problems working with him in the future, just as it happened before with Bob Talbot.

But it was something else Pipin said what reopened my by-now dormant suspicions. It happened when Pipin and I were located on the bridge of the *Ares,* three levels above the ship's main deck, where Cameron was briefing his people before launching the two apple-green mini-subs. The two-seat submersibles were to be tested and certified that day, for insurance purposes to one thousand meters of depth.

THE LAST ATTEMPT

While observing Cameron from the bridge, I listened in awe to Pipin's remarks about Cameron and his bulk of pages outlining the plan for the day's activities to his staff.

"Can you believe that guy?" Pipin said while pointing at Cameron. *"He's using an encyclopedia to tell his people what to do."*

"Pipin, that's the way it's done."

"Ha! What if he looses one page, they'll cancel the whole operation? Oh, yes, I'm going to have problems with that mariconeria."

"That's called a checklist," I said, *"and even the army of the United States, before invading Iraq, used one of those."*

Pipin looked back at me with a menacing smile, and while pointing his right index finger to his forehead, he added,

"Here is the only checklist I'll ever need, and it's infallible!"

Atrocious words uttered by the person whose *"infallible"* checklist neglected the tank of his now deceased wife. But with Pipin's statement I wondered, once again, if he had really forgotten to fill Audrey's tank, because if his "checklist" was indeed infallible, then the tank must have been empty for a reason other than a tragic mishap.

Credit: Carlos Serra

A comment made by Pipin at this moment, stirred my concerns again about Audrey's empty tank.

As much as I hated having to think about wrongdoing from Pipin's part, his words truly pinched a nerve. I had given him loyalty and friendship, supported him through the aftermath of Audrey's death. I had given him the benefit of the doubt time after time. I even accepted, silently, when Audrey's dad grumbled for the lack of safety divers in the water to protect his daughter, although it was all his doing.

Furthermore, I had proposed Pipin, weeks before departing to the Dominican Republic, to bring more technical divers. In Miami we had plenty to choose from but he refused, claiming that it would cost too much and that it was too risky for the divers, especially if we didn't know their credentials. That's when I reminded him of Mike, an FBI agent who is also a technical diver and already knew his credentials.

Mike had helped us in Fort Lauderdale in May 2001, when Audrey did her 130 meter record-dive. He did an excellent job, not only by descending to 120 meters to protect Audrey, but covering the deepest safety diver, Cedric, who was at 130 meters. And yet, Pipin refused to bring Mike onboard, even though, most likely, Mike would have asked for lodging and airfare only. The hotel was already providing the rooms and we would only have to pay for a nicely discounted air-ticket from *Mexicana*.

Even to these days my skin resembles a *Thanksgiving* main dish when I think of the depth where Audrey lost consciousness before dying; 120 meters. Exactly the same depth where Mike would have been placed based on our previous experience with him in Fort Lauderdale.

Chapter 18

PUTTING THE PIECES TOGETHER

SEPTEMBER 2003

Up to this point, Pipin had been quieter than a meditating monk, but with the book project on the works and the prospect of a movie, he became increasingly eloquent with his statements. He seemed confident that no one could ever finger-point him in regards to Audrey's death, so I started to listen carefully.

As Pipin's statements became less restricted, so were his accusations against Wiky. By this time, he had started to express Wiky's alleged responsibility around the diving circles of Miami.

On an early day on September 2003, Wiky called my cell phone. I looked at the caller-ID wondering what Wiky wanted this time. He had called me only a couple of times during the previous year but always related to Pipin's accusations against him. It wasn't any different this time, only that I was not aware of Pipin's reenergized incentive to blame his former safety diver.

When I answered, Wiky was outraged. He wasn't too happy the previous times, but now he was fuming. It took me a while to calm him down enough to understand what he was saying. Finally, more relaxed, he told me,

"Pipin went to Mayito's dive shop," who is a mutual acquaintance of Pipin and Wiky, *"and said that Audrey died because of me. That if I would have been down there to receive Audrey from Pascal, instead of cowardly leaving my post, she would be alive today."*

For Wiky that was it. Wiky and Audrey were reciprocally fond and Audrey's passing had been devastating for him. On top of that, Wiky shared with me a piece of information I hadn't even considered until then, and for which I didn't know of Wiky's awareness on the matter.

So I went to Pipin's house to confront him, but as soon as Pipin opened the door, he greeted me saying,

"Hey, Carlos, parking-meter and I went to a hotel in South Beach last night and..."

"Pipin," I interrupted. *"I'm not here to listen to your fantasy-driven, sexual adventures with Salma Hayek."*

"What is it?" he asked curiously, noticing my impatience.

Right after sitting down in his living room, I explained to Pipin, once more, that if he didn't stop accusing Wiky for Audrey's death, he would get into a lot of trouble. Now reflecting apprehension in his face, Pipin asked,

"What kind of trouble?"

"Wiky told me that he would tell everyone about Audrey's request to divorce you."

"What!" he burst out. *"Wiky is a liar, he has nothing against me..."* then he hesitated for few seconds while I kept attentively observing his reaction. Rubbing his head he continued, *"There is nothing he can say ... ese no sabe ni pinga ... there was no divorce, that's a lie!"*

Then I added more fuel to the fire,

"Wiky is not lying. Audrey had told me exactly the same."

Now he looked shocked, in awe, perplexed, as I've never seen him before. He paused for a moment seemingly rearranging his thoughts as he continued rubbing his head, and that's when I kept pushing,

"Audrey told me about the divorce request the day she made the one hundred and seventy meters practice dive. We were at the lunch buffet while you were waiting at the table. Instead of being happy for what she had just accomplished, she seemed awfully sad, and when I asked her what was going on, she told me that she had asked you for a divorce; that she couldn't be with you any longer. So, Wiky can't be lying because with the exception of my wife, I've never mentioned Audrey's divorce request to anyone."

Now instead of coming at me in rage, as I had expected, Pipin started to insult Audrey. He said the most vicious epithets a person can say to a woman, not uncommon, but I would have never expected it against Audrey. In respect of her memory, those words will not be reproduced in here.

"She's a .... How could she do this to me, talking about private matters with someone else? She's a .... She betrayed me!" he said angrily.

After pausing for a moment, his reaction and comments changed dramatically; he settled down and left me puzzled with his bipolar-like sudden change.

"After everything I did for her ... this record shit in her honor doesn't make any sense anymore ..." and after another brief pause he said, *"She never told me about a divorce. If she said it, I didn't know anything about it."*

Now he went into his characteristic denial, because the day of the record, when I approached their hotel room, divorce is one word I heard from the fight they had.

Pipin's reaction was quite unnerving, but also an eye-opener. Audrey had only expressed her intention to eradicate her anguish. The signs of misery in her relationship with Pipin were irrefutable. She had spoken with two friends about getting away from the source of that misery; so where is the betrayal part on that?

More attention-grabbing is that he denied discussing divorce with Audrey and called Wiky a liar, but only until I said that Audrey had told me exactly the same. Pipin knew that I wouldn't lie in such delicate matter. I wouldn't make that up; so instead of continuing with his denial, he went ballistic on Audrey because a potential motive had been left behind; left behind by Audrey.

That's when my blurry suspicions on Pipin started to take shape, turning into a snowball effect revolving faster down the hill every time he opened his mouth. Until this point, I had considered the divorce issue a personal matter and never linked it with her empty tank. But Pipin's reaction made me realize how potentially naïve I had been. But that wasn't all.

THE CARROT AND STICK APPROACH

After relaxing from his wild eruption, he came out with something that made a warning-light go off in my head,

"Carlos, how much money do you still owe in your house's mortgage?" he asked.

"About seventy plus thousand dollars."

"I though it was around forty thousand, only."

"No, Pipin, the statement comes every month with the balance on the principal; believe me, it's a little over seventy thousand. But why are you asking anyway?"

"Well, I was planning on giving you a bonus once I get paid for the movie. I'll pay your mortgage so that your kids have a secured home to live in," referring to Alexander but also my newborn, Christopher, who was only few days old.

Just minutes before Pipin was placed between a rock and a hard place when I acknowledged Audrey's divorce request. Now all of the sudden, Pipin the philanthropist was offering to pay my mortgage.

He even touched my tender spot, my kids, to make me envision the kindness of his offer. But this time I had an armor of mistrust to repel his stratagem. Pipin's charm wouldn't work this time.

Feeling like the horse chasing the elusive carrot, I gave him a condescending,

"Thank you; that would be nice," and soon after, I left.

While driving southbound on US1, a depressive commotion overwhelmed my senses. Someone had just pulled the veil off my eyes, and by squinting to see through the shinning and glamorous life of travel, fancy hotels, money and tropical beaches, I finally looked into the ugliness of human ambition at its worst. I was now seeing another entity, a heartless and remorseless creature dwelling within the person I loved as a brother and supported as the best of friends.

Being stopped by a red light, I hit the steering wheel with a fist, in frustration,

"How could I have been so stupid?" I asked myself repeatedly. *"I'm an idiot. Ricardo Hernandez is right. Wiky is right."*

Then a horn blasted from the vehicle standing behind me. A hysterical woman waving hands was reflected in my rear mirror. I looked forward and the green light was on. I was blocking her and everyone else behind. I should have pulled over because I was weeping, once again. I couldn't stop thinking of Audrey and how she probably felt on those last days. When she opened her eyes for the last time, she was submerged in a cold and lonely abyss. She had seen the cruel reality at last, but only too late.

When I finally made it home and parked in front of the house, I had no idea on how I got there. Forty-five minutes of mostly unaware driving had passed. My conscious kept thinking of Audrey and her senseless death, while my unconscious did the driving.

"I can't go on like this," I told myself. *"I must depart from Pipin and yet I still need to put the final pieces together."*

By now I was getting convinced, the tank had probably been left deliberately empty, but I still needed a motive. Pipin got a good deal after Audrey's death but the money wasn't large enough to believe that was his motivation.

If Audrey wanting to divorce him was his motive, why would he take provisions to rescue her from an eventuality that, curiously, only Pipin had anticipated. So why try to kill Audrey while looking to save her at the same time?

"I'm missing something," I recall thinking. *"There are too many things not connecting in a logical manner."*

Chapter 19

THE BEGINNING OF THE END

STILL SEPTEMBER 2003

*H*BO's *Real Sports with Bryant Gumbel* came to Miami. They wanted an interview with Pipin and some of the people from his entourage, to look into Audrey's death and the saga caused by it. But they would also interview someone from the outside; someone who wasn't even present when Audrey died.

By now, Ricardo Hernandez had amplified the tenor of his accusations against Pipin and me over the internet, creating this way tremendous controversy. He even claimed that I must have been the writer of Pipin's statements refusing to give any details about Audrey's death ever since Pipin was *"intellectually challenged"* to do it. But no, I didn't write the statement and even argued with Pipin for such declaration.

Since the times when Ricardo was the company's general manager, he knew of me as the source of ideas and the architect of business stratagem to raise the company from the red-ink pool where I found it. In less than a year, I had turned the company around and made it profitable.

Consequently, Ricardo assumed that if Audrey had been killed without a smoking gun on sight, sort of a perfect crime, and having selected the Dominican Republic due to *"more lenient laws"*, as he once claimed, I had to be the evil brain behind the plot.

What Ricardo didn't know is that although I didn't believe Pipin to be intentionally responsible, I was committed I was to find the truth. And in one regard Ricardo was wrong; Pipin may be many things, yet being an idiot is not among them. Actually, he's the embodiment of street-smart. But due to his controversial position, Ricardo was to be interviewed by *HBO*, too.

The show's producer, Michael Sullivan, arranged for a first interview at the *Mandarin Hotel,* located in Miami's Brickel Key. The reporter was a prominent correspondent and 6-time Emmy Award winner for investigative reports; his name, Bernard Goldberg. I smelled trouble for Pipin right away. In the end, they only interviewed Ricardo Hernandez, Wiky, Pipin and me.

Pipin and I were interviewed the same day; September 12, 2003. Pipin in the morning and I had my turn in the afternoon. The interview was planned separately, but Pipin wanted for me to accompany him. Once at the hotel, we were told about doing the interview one at a time. So I went back home and returned at 12:45 p.m.

Somewhere around noon, when I was on my way to the hotel, Pipin called me at my cell phone claiming that *"the interview went fine".* But having become an expert in Pipin's deceptive tone of voice, I didn't believe him, and whatever the questions he had received, it made him nervous. That's when he asked me what I was going to say.

"How would I know, Pipin. I don't know what they are going to ask me."

"Well, brother, call me as soon as you finish, okay? He said with an increased edginess in his voice.

He was perceptibly concerned about my side of the interview. Our recent arguments were quite disruptive for him, especially having me asking more direct questions regarding Audrey's death. He probably also noticed how my attitude towards him had changed. I avoided much contact with him, and had stopped having our customary lunch at his house.

Once in the room with *HBO's* staff, I got a bit nervous with the setting. Spotlights, floodlights, umbrellas, cameras and wires can make your legs tremble if you are not accustomed to it, and I was not. Bernie Goldberg, however, who had just invited me for lunch few minutes before, started the interview with informal conversation, making me feel relaxed and welcomed. By making jokes to one of his assistants during lunch, he had started to work on me. His experience became evident.

Not long after the interview was over, and while I was heading back home, Pipin called me at my cell phone, once again. He wanted to know of the questions they asked.

"There was one tough question, but I was expecting it, anyway."

"What question is that?"

"If I believe that you've killed Audrey."

There was no immediate response from Pipin. The pause was long enough to make me wonder if he was still on the line. Then his reaction finally came.

"And what did you tell them."

"Well, that I don't think that you intended to harm Audrey."

Then another pause . . . 5 seconds . . . 10 seconds . . . 15 seconds . . .

"Pipin, are you still there?"

"They never asked me anything like that," he said.

"What did they ask you, then?"

He claimed their questioning was all related to the great love Audrey and he felt for each other, and his future plans working with Jim (James Cameron). He alleged never being asked anything related to the *"accident".*

THE LAST ATTEMPT

"Pipin, these guys came all the way from New York City to investigate and report on Audrey's death, and they didn't ask you about what happened?"

"No, they didn't."

I decided to leave it that way. Performing a polygraph test on Pipin would only send the needles off the chart and he'd still deny the obvious. On the other hand, Pipin changed the subject and expressed his concerns about the interview with Ricardo Hernandez and Wiky, particularly the latest one.

"I wonder what that fat dick-sucker is going to say."

"We don't have much control over that, Pipin. Do we?"

"I'm sure he's going to say all kinds of shit about me."

"But if you have done nothing wrong, then there is no reason for you to be concerned."

"Audrey is dead because of Wiky," he said. *"If he would have been in his post at ninety meters as I told him, she would be alive today."*

"No, Pipin," I said firmly, *"Wiky was there, only that he couldn't get any deeper without killing himself. Audrey would be alive today if the damn tank would have been filled . . . and you left it empty, not Wiky."*

"But, Carlos, that wasn't the first time it happened. The tank had been empty before," he finally acknowledged.

"Yes, and always when you refused to fill it, like it happened in Hawaii with Wendell, but it never happened in an actual record attempt, and much less when going to one hundred and seventy-one meters of depth, for God's sake!"

> Note: Wendell Ko is the former captain of the Hawaiian spearfishing team, winner of the 1999 U.S. National Championship. During a freediving course Pipin and I taught in Hawaii, Wendell rode the sled to forty meters and found himself without air in the pony-tank. After two students having used the sled before Wendell, I warned Pipin about the pony-tank being near empty. *"No, there is enough air for one more dive,"* he said. But there wasn't. However, as the well-trained apneist he is, Wendell pulled himself up the line, unharmed, all the way to the surface.

"Well, Wiky wasn't down there to assist Audrey and give air to her," Pipin dodged.

"But Pascal assisted Audrey and she didn't get air from Pascal. So why are you taking it with Wiky?"

"Pascal is another dick-sucker," concluded Pipin.

Once my conversation with Pipin was over, I called Wiky to set up a place and time to meet with him. It would be the first time I would see him since he had left Pipin's house, almost a year ago. But with Pipin's final acceptance of the empty tank and obstinate resolution to blame Wiky, he furthered my suspicions.

"I think he was aware of the empty tank before Audrey descended. I must open Pandora's Box," I reflected.

Even though I was afraid to find greed, envy, hate, cruelty and despair just like in the mythical story, I had to dig deeper. I needed to obtain as much information I could about Pipin's shady side, and if somebody knew that side, it had to be Wiky. So I invited him to convene.

SEPTEMBER 15, 2003
THE EYE-OPENER MEETING WITH WIKY
THE DIVORCE REQUEST

Wiky accepted right away, stating that he had been looking forward to meet with me for a long time. On the evening of September 15, Wiky knocked on my door. By now, my wife was getting a bit nervous with my determination to uncover the truth.

Adriana never was particularly thrilled with Pipin, but after Audrey's passing, she was simply reluctant to hear anything related to him. Consequently, Wiky and I headed for the trendy *Bahama Breeze* restaurant located on Kendall Drive, right off the Florida's Turnpike, to steer clear of my wife's uneasy feeling.

Seating at the bar, Wiky asked for a cup of coffee. My shaky hand, however, revealed the need for something stronger to ease my stress. Not being much of a drinker, a beer would be strong enough.

"Okay, Wiky; I need some answers. How did you know about Audrey's request to Pipin for a divorce?"

"She told me."

"When was that? Do you remember?"

"Of course I do. I'll never forget that day. That was the day Pipin and you went to coordinate the catamaran for the last time."

"That was on Thursday before the event."

"That's right, and I found Audrey seated alone by the pool where we always met at night."

"Okay, that's the pool of the Palace."

"She was giving her back to the pool, facing a wall and when I got closer to greet her, I noticed that she had been crying."

"Did she tell you why was she crying?"

"Ha, papito, I almost fell to the ground right there when she said, 'I'm going to divorce Pipin. I can't continue with him.'"

"Hmm, she had told me so the day before, Wiky. But until now, I always downplayed the issue or, at least, I didn't connect it with what happened with the tank."

"Carlos, let me tell you what I told Audrey that day, 'Are you crazy? No one abandons the madman; he abandons people, but you never abandon him.'"

"That's probably why he's blaming you for her death."

"Exactly! Not only that; I told Audrey to better take an airplane and leave immediately. I even offered to take her myself."

"And what did she say?"

"That she couldn't do that because the event was to close to cancel it."

"*But, Audrey,*" Wiky affirms having told her, "*You are not safe if you proposed divorce to him. You better pack your stuff and leave the Dominican Republic, now!*"

Wiky, now alarmed, invited Audrey to his room to speak privately. She had started to cry again and Wiky was afraid that someone, especially Pipin, could see her weeping.

THE BRUISES

Once in Wiky's room, she expressed her intention to divorce Pipin because she could not handle the abuse any longer. That's when Audrey showed Wiky her chest. There were bruises in her breast that according to Audrey were caused by fist punches. Wiky was astonished, he had known Pipin for over fourteen years and knew of his rude nature, but now he was presented with the evidence.

"*There is more,*" said Audrey while lifting her shorts' bottom part showing her buttocks to Wiky. More bruises appeared before him. Wiky, after observing the blacks and blues, insisted,

"*Audrey, you must leave the Dominican Republic. After fourteen years, I know Pipin. You must go!*"

Wiky offered to take her to the airport if she was willing to take the step, but she wasn't. She persisted that the record was a great responsibility and could not stop it now.

Audrey probably felt the pressure of having the journalists already in place. The resort had made a great effort in providing the lodging for the crew. She wouldn't do that to the team itself; they all had worked too hard, even though they would have supported her, regardless.

Then the embarrassment, with all the potentially unpleasant headlines, was probably too much for her to handle. And most importantly, she wouldn't fail Pipin. Although leaving him was a logical course of action, she wouldn't leave him dealing with the clutter. For Audrey, quitting was not an option.

But the most compelling part of Wiky's statement was the bruises. I had seen them in Audrey's chest the day she died while practicing CPR on her. I presumed that it was the consequence of a rough CPR given in the boat by either Amaury or Matt while being transported to shore, but now it didn't seem to be the case.

There was no way for Wiky to see the bruises the day of the tragedy, because during the time we were dealing with the emergency, Wiky was still in the water decompressing. The last time Wiky saw Audrey was at depth, when Pipin carried her up and passed in front of him. He didn't get to see her again. How could he know about the bruises, then?

Audrey must have showed them to him, meaning that the bruises were there before she died. This could explain why Audrey, the day of the event, unlike the previous two weeks of practice, came out of her room covered.

CARLOS SERRA

THE WITCHCRAFT RITUALS

Wiky continued by explaining the meaning of the red bandana Pipin had asked Audrey to wear around her right wrist. Apparently, by wearing a bandana, Audrey had been marked; a way for the gods to identify the person for which the divine entities have been consulted.

Audrey also performed, under Pipin's command, some bizarre ritual with a banana. She peeled the banana and threw the peel in the water before starting the event. Apparently, by throwing the peel in the water, Pipin had *consulted* one of the underwater spirits he worships; Olokún, most likely.

If the banana-skin sinks, it should take the bad influences down with it. If it floats, the bad influences shall remain present and have a negative influence over the person for whom the gods have been consulted. Audrey threw the peel while seating on the edge of the catamaran and just before entering the water. A video taken from another boat by a friend of Wiky shows the moment she did it.

Another point brought up by Wiky is that a week later, Pipin took Audrey's ashes to his room to "sleep" with her. It happened the night of the vigil; the day before spreading the ashes in the ocean.

Wiky said that in Pipin's cult nothing is more powerful than using human remains as part of the rituals. He even mentioned the possible addition into food to have people eat the remains as a way to control them and obtain the favor of the gods.

That's when I started to breathe fast and sweat cold. Wiky coincided with something my sister-in-law, Elizabeth, had told me before, forcing me to stop my daily lunches with Pipin. My determination to find the truth, coincidentally, increased right after having stopped those lunch meetings.

"And if you see Pipin wearing white clothes, be aware; he's cooking something," Wiky warned me.

Pipin dressed a white shirt the night before Audrey's fateful dive. Nothing special about wearing a white shirt, but the noteworthy aspect of it is the figure of an Aztec sun printed on the front and back of the garment. This particular figure represented, in the old Aztec culture, the Sun-God of sacrifices.

Although I've never been inclined to believe in such things, the fact is that Pipin does, beyond reasonable doubt.

UNFAITHFUL NATURE

Wiky continued with a synopsis of Pipin's ambivalent moral fiber. Actually, he went over a subject for which I was already aware, and one for which Pipin has never attempted to hide.

I even witnessed two of his escapades with two different students; one in Hawaii and another one in Spain. I found out simply because Pipin made it obvious. It was a matter of pride for him, I presume.

THE LAST ATTEMPT

Wiky mentioned a German lover who lives in South Beach; a blonde and slim lady in her mid to late 30's who produced a documentary of some sort with Pipin few years ago. But that wasn't news for me. I had become aware of the woman and had even met her not long ago. She had started to work with us at the office soon after Audrey's death and was driving Audrey's SUV, provided by Pipin.

"She has no means of transportation other than a scooter," replied Pipin when I asked, back then, why she was driving Audrey's vehicle. I didn't know anything about her yet, only that she was working for us. It took me a while before realizing who she really was.

Only few weeks after Audrey's passing, I paid a visit to Pipin at home to check how he was doing, and he was doing well. Unexpectedly, I saw the German blonde posing as the lady of the house. Although Pipin made a futile attempt to conceal the obvious, it became evident that the newest addition to our company was indeed subtracted from the old list of Pipin's mistresses.

Feeling troubled by her presence and stand, I left the house shortly after. In my mind, Audrey was still the lady and rightful owner of that residence, as it was too soon for me to accept someone else and especially under those circumstances.

The hideous side of that issue is that Audrey, in life, was aware of Pipin's most steady *friend* and despised her like no one else. In fact, Audrey knew about Pipin's escapades and even accepted it with resignation, but for her, this particular woman was a more threatening rival due to the permanence of their relationship. Even to this date, they both continue to work together.

"But, Wiky, I fail to see the connection between Pipin's extramarital affairs and Audrey's death."

"Carlos, I know how Audrey and you shared a very strong bond. So let me ask you this; can you imagine Audrey having to deal with all of that?"

"No, not really. I know she accepted it with certain degree of resignation, but I know how sad that made her."

"That's the point . . . she had enough. That's one of the reasons why she wanted to divorce him. But to divorce Pipin? Ay, papito . . . forget it!"

THE TANK AND THE TRANSFER WHIP

When I decided to ask Wiky why he was so certain that Pipin had left the tank empty, he dropped a bomb-shell; a new and undisclosed piece of the enigma. And this one would bring another upsetting factor to the equation.

"Because," responded Wiky, *"I'm the one who brought the scuba tank and the transfer-whip to fill the pony-tank, aboard the catamaran."*

"What? You arrived to the catamaran only a minute or two before Audrey and me. Are you sure about that?"

"Totally, I'm the one who brought the whip on board."

"But, Wiky, I've spoken with Matt Briseno and he says that the tank was already onboard when Audrey, you and I arrived to the catamaran."

"*No way,*" claimed Wiky energetically. "*Matt must have seen another tank. Remember, we had dozens of cylinders there. But the one to transfer the air, along with the whip, I'd brought them with me.*"

"*Are you positive about that?*"

"*Completely!*"

"*But, that doesn't make much sense. The tank and the whip should have been taken by Pipin when he parted to the catamaran over an hour before we got there.*"

"*That's why I knew,*" insisted Wiky, "*that he hadn't filled the pony-tank. I'd found the whip in the dive shop's warehouse, laid on the floor and hidden behind the big plastic bow where we put the parts for the sled.*"

"*Hidden, you say?*"

"*Yes, it was hidden,*" he insisted with resolution. "*It was as if someone placed it behind the box, not to be found.*"

"*When did you find it? When was that?*"

"*That was just minutes before taking the boat transferring us to the catamaran. I was doing a last minute check just to make sure I hadn't forgotten anything. Then I found it.*"

"*That only means that Pipin had spent over an hour in the catamaran by then and the sled had been rigged and ready, but the pony-tank hadn't been filled yet.*"

"*Exactly,*" said Wiky effusively. "*That's why I insisted so much for him to fill the pony as soon as I got there. I knew he couldn't have filled the pony-tank. Without the transfer-whip, it was simply impossible for him to have done it.*"

Furthermore, when Wiky brought the tank and the whip near the area where the sled was assembled, Pipin, in rage, told Wiky to go away with the rest of the divers. When this happened, Pipin was in the water already, next to the sled, and waiting for Audrey. But Wiky, knowing the importance of filling the pony-tank, persevered,

"*Here are the tank and the whip, Pipin, to fill the pony-tank in the sled,*" said Wiky once again while pointing at the sled, but Pipin continued to hurl Wiky away.

That's when Wiky departed to the other boat tied next to the catamaran, where the rest of the safety divers were assembling their gear. Thus the tank and the whip remained in the same spot where Wiky left it. Pipin simply ignored Wiky's petition to fill the tank for Audrey.

Until that day, September 15, 2003, when I met with Wiky, I had thought that the tank and the whip were already in the catamaran. That Wiky had taken it from another spot within the vessel and then presented it to Pipin just to make sure. This double-check was common in Wiky, as it is in most scuba divers—especially instructors—due to the standardized training they undergo. Therefore, I assumed that Pipin's upset reaction was for asking something so basic but so vital at the same time; a nurse never asks a surgeon if he washed his hands before operating.

Although there is a discrepancy of opinion between Matt, who claims the tank was already on board, and Wiky, who maintains that he brought it from shore, one aspect remains undisputed; Pipin had the chance to fill the pony-tank when Wiky insisted. But he did not.

THE OTHER DEATHS

Wiky also warned me about a subject that it's been kept quieter than a tomb; a burial place with other five deaths connected with Pipin.

"... Audrey is just one more," said Wiky. "There are many others before her."

"I know of Massimo and Pepe, and there is also a doctor in Key Largo, but who else?"

"The first one is a Canadian tourist in Cuba that Pipin was guiding underwater. There is also a spearfisherman in Cuba hunting with him."

"Oh, yeah," I assented, "Pipin had told me something about it, and I think he even wrote it in his Ninety Miles book. He said something about a shark eating him."

"Well, that's what he says," continued Wiky. "But there was a doctor in the Florida Keys."

"Yes, that's another one," I remembered. "I was working in Dixie Divers of Key Largo when it happened."

"But, Carlos, are you aware of what people say?"

"What is it?"

"That Pipin owed the guy a lot of money. How convenient is that?"

"How much is a lot of money?"

"They say is something like forty or fifty thousand dollars."

"Whoa ... that's indeed a lot of money, but can that be proved?"

"Of course, you just have to ask the doctor's family."

"Hmm, I didn't know anything about the money."

"Carlos, papito, you have the Canadian tourist, the spearfisherman in Cuba, the doctor in the Florida Keys, Pepe, Massimo and now Audrey; they all died with Pipin next to them. So, make no mistake; if you are next to Pipin an accident may, by coincidence, happen to you. Just don't contradict him or piss him off."

"I think that 'coincidence' already occurred with me."

"What? When was that?"

"It happened in the Dominican Republic during a practice dive before you arrived. He pulled my regulator from my mouth and took my tank away while underwater."

"To try something against you he must had been very upset. You are the only one he ever respected."

"Yes, he was upset. He made a fool of himself in front of everyone and I embarrassed him even more."

"Ha, you see? I know him too well."

"Interesting," I reflected, "they all died in the water; coincidentally, where Pipin feels safe."

"Yes!" exclaimed Wiky. "That's where he feels protected by Olokún."

"But, Wiky, something doesn't add up."

"What is it?"

"Leaving aside the empty pony, why wasn't Audrey breathing from one of Pascal's regulators?"

"That's a good question to ask Pascal, isn't it?"

"Uh-hmm, I'll speak with him in Cabo."

"What," jumped Wiky, "are you going to Cabo for Pipin's record? Are you out of your mind?"

"I need to get some answers from Pascal about what truly happened down there between Audrey and him. There is something about it that's been bothering me for a while."

LATER THAT NIGHT

Wiky has always been known for spicing up stories or adding his own flavor to reality, especially when it comes to hilarious anecdotes, but that didn't seem to be the case this time. The level of details he provided, plus the impossibility to have made-up specific elements, clearly indicated that he was not adding his Cuban seasoning. Besides, the subject was neither anecdotic nor hilarious.

Once back home, my wife and kids were asleep. Sneaking inside the sheets, I tried not to wake her up, unsuccessfully though, because even through the darkness of our dormitory, I saw the unforgiving stare. Then Adriana turned around to face the crib next to her side of the bed, check on Christopher and fell asleep, once again.

That's an icy gaze I deserved; she had given birth to our second son only eleven days ago. Consequently, the little sleeping time she could get was not only precious, but guarded with an attitude.

Then I kept observing the spinning blades of the ceiling-fan in a futile attempt to self-induce my sleep. I'd successfully done it many times before, but not this one.

Wiky's account kept reverberating in my mind when, suddenly, a petrifying commotion assaulted my body; a bloodcurdling tingling slithered down my spine. It was the kind of eerie feeling you get when presented with a supernatural presence.

Although I try not to put much faith in such things, some inexplicable experiences in the past have made me familiar with this hair-raising sensation. Actually, the last time I felt it, I was standing on the beach of the hotel during the wee hours of Tuesday 15, the third day after Audrey's death.

The unnatural feeling made me jumped off from bed, and while seated on the edge, I looked at the clock on top of the nightstand and read 3:33 a.m. The feeling intensified. That's exactly the same time I had on my watch that night on the beach when an awful possibility, a possible answer to one of the enigmas crossed my mind.

I remember it because I was born on the third month, March. I was 33 years old when I moved to the U.S. My diving-instructor number contains three 3's, and 3 has always been my favorite number. But if divine signs of some sort exist, maybe it was time for me to see them and I knew that my month of birth would have nothing to do with it.

THE LAST ATTEMPT

In fact, it reminded me of the number of people who, before Audrey's dive, had asked Pipin if he had filled the tank or attempted to fill it. I had also asked him thrice after the tragedy if he had filled the tank, and all three times he claimed having done that.

Then I left my wife and kids sleeping placidly and went to the living room downstairs to reflect about the situation. I didn't turn the lights on. I just sat down on the couch to think. But with memories overflowing my mind, a surge of sadness and anguish took over me. Just when I thought I was overcoming that point, I shed tears, again.

The meeting with Wiky reopened old wounds and opened some new ones. I have now come to realize the deepness of Audrey's misery, and even though she had told me about it, I failed to hear beyond the words. I had failed to listen to the shriek for help that came out straight from her soul.

"... just hang in there," I told her moments before, *"focus on your record today, and tomorrow will be another day."* But for Audrey, there wouldn't be another day.

Only two weeks before going to Cabo San Lucas, in Mexico, to help Pipin with his record dive, and there I was debating in the silent darkness of my living room if I should continue to support him or cut my ties for once and for all.

Every time Pipin would raise his voice in rage to her, she would assume a defensive posture, as if he was going to hit her. But he never did, at least not in front of me. And Audrey, in the many times we shared laid-back conversations, never confided me with such thing. So I honestly can't say if she ever got hit or not. But I did see the bruises Wiky mentioned and they were not caused by the initial CPR Audrey received.

The psychological mistreatment, on the other hand, was already evident, and Audrey and I talked about it many times. I had seen Pipin calling her names, diminishing her self-confidence by constantly implying that she wasn't smart. He kept reminding her that if it wasn't for him she would be nobody.

Not long before heading to the Dominican Republic, on the way to their house for our customary lunch-meeting, Pipin called Audrey, who was seated in the back of my SUV, *"fat, old and ugly"*.

At first, I thought he was just kidding; I even remember saying, lightheartedly, that I would never have the courage to say just *one* of those adjectives to my wife; much less all three within the same sentence. Pipin, however, continued with denigrating expressions and threats about leaving her to find a younger and better looking woman.

The puzzling part is that Pipin didn't seem to be upset or mad. He appeared to be using humor, cruel and gruesome, perhaps, but humor, nevertheless. In any case, the subject came out of no where and it was quite inaccurate. Audrey not only was slim and attractive, she was in the best shape of her life and had just turned twenty-eight years of age. Pipin was passed forty and for me that was the humoristic part. But when I turned around to see Audrey, her face was down like a goat ready to be slaughtered. Only then I realized that it wasn't funny, at all.

Audrey was a docile wife who submissively accepted cheating and maltreatment, but from time to time, she would resist the nonsense and fight back. In one occasion Pipin reacted sarcastically and said, *"I guess I have given you a long leash; I'm going to have to shorten it,"* and the following day, Audrey would come back to the office quieter than before and hide within the confines of her desk.

Pipin in his treatment with Audrey alternated roughness and cruel expressions with smoothness and kindness. It was a debilitating and systematic scheme to exert control, and it worked. It's been working since the cavemen used a wooden mallet to hit their consorts on the head, a caveman with a *Nike* outfit in this case. It was an uncomfortable situation for me to witness, but I accepted it as a private matter.

Pipin had been, however, utilizing this systematic method to control not only Audrey, but the staff as well. Occasionally, he would present himself as a magnanimous friend; a person with the charm of a prince and the conduct of an angel. In other instances he would be aggressive, almost violent; a totally hideous and uncontained monster.

If the *sweet and sour* approach didn't work or the circumstances called for a harder approach, he would use his *concealed punishment*; just like the day he removed the ladder from the boat to give Wiky a lesson. Or like the day when he, sneakily and unlawfully, downgraded me to vice-president of the company when renewing the corporation with the state of Florida in May of 2002. This last maneuver happened right after I complained to him for having declared to the press that he was the president of the company.

"Pipin, going around declaring that you are the president of the IAFD, not only diminishes my credibility and effectiveness to negotiate for the company," I said in recriminatory tone. *"It's also a lie."*

His answer was a muted look with piercing eyes. A month later, I was downgraded with neither my consent nor knowledge. Actually, I didn't find out for almost a year, and when I confronted Pipin about it, he claimed that Audrey had made a mistake and signed the papers with his name. Audrey was already dead.

But having me illegally removed from a corporate position pales when compared to what it could be the ultimate punishment ever committed; an empty tank.

If Pipin was looking to punish Audrey for requesting a divorce, an empty tank should put her back in place. For months, that theory was unthinkable, but by now it had become a repulsive option. The shocking revelations provided by Wiky regarding private matters plus details concerning the equipment, were getting me closer to a conclusion. But I still needed a way to prove it.

"If I go to Cabo for his record attempt," I debated in the stillness of my house, *"I'll have a chance to speak with two other key witnesses; Pascal and Tata."*

With neither one of them I had had the opportunity to talk about the tragedy ever since it happened; particularly Pascal. He was crucial in determining what happened after Audrey and Pascal in the sled's video, came out of the screen.

In addition, I would get the opportunity to see Pipin plunged into the element in which the egotistical ogre within takes over; another record and the attention that comes with it. Since James Cameron's presence had been announced, Salma Hayek confirmed

THE LAST ATTEMPT

her assistance as well, most likely to secure her leading role in the movie as Pipin had promised.

"Pipin's ego should be at the peak of its potency," I thought. *"That's when his tongue may betray him."*

On the other hand, I still had some concerns about his own welfare; another undersupplied organization and he could also die. Somehow, I wanted the truth, but I didn't want for him to be harmed via his own *cowboy-style* performance.

For that reason and despite the tense relation with him at this point, not to mention my reservations about his ultimate responsibility for Audrey's demise, I decided to go to Cabo San Lucas. Despite its distance from Miami, I felt the truth was just around the corner.

Chapter 20

THE POINT OF NO RETURN

Before departing to Mexico, I kept regular contact with the *Secretaria Municipal de Turismo de Los Cabos (Los Cabos Municipal Secretary Office of Tourism)* and requested enough medical logistics to ensure ample and adequate treatment in case something would go wrong with Pipin, or any of the safety divers.

Sara Tapia, the Secretary's Director of Business Links, was receptive and helpful. She found a local clinic in Cabo San Lucas, *AmeriMed*, willing to provide free of charge, the list of items I had requested. The list included:

- Two paramedics on board the days of practice.
- One Doctor and 4 paramedics the day of the main event.
- One Defibrillator with a certified technician for its operation.
- One or more oxygen kits to assist two people simultaneously for at least two hours.
- One Recompression Chamber on alert the days of practice and main event.
- Local Coast Guard on alert.
- Local Police Department for crowd control.
- One Helicopter for fast evacuation.
- Stretchers.
- Two fully equipped First Aid kits.

"This time everything will be coordinated the way it should be, just like I did for Audrey's record in Fort Lauderdale."

Pipin, in contrast, crushed my optimism the moment I showed him the list I had emailed to Sara Tapia.

THE LAST ATTEMPT

"Okay, you take care of that medical shit, but I'll take care of the safety diver's coordination."

"Here we go again, Pipin. What's your plan now, no safety divers to cover the distance like in Audrey's event?"

"No, we'll have safety divers, but I can arrange for them in Cabo. There are plenty of them down there."

"But, Pipin, those dives are not for technical-diver wannabes, and we have some of the best technical-divers in the world right here in Miami."

"No, those Mexicans are good, and these guys in Miami would cost a fortune."

"And how about the gases needed to make Trimix . . . can that be done in Cabo?"

"Oh, yes . . . there are lots of places in Cabo to do that."

Once again, I did find myself dealing with a broken promise from Pipin's part. He wouldn't let me coordinate the event. Now he was actively involved in all aspects of the organization, except for the medical part. And I let it be. I wasn't eager to exchange blows with him anymore, in the first place. Secondly, he had done two previous events in Cabo, so he should know the logistics of the place. And finally, my key objective wasn't Pipin's record attempt, but to obtain the information needed to conclude my personal investigation about Audrey's death.

However, something for which I had been suspicious for a long time and confirmed by Wiky, came to mind.

"Pipin never places divers in certain range to avoid be seen in the way up. The hose that provides air to the lift bag is always loose. It's easy to pull the hose out from the bag to breathe from it."

This brought my recollections back to Cozumel in January 2000, when Pipin did his record dive of 162 meters. No divers were placed between 100 meters and the maximum depth where Pascal was. Actually, Pascal was initially located in 140 meters and banged his tank, warning Pipin that he was close to his target depth. Then Pascal immediately descended to 160 meters to watch over Pipin, just like he did with Audrey. The moment Pipin started his ascent, a whole gap of unsupervised sixty meters existed, with only a tank full of air and Pipin holding on to it.

Factors like no video recording the ascent, no divers to witness, an athlete who has candidly breathed compressed air before in an attempt to one hundred and fifty meters (Cayman Islands-1997), a pony-tank full of air, and a lose hose attached to it, silently shout a potential cheating. The lack of divers and/or video to document his ascent, unlike any other *No Limits* athlete, is a blueprint for Pipin's records, which lays a fog of disbelieve over his performances.

SUNDAY, SEPTEMBER 21, 2003
CABO SAN LUCAS, MEXICO

The crew arrived to Cabo just in time to witness the fury of a hurricane. Indeed, hurricane *Marty* hit the coast of this tourist destination the same night of arrival. Since then, the entire southern tip of the peninsula of Baja California remained in a chaotic state for days. Loads of mud avalanching from the northern hills eventually became dry dirt, covering the small town with a thick blanket of filth.

Even the crew from the movie *Troy,* with Brad Pitt, Orlando Bloom and Peter O'Toole, paid the consequences. They were in Cabo at the time filming the legendary epic-story of falsehood and betrayal. The movie set suffered millions of dollars in damages.

But with the hurricane gone, the high temperatures remained, as another after-the-storm related factor affected the town's regular life; power outages, bringing with it further inconveniences. Without air conditioning, Internet connection and the lack of diversity on the menu, we felt like penguins in the desert; out of place, clammy and disoriented. Not to mention the funny walk due to the sweatiness of unmentionable body parts and the stickiness of certain hidden garment.

About a week after the storm, nonetheless, the streets of Cabo started to look a lot cleaner and the blackout periods became shorter every day. The town was getting, slowly but surely, back to normal.

Pipin's crew, with the exception of Tata, Pascal and me, was comprised of new faces. Wiky wasn't there, of course. Pipin would have to assault *Fort Knox* to collect enough funds to persuade him. Similar situation occurred with Matt Briseno, who wanted no part in any of Pipin's events, ever.

Instead, Pipin obtained the help of two other Cubans and a former helper named Guido Brasse. Guido seemed to be in his late 30's or early 40's, who despite being born in Switzerland, lived and studied in Germany. Being tall, slim and blond, and with a pony-tail that makes him look younger, his pose is that of a consummated bachelor. He had helped Pipin in couple of world records before, but mostly as a photographer. I've met Guido back in January 2000, in Cozumel, during Pipin's last solo-world-record before this one, but my interactions with him were limited back then.

Guido brought with him a couple of additional helpers this time; Chris, a Canadian technical-diver and videographer, and Eric, also a diver and assistant photographer. Chris, like Guido, is also blonde but with short hair and shorter in height. He seemed to be in his early 30's, while Eric, much younger looking, couldn't get a *Diet-Coke* without a picture ID.

All three were friendly, but the lack of fluency in Spanish in one side and the lack of English on the other, restricted their exchanges with the Latin side of Pipin's group.

The Cuban helpers were also much less sophisticated in outlook that the Anglo-Saxon counterpart and that kept an invisible, yet perceptible line of idiosyncratic dissimilarities between them.

But, in spite of Guido's easy-going personality, shortly after arrival, apprehension presented itself as a dark cloud on a clear sky when Guido, in recriminating tone, asked me,

"*Are you here just to take pictures?*"

We were at the *Cabo San Lucas Marina* inspecting a barge to be used for the event. I was taking pictures from the dock while Pipin and the rest of the team were aboard. That's when Guido came with his recriminatory inquiry. But once I clarified what my duties were, including taking pictures for the press and the internet report, he settled down.

And yet I immediately recognized Pipin's mark, as he always finds the way to put his own words into somebody else's mouth. Phrases like, *"You are not here on vacation,"* or *"Did you only come to take pictures?"* were part of his trademark axioms, repeated over and over throughout many events to his staff.

So I looked to the floating platform and saw Pipin semi-hidden behind a panel, gazing at Guido and me. He had just manipulated Guido the same way he had done many times before with others.

By now, Pipin's behavior was pitifully unsurprising. His favorite policy of *Divide and Conquer* as a way to rule was in place, but it was been used against me this time. I knew that early that my stay would be shorter than anticipated.

Later that same day I had my first harsh encounter with Pipin. He had come to my room to check on my coordination for medical support.

"Not only we have the doctors and the clinic, but we also have a recompression chamber available at no cost."

"Aha," he assented with disdain. *"What else?"*

"I had requested paramedics for the days of practice and paramedics plus a doctor for the day of the event. Instead, AmeriMed is providing us with doctors and paramedics for the practices and the day of the event, as well."

But Pipin's reply immediately shocked me.

"I don't want any doctors there."

"Coño, here we go again. Have you lost your mind?"

Then I turned to my roommate, Domingo Palma, who had come as a videographer, to ask him if what I heard was correct. Domingo didn't say a word. Smartly, he decided to keep himself out of it. I explained to Pipin that he either will have the doctors there or I was gone.

"After what happened to Audrey," I said, *"the eyes of the world are going to be over this record. What's the message here, that we didn't learn anything from her death?"*

At this point Pipin had started to rub his head and show his feature grimace.

"Oh, let me guess, you are going to bring Doctor Sam again, right?" I said with caustic tone. And that's when I pinched a nerve, because *Doctor Sam* was Audrey's *"Personal Doctor"* in the Dominican Republic.

He's the one I kept asking for when Audrey was placed moribund in the catamaran in front of me. The same Doctor who never appeared. *Doctor Sam* was in another boat as a mere spectator, and there was a reason for that. Pipin had conveniently "forgotten" to mention that *Doctor Sam*—whose real full name I rather keep undisclosed for obvious reasons—was a dentist from Miami and a friend of his who specializes in endodontics.

The "doctor" was unaware of Pipin's stratagem, although he was introduced to everyone by Pipin as *"Audrey's personal Doctor"*. And that included me, because I didn't become aware of this particular charade until the day after Audrey died.

CARLOS SERRA

While searching for the doctor around the hotel to confront him for his desertion, I found Tata instead, and when I asked for *"Doctor Sam",* Tata told me who he was.

Pipin's deception had denied Audrey the possibility of having a real doctor on board. It wouldn't have made any difference anyway; when Audrey came out of the water she was beyond hope. But under other circumstances, that could have been the difference between life and death. What Pipin did was disgraceful, and now, a year later in Cabo San Lucas, he wanted to repeat the scenario.

"I'll be fine; I won't need a doctor. Nothing is going to happen to me . . ." Pipin said obstinately, while dodging *"Doctor Sam"* as a subject.

"Oh, sure, I know you are superman. I know your underwater gods protect you and all that kind of crap. But what do you say about the other guys? Have you thought about them? Or what if I suffer a heart attack after listening to so much bullshit from you? I want doctors and paramedics there this time, damn it, and that's final!"

"Okay, Carlos," he said with condescending tone. *"If it makes you happy you can have doctors there. But make sure you keep them away from me."*

After Pipin's irrational position, I got certain that I wouldn't make it to the end. Many weird things were happening. The atmosphere was incredibly tense. The groups were alienated in four; the Cubans, Guido's team, Domingo and I, and Pipin, who was either by himself or with Tata keeping him silent and devoted company.

By now it was clear, the discrepancies between Pipin and I had eroded whatever friendship was left and I preferred it that way. I was getting to a gruesome conclusion about the real motives for the tank in Audrey's sled to be empty; especially after a conversation I had with Tata the following afternoon.

We had all finished lunch. The team had left the hotel to complete some tasks related to the event. Only Tata and I remained behind at the *Los Patios Hotel's* restaurant, and that's when I went directly into Audrey's tragedy. Almost a year had passed and we didn't have the chance to cross-study the event.

In abstract, Tata confirmed what Wiky had told me regarding some grisly aspects of Audrey and Pipin's relationship. Now I had a better idea of what Audrey avoided saying in the boat the day she died.

Surprisingly, Tata was also convinced that Pipin hadn't forgotten to fill the pony-tank. So if I had any doubts about Wiky's statements, now I had more conclusive testimony. Particularly since Tata continued to support Pipin and didn't get along with Wiky anymore. Pipin had managed to disintegrate their friendship.

Tata's testimony was revealing, but what really brought me to a point of no return was a conversation with Pascal. It happened the following afternoon. Domingo and I were chatting in our room's balcony when I saw Pascal walking to his room, but I invited him to come to mine, instead. Once inside, I went straight to the point,

"Pascal, a whole year has passed and we haven't really talked about what happened to Audrey. I'm actually surprised to see you here . . . can you tell me in detail what happened down there?"

THE LAST ATTEMPT

"Well, Carlos, ah . . ." he seemed hesitant, *"Audrey was fine, she had air in the tank . . . ah, not much but she had enough . . . she opened the valve and started to ascend . . . then, hmm . . ."* hesitating once again, *"the sled got stuck about five meters up and that's when I went up to help her."*

Pascal's statement was beyond belief. He was totally contradicting the sled's video.

"Pascal, that's weird, that's not what I saw in the video and I have seen the video a hundred times . . ."

"What?" He interrupted nervously. *"Have you seen the video? Is there a video?"*

"Of course there is a video, Pascal. There is always one, and what you just told me it's not what I saw in it."

"Well, Carlos . . ." he chuckled nervously, *"a whole year has passed, I don't remember exactly what happened."*

"Lucky you, Pascal, because I will never forget that day," I said with a reproachful tone. I was now getting a really bad feeling about him, too.

"One more question, Pascal. Why didn't Audrey breathe from one of your regulators? Did you ever offer one to her?"

"No, we had arranged for her to ask for it if she needed it. She never asked." Then, claiming to be in a hurry, Pascal left the room.

Before closing the door behind, he told me that we could talk more in detail another day. But I know he didn't mean it, because he later avoided me like a disease.

This conversation with Pascal was shocking but revealing at the same time. Pascal was lying, bluntly. That tale about having forgotten because a year had passed, I wouldn't buy it in a hundred years. I still have recurrent dreams about that day and can give an account, almost minute by minute of my ordeal with Audrey; from the moment she was placed unresponsive in front of me until the day we came back to Miami and afterward.

But what resulted quite unsettling was Pascal's reaction to the video. The video on the sled was *a must*, so why would he ask if there is a video? Now another aspect of my meeting with Wiky came up in an unexpected way.

Back in September 15, 2003, Wiky said something to which I didn't pay much attention to. He claimed that Pipin, before releasing Audrey's sled, tried to turn the camera off. But since Wiky had made an improvised repair in the On-Off mechanism, the switch could turn the camera on but couldn't be turned off. Wiky insisted that Pipin didn't want the video camera to work.

With Pascal asking, *"Have you seen the video? Is there a video?* Wiky's allegation makes sense. If Pipin had convinced Pascal to stick with him, with the strange story that Audrey went up by herself but later got stuck, the video *should not* exist. But I had kept the video jealously for a whole year, and always got my attention that Pipin never asked for it. Furthermore, in mid 2003, there were rumors in Spain that the video was made public on national TV. When I addressed that rumor to Pipin, he told me convinced,

"That's not true; they don't have shit!"

CARLOS SERRA

"How do you know, Pipin? Angelo brought the video from the Dominican Republic and had it for few days before I asked for it. It belonged to the IAFD, so I wanted it back. Maybe a copy of it got out in the meantime."

"There is no video, Carlos," Pipin told me with absolute confidence.

Interestingly enough, I had the video in my possession. I didn't want for such an important piece of evidence to disappear.

Now I started to believe, after the talk with Pascal, that Wiky had a point. Maybe Pipin was convinced that he had turned the video camera off. The only evidence from the outside, to know if the camera is on or not, is a little red light inside the viewfinder. Inside the housing, however, it's hard to see the tiny light.

In addition, there was a combination of factors to possibly impede Pipin to see the light. Those factors are; the intricacy of the housing design, the alignment between the housing's viewfinder and the camera's viewfinder, the water movement at the surface, and the limited vision provided by the diving mask.

All the same, there was a way to find out if Pipin tried to shut the video off, but it would have to wait until my return to Miami. The other two divers videotaping at Pipin's command, could have filmed Pipin at the surface before Audrey's descent. *"I'll have to check those tapes in detail."*

Not long after my conversation with Pascal, another issue roofed the staff with a cloud of concern. Pipin said that for the day of his record attempt, everyone would be filming on the surface. That left only one diver in scuba in 30 meters, Tata in the surface, Pascal at the end of the line (171 meters), and his buddy, another French diver called Hubert, who had planned to be in 150 meters; 20 meters above Pascal.

With no one between 30 meters and 150 meters, Pipin had 120 meters of plain water, a huge gap with neither protection nor witnesses. The more irrational Pipin sounded, the more sense Wiky's allegations made.

Another aspect is how visibly unhappy Pipin was with Pascal for bringing additional help. Hubert was not on Pipin's initial plan, so he extended the gap in the way up by removing the shallower divers.

To increase my reservations about Pipin's record even further, he also told me of his plans to deny James Cameron the setting of a camera system the renowned director had designed. To film Pipin's descent and ascent, two cameras would ride along two separate cables descending parallel to the sled.

"That's great," I said. *"For the first time your dive will be recorded in its entirety."*

"No, I don't want that."

"Why not?"

"Those cables Jim's planning to set may get on the way of the sled."

"Well, that didn't seem to be a concern for you in the Dominican Republic, right?"

"What do you mean?"

"The deco-line; do you remember that episode?"

THE LAST ATTEMPT

Pipin looked at me with his eyes on fire, but before letting him puff lava like a Hawaiian volcano, I continued,

"Besides, I'm sure Cameron is coming up with something to keep the lines and his cameras away from the sled. It's not like he's inventing the wheel. It's been done before."

Now Pipin looked puzzled.

"What? Nobody has done it before."

"Not underwater, perhaps, but haven't you seen the Olympics? In the track and field competitions there is a camera running in parallel to the athletes. The same happens in car racing, dog racing, horse racing, and so forth. Cameron is just applying the same principle but below the surface."

"Well, I don't want it anyway. It'll be too distracting and may affect my concentration."

"How many times have you said that once you are on the sled, your focus is like the one of a Tibetan monk, Pipin? You've claimed that not even a train running next to you can distract you."

"Well, I don't want that shit next to me."

"You don't want to appear on camera? That's new."

At this point, and becoming visible irritated by my insistence, Pipin started to rub his head. So to lessen the pressure, I added,

"Well, we shouldn't worry about it. Cameron already said that his design may not be ready and fully tested for your attempt. He may end up not using it, anyway."

But I had just confirmed what I was afraid of; Pipin will not accept any type of filming of his ascent, not even if it was filmed by the acclaimed James Cameron himself.

SEPTEMBER 28, 2003

The whole team was having dinner at the *Baja Cantina Restaurant,* located at the *Cabo San Lucas Marina.* With us were two special guests, a lady and a gentleman from *Lightstorm Entertainment*; James Cameron's production company.

While waiting for food to be served, Pipin was put on the spot by the lady, a middle-age and fair-skin American producer, by asking Pipin for his alleged trip to Tibet. A bewildered Pipin, not knowing what to say, became stressed out and looked out for my help,

"Ah . . . Tibet . . . Carlos, how do you say Tibet in English?"

He wanted me to cover for him; to save him from the embarrassment as I had done many times before, but I wasn't keen to do it this time.

"Pipin, it's exactly the same. Now, what she's asking you is where in Tibet were you?"

Pipin got visibly upset with me but chuckled nervously to them, not knowing what to say. The situation worsened when the lady from Cameron's staff said that she had been in Tibet and was familiar with the *Dalai Lama's* motherland.

CARLOS SERRA

The lady, who standing didn't extend much more than five feet from the floor, had something bigger than Pipin and his tall complexity; knowledge. Now Pipin was in deep trouble; he couldn't lie to her.

I kept observing his reaction closely, perceiving his aggressiveness intensify. But neither admitting nor denying having gone to Tibet, he changed the subject and got into meditation as a topic. The second person, the gentleman from *Lightstorm Entertainment*, soothed the situation by complementing Pipin and his so-called ability to control his own body and mind.

"Ah, here is another one," I thought, *"who knows how to get on Pipin's better side."*

Pipin, however, remained in discomfort; he'd been caught in his *Tibet* scheme and knew it. He responded to the compliments by saying that nothing in his surrounding could bother him; that he had absolute control over his emotions, and stress was something unknown to him.

Then a puzzling paradox occurred, at least for the two people from *Lightstorm*, because Pipin was visibly edgy. He had just said that stress never got to him, but he was clearly upset.

"Everyone is envious of me for what I have done. Especially those around me, whose only ability is to write, work with computers and make letters."

It didn't take much for me to figure it out; without saying my name, he was talking about me. I wrote the *IAFD's* training manuals and the website's daily report. I also wrote the articles for our *FreediverPro* magazine; the magazine I had produced just before Audrey's event.

Additionally, I had written many articles for specialized magazines in the past, as well. I do all the writing in computers, and I was the one always giving him guidance on how to solve problems with his laptop, a state-of-the-art computer that Pipin couldn't get to manage too well and acquired through *Hialeah Enterprises*. That's a phony name I used to identify a company directed by a friend of his, but for some mysterious reasons, it's not listed in the Yellow Pages or the local Chamber of Commerce.

Regarding the *"letters,"* it was a clear allusion to all the agreements, contracts and other documents related to classes, sponsoring and events I had made. Besides diving, to which he didn't refer to, he basically mentioned the main bulk of my duties. And of course he wouldn't mention diving. Since I hold the highest and most respected title in the scuba diving industry, with PADI, the largest training agency in the world, that's the one aspect for which he always felt somewhat relegated.

During the many trips we did together, the moment I pulled my certification card in any dive resort to either rent some gear or book a dive trip, Pipin noticed how that simple plastic card with the title *Course Director* printed on the front, would bring immediate deference and red-carpet treatment. In the diving world, people know what it takes to get there, diving instructors in particular. So they only acknowledge the endeavor for making it to a level for which most career-oriented divers will never reach. For Pipin, however, I was thieving attention away from him.

THE LAST ATTEMPT

As Pipin continued with his remarks, something he said to both of James Cameron's producers, waved a red-flag right before my eyes.

"I have a surprise for someone. Something I'm going to say during the press conference. I've written a letter and I'm going to make it public for the press. It will settle things for once and for all."

"Hmm, I can only wonder," I reflected, *"if he already knows about my conversations with Tata and Pascal."*

After dinner, we all walked out to the parking lot, and before we boarded our respective vehicles, the female producer said to Pipin while rubbing his back,

"Don't worry, sweetheart; there are a lot of envious people everywhere. But you are the greatest."

"Interesting," I thought. *"These people want their movie deal no matter what, but what about Audrey? No one seems to care for her anymore. No one wants to know what happened to her. Let's make some millions while Audrey's ashes are all over the Atlantic, right?"*

As I was looking to get a lift back to the hotel with the Cuban side of the team, Pipin called me to ride with him. We had come together but I truly wanted to keep away from him.

"Shit!" I whispered. *"Well, let's see what he wants."*

He drove back to the hotel. Domingo Palma accompanied us. But after few minutes of awkward silence, Pipin asked.

"Is there any news from the office?"

"Yeah, Salma Hayek confirmed her presence via email. She will be here the eleventh, the day before the attempt."

"Email? Do you have Internet connection in your room?"

"Not yet," I replied. *"I went to a cybercafé in Cabo's downtown."*

Amazingly, and in spite of his recent remarks, Pipin's attitude towards me did not indicate resentment or bitterness. Instead, he went once again into his favorite topic lately; his sexual adventures with *"Salma"* or *"the parking-meter"*. But to cut the annoying subject I repeated myself,

"Pipin, I've told you before, if you fucked her; congratulations. But, if you didn't, and you are just daydreaming about it, you need psychological evaluation . . . urgently, which I believe you need it anyway."

Domingo, who was seated right behind Pipin, remained silent. He was working for us in the making of a documentary I had proposed months ago. I had also proposed Pipin to hire him to film it, as a way to help Domingo. He had been unemployed ever since Pipin had fired him over a year ago, before Audrey's ordeal. Being a hardworking man, a creative mind and Venezuelan born, just like me, I felt compelled to help him in any way I could.

Smartly, Domingo wouldn't say a word that could create a situation with his once-again boss. He is easy-going and laid-back, and conflict is against his nature. In fact, his physical appearance conceals his real personality; being short and plump, with straight black pony-tailed hair and a goatee, he looks more like a *Mexican Charro* than the intellectual he actually is.

Domingo is a film-maker, a writer, a person who enjoys arts, but as for diving, only in a hot tub. He was in Cabo to film the entire event; therefore, he wouldn't say a word in front of Pipin.

Just before arriving to the hotel, Pipin said that he didn't want any doctors. Once again, I was listening to Pipin's mind-boggling demand, but it would be the last time. If Pipin didn't want any doctors, paramedics and the appropriate equipment to preserve his life, I had nothing to do there. I couldn't keep my name connected with another potential disaster, at all.

And to make my decision definitive, just after entering my room, I received a phone call from my wife. She was concerned about my stay with Pipin in Cabo. She had asked me not to go and to stay away from him. But now she was more alarmed than ever.

"Carlos, can I give Wiky the hotel's phone number and your room number? He's been calling asking for you and wants to talk to you, urgently."

"What does he wants?"

"He didn't give any specifics, but he insisted that you must leave Cabo San Lucas right away . . . and you should!"

"That's okay. Give it to him," and not long after . . .

"Carlos, papito, I'm glad to hear your voice. Oye, you must leave the madman right now. Take the first airplane away from him."

"What is it, Wiky? What's going on?"

Wiky claimed that Pipin had made some private and public statements before departing to Cabo San Lucas, blaming the 90 meters diver for his wife's death.

"Wiky, I promise, once again, that I won't let Pipin put the blame on you."

"Yeah, but that's not all. He also said that he had changed the IAFD's directors to avoid happening to him what had happened to Audrey."

"What? Where did you hear that?"

"I saw it on the television. Carlos, the directors of the company are you two; nobody else. He's not going to remove himself. He's talking about you."

Indeed, the only director he could have changed was me. I couldn't, however, confirm the allegation in this last matter, but it made no difference at this point.

When I told Wiky that I was ready to leave Cabo, in any case, he asked for details about why Pipin and I were antagonizing.

After explaining, he claimed to know how mad Pipin was with me because I had continued to search for answers; that Pipin would find a way to stop me.

"Keep in mind," Wiky said, "that Pipin and I know the same people, and he talks a lot. So I always know what he says or what he's doing. You must leave Cabo!"

"I don't think he is stupid enough to attempt anything against me, Wiky. If anything happens to me, everyone will be looking at him."

"What? Are you crazy? Six people, Carlos; six! Besides, with a couple of thousand dollars and three Mexicans, the coyotes will have a banquet with your body in the desert behind Cabo. You'll never be found!"

Wiky sounded a bit over-the-top, but I wouldn't risk it, regardless. In the end, six people had crossed-over with him, one way or another, linked to them.

I immediately made the changes in my flight and by October 3rd I was ready to go home. I will finally leave Cabo without giving Pipin any notice, and that actually saved me from additional troubles. Pipin had prepared another odd covenant with the Hotel owner that could have cost me plenty.

OCTOBER 3
9:00 A.M.

Pipin had already come out of his room and was waiting for me at the lobby. I told him that I wouldn't be joining them that day because I had some personal and important matters to solve. He insisted on asking what it was, but I refused to tell him. I wanted to depart without giving him a chance to do something to stop me, although I couldn't suppress my anger.

He became aware that something was happening. I insisted for him to go and practice since he was behind on his training schedule. When he finally left the hotel, I went for breakfast. I still had to wait one hour for the driver to come, pick me up and take me to the airport.

Minutes later, the hotel's owner joined me at the table. He said that according to Pipin, I was the person responsible for the finances. Furthermore, that Pipin wouldn't pay for invoices not signed by him. That was interesting because for a whole week, Pipin endorsed me all the invoices to sign.

"No way," I exclaimed. *"Pipin is to pay for consumption for the restaurant and the lodging, for him and for the entire group."*

The owner agreed; that was the original deal, anyway. The one with the company's checkbook was Pipin, not me. The owner, however, seemed puzzled and a bit concerned. Although I was as surprised as the hotel owner, Pipin was trying to do something not entirely new to him.

Back in 1989, after a record attempt he did in Italy, Pipin left his Cuban helpers hanging with the hotel and meals tab while he flew back to Cuba. That's a story Wiky had shared with me before, only that it was happening to me now.

The hotel expenses, nevertheless, weren't all. Pipin had also made a written statement to be read at the press conference before the attempt, planned for October 11. In his statement, he blamed me for Audrey's death after having delegated on me the task of *"event coordinator"* the night before.

That's when it hit me like a thunderbolt. One of the riddles had been answered. Pipin was ready to pull his hidden ace from the sleeve; the same one he didn't have to use in the Dominican Republic when he, supposedly, *"delegated"* on me the coordination of Audrey's event.

Pipin had planned to discredit me in front of the press, with me right there. That would have been a bold move, especially for Pipin, because up until then he was contented with going around my back. To my luck, I was leaving Cabo before the press conference would take place.

That's the same statement he had mentioned to *Lightstorm Entertainment's* producers. I read the statement on October 3rd, the same day I departed Cabo San Lucas. Pipin had it saved in his laptop. The document, by the way, was saved on a date previous to our trip to Cabo, and was evidently written by somebody else.

He couldn't have written this one. It's his language style, but the structure is some one else's. I guess he found somebody to write his letters. Well, I wish good luck to whoever that is; because I'm out for good."

Finally determined to come forward and expose Pipin for what he had done to Audrey, I boarded the taxi few minutes later and headed for the airport. Even though I still didn't have the smoking-gun, I had to speak out; tell what I knew and clear Wiky's name for once and for all. It was about time.

Chapter 21

A True Master Speaks Out

OCTOBER 3, 2003—
LOS CABOS INTERNATIONAL AIRPORT

Humidity was almost at one hundred percent but it wasn't raining. The temperature was around 35 degrees Celsius (95° F), but it was mid-morning. Although more than three hours had passed since I showered, my hair was damped. It was pure sweat dripping profusely down my face, yet I was not exercising; I was calmly seated at the airport waiting for my flight to Miami via Mexico City.

The installations were modernly designed with wide open spaces and ample windows. This feature provided a magnificent view of the airplanes and their aerodynamically designed noses pointing inside, just few meters away from the glass.

These same windows rose up vertically for ten or twelve meters to later become part of a vaulted ceiling of glass and concrete; plenty of sunlight could spread around the hall and bounce back off the white walls, floor and columns. Even under the limited shade available, sunglasses are needed and a suntan is possible.

With *Frigidaire* working, the airport must be a delightful place, but I was feeling like a chunk of meat inside a cannibal's cauldron in New Guinea. The airport's air conditioning system had stopped running during the hurricane, making the heat unbearable.

But the heat wasn't as bothersome as the circumstances of my sudden departure from Cabo. By leaving, I was cutting my ties with Pipin, permanently; no more friendship and no more business together. I felt as if the last three years of my life had just been thrown into a waste basket. My only consolation was, *"at least I'm still alive,"* and that's something Audrey couldn't say anymore. A selfish feeling, but very human, I guess.

Pulling out my handkerchief to wipe the sweat from my forehead, I started to reflect about the downward spiral of events that brought me to this point. Pipin was only days away from attempting his first solo-record since Cozumel in January 2000. I partnered him only days after that event and he never did another one ever since.

Giving different excuses, he had canceled the attempt twice before, but I knew it was fear. He can't do these records any longer; not without paying a dear price, further brain damage or even death. But when Cameron came into light with his movie proposal, Pipin decided to do it in the anniversary of Audrey's death. If someone knows how to draw attention with an emotional exploit, that would be him.

At first, Pipin just wanted to break Audrey's last record; her practice dive to 170 meters which I had recognized as the official *No-Limits* World Record for the *IAFD*. It took me some serious convincing to make him understand that he should do the dive to the same depth as Audrey, and to honor her memory before breaking her record. That only then he should continue with his record-breaking career. Somehow he listened.

Now in Cabo, I wasn't sure that he could make the dive. An attempt exceeding three minutes, and his chances would become exponentially slimmer with each additional second.

That's because Pipin's capacity to hold his breath is one of the shortest I have seen in most well-trained freedivers. Tanya Streeter, for example, performs her records in about three and a half minutes and comes out of the water, fresh. Pipin doing that time would be disastrous. To prove it, there is a long list of blackouts he had suffered; the Cayman Islands, Aruba, Cozumel, the Canary Islands, and each one of those occurred while attempting much shallower depths than 170 meters. Then I recalled,

"Ah, of course he's going to do it, just as he always does. No divers, no witnesses, no video, no anti-doping test and the tank. The same tank responsible for Audrey's death is going to be full this time and used to perpetuate his legend."

That brought my memories back to a conversation I had few years ago with the father of contemporary freediving and the most respected figure in the sport.

JACQUES MAYOL'S OPINION ON PIPIN

I had the honor of meeting Jacques Mayol few years ago when I still had the dive shop in the Florida Keys. To this day, I treasure his autographed book which I had acquired not long before meeting him.

When I saw Mayol's signature, something that immediately caught my attention was the extraordinary resemblance between Pipin's signature and his. Needless to say, however, that Mayol had been signing the same way for years before Pipin was even born.

Mayol was an exceptionally open person and very pleasant to talk with, but the moment I mentioned Pipin, his mood changed rapidly. His salt-and-pepper hair and wrinkled face, symbolizing with dignity his years of experience, was abruptly transformed into an unpleasant grimace. He even immediately admitted how disgusted he was by the way *"the Cuban"* was hurting people and freediving alike.

THE LAST ATTEMPT

Actually, Mayol was one of the very few with the courage to openly denounce Pipin for his actions. For instance, in his book *"Homo Delphinus—The Dolphin within Man"*, Mayol refers to Pipin's performances as, *"Sheer Stunts"*.

He also reiterates a statement given by the Editor-at-large of *Sport Diver Magazine*, Pierce Hoover, who referred to Pipin's records as, *"A Circus Act!"*

In an article for *Outside Magazine* written by Paul Kvinta (October 1998), Tec Clark, director of the *YMCA* scuba program and U.S. representative to the *Confederation Mondiale Activités Subaquatiques (CMAS)*, declared the following,

"Pipin's a freak show . . . Sitting on a sled isn't freediving. It is stunt diving, and it's dangerous."

Years ago, *CMAS,* the oldest international diving body, alarmed by a small group of *No-Limits* athletes whose performances started to go deeper than 300 feet, stopped endorsing *No-Limits* and tagged this type of performance as *"human applied experimentation."*

There are many respected personalities of the diving arena who explicitly oppose Pipin's so-called "records", but the most open to point out Pipin's dives as *cheating* is Mayol.

The following are unaltered excerpts from Mayol's book kindly authorized by his publisher, Maurizio Candotti Russo, Vice-president of *Idelson-Gnocchi Publishers*:

". . . until the Cuban began cheating a bit and halfway down started breathing compressed air from a small tank mounted on his vehicle's frame."

Then he continues,

"The media and public didn't understand and continued to fall into the trap. Mr. Pipin knowingly pulled the wool over their eyes and today touts himself as the unbeatable breath-holding champion."

Then Mayol conveys his inspection on Pipin's so-called *love* for the ocean by stating;

". . . who loves the sea so much that he dives with his eyes shut and only has one idea in his head; to reach the end of the cable to eliminate the 'suffering' from the descent as quickly as possible . . . which obviously proves that he doesn't like it so much 'down there'."

Although the observations from Mayol may sound as the bitter outburst of a jealous rival, it's important to note that Mayol had been retired for years when Pipin came to light. In addition, Mayol had helped other freediver champions like Umberto Pelizzari and an American athlete named, Meghan Heaney-Grier, at one time the U.S. Record holder for Constant Ballast with 165 feet.

Therefore, as a fervent lover of the ocean and freediving, and a willing helper of new talent, Mayol's words evidently came from the heart, not jealousy. He was sincerely concerned about the adverse publicity Pipin would bring to the sport he loved, and with the same honesty, Mayol didn't even try to hide his dislike for Pipin and his deeds.

"Obviously, I hold a grudge against 'the greatest breath-hold diver of all times', first for personal reasons that I do not have to divulge here and for professional reasons related to the dignity of the apnea world."

Mayol followed his statement by addressing Pipin's reputation among the experts:

"One needs to read between the lines of the different articles published in reputable technical journals to realize that Pipin has a bad reputation, which can only harm breath-hold diving's reputation. But I prefer not to dwell on this. The truth about such characters always surfaces on its own, and that will surely happen in this case."

After citing some of the people who had died, *". . . during some of Pipin's 'circus acts' at sea,"* Mayol finishes with some lapidary words,

"You can't fool with the ocean or cheat with the sea!"

Mayol not only wrote about Pipin in his book. He also shared his sentiments with close friends, and one of those friends is the *Director of the Marine Mammal Division* at the distinguished *Harbor Branch Oceanographic Institution* in Fort Pierce, Florida. His name is Steve McCulloch.

"Jacques always said . . . and I (McCulloch) quote, 'Pipin is nothing but a Cuban Kamikaze. He is NOT one with the Ocean. One day she (the ocean) will punish him for forcing himself on her. One day it will happen, when he least expects it'."

Mayol's disappointment came from the fact that freediving is, for the true apneist, more a spiritual activity than a competitive sport. Breaking records was for Mayol a way to discover his true limits and rediscover his inner-self. Admiration, fame and glory was only a side effect; not an ambition. But there is another great champion who nicely describes what true freediving is all about, and that's multiple times world record-holder, Umberto Pelizzari.

"From the depth of 100 meters and more, headlong in the abyss, the heartbeat gets slower, the body disappears, and all the feelings take a new form. The only thing that remains in us is the soul. We take a long jump into the soul, which seems to absorb the universe. Every time I ascend, I am making a choice: it is me who is re-discovering myself in my human dimensions, meter by meter, to come up to see the light again. It often happens that I am asked what is there to see deep down in the sea. Maybe the only possible answer is that one does not descend this way to look around, but to look into Himself. In the deep I look for myself. This is a mystical experience bordering on the divine. So deep down, I am immensely alone but inside it feels as if all humanity is with me. It is by being human that I surpass the limits we set for ourselves and diving makes us one with the sea and its surroundings. It is here that I become one with the sea and discover my true self."

Mayol, through his friend McCulloch, also confirmed something only known by those directly involved with freediving at the top level or those close to my partner; that Pipin is *not* into yoga or meditation; he's just impersonating Mayol's authentic connection to the mystical Easterner life style.

McCulloch says; *"Another example that Jacques pointed out was Pipin's refusal to accept that yoga and controlled breathing and meditation were useful practices in the field of breath-hold diving. Pipin bragged about his large lung volume capacity . . . Pipin discounted Jacques' Yoga style and methodology and even criticized Jacques at some point. Then, after a free diving accident in the Keys where one of Pipin's students drowned, he suddenly began taking on Jacques' yoga approach and incorporated these techniques into his own (Pipin's) teachings. Another example of how Pipin "ripped-off" Mayol's innovations."*

THE LAST ATTEMPT

Steve McCulloch is a distinguished member of the scientific community, and as a close friend of the late Jacques Mayol, and director of the *Marine Mammal Division* at the *Harbor Branch Oceanographic Institute*, his words are as rock-solid as the reputation that precedes him.

The *HBOI* is a state-of-the-art research organization dedicated to the most advance investigations in the area of aquaculture, biomedical research, engineering, marine education, marine mammals, marine operations and marine science.

During my short dialogue with Mayol, he described how Pipin did his "stunt" dives and mentioned the pony-tank with the loose-hose trick, the lack of divers and the lack of video for his ascent. Speaking of people with *wool over his eyes*, I didn't believe Mayol back then. I just couldn't accept my friend, sport hero, and eventual business partner to be as authentic as a three dollar bill.

Mayol even said that Pipin was a disgrace for freediving and was afraid that he would be, one day, responsible for more deaths. At the time Mayol knew about Pepe Fernandez and Massimo Berttoni, the scuba safety divers who mysteriously died during two of Pipin's attempts in the past.

Even before Audrey's tragedy, Pipin had the dubious honor of being the only freediving athlete ever to lose not one, but two people during his events. Now his most authentic record has mounted to three and that's an impossible endeavor to beat, unless *Son of Sam* gets out jail and dedicates himself to break freediving records.

Pepe and Massimo were both scuba divers, but Mayol was expecting a freediver next time; either a Pipin copycat or somebody under Pipin's coaching. It gives me a hair-raising sensation to remember Mayol's prophetic words.

I also remember asking Mayol about a picture in his book. It is a photograph of Angela Bandini, the young Italian freediving champion with Mayol himself by her side. The photo was taken while practicing for the world record she did in 1989, beating Mayol's official record and Pipin's unofficial record. The picture was printed in the same page where Mayol referred to Pipin.

I asked him if it was a subliminal way to vindicate Angela Bandini for false allegations of *"unknown"* origin made against her performance in 1989, and his answer was,

"You are very perceptive young man . . . very perceptive."

No need to be perceptive, though. Mayol's book is a Coffee-table format and contains 360 pages. The one picture in the book of Angela Bandini's defamed world record is precisely in the same page (265) where Mayol dissects Pipin. Anyone knowing the story could have come to the same conclusion, and that's probably the *"personal reasons"* to hold a grudge against Pipin as he wrote in his hardback.

By the way, in his book Mayol mentions most of the world-class freedivers at the time, but the only one he wrote about in an unenthusiastic way was Pipin.

Mayol concluded our improvised meeting with the following prophecy:

"Someone will suffer a serious accident one day, or perhaps even die while attempting to break Pipin's record in an honest way."

Besides Audrey, Mayol's prophesy became true when German freediver Benjamin Franz suffered a near-fatal accident while trying to break Pipin's *No-Limits* record only few months before Audrey's attempt.

"SU ATENCION, POR FAVOR..."

The public announcer at *Los Cabos International Airport* brought me out of contemplation. They were finally boarding the flight to Mexico City that would connect with my final destination; Miami. As I walked towards the airplane, I kept looking behind my back. Wiky had told me so many creepy stories about Pipin that I started to feel paranoid.

Once inside the aircraft, I started to reflect about what I should do next.

"Although I still don't have anything conclusive, I must come forward. I must say everything I know about Audrey's death and clean Wiky's name. The poor guy has gone through enough already."

However, I wasn't sure about disclosing the way Pipin performs his records. I was concerned that people would take it as a personal vendetta and a discrediting plot, because in the end, it was the greatest mass-murderer, evildoer, cheater and myth-crafter of the 20th century, Adolph Hitler, who said, *"The great masses of the people will more easily fall victims to a great lie than to a small one."*

Even nowadays, there are people who still reveres the mono-testicle dictator the same way some people truly believe Pipin to be the greatest freediver of all times.

The fact is that Pipin has been performing a stunning show; an incredible magic act, an illusion that not even Harry Houdini or David Copperfield could have executed so brilliantly. But it was also Hitler, who said,

"Great liars are also great magicians!"

I never really understood the deeper meaning of that phrase . . . until now.

Unexpectedly, I realized the similarities between Pipin and Hitler. This likeness include crafted mythical stories about themselves; liking the occult and the esoteric; believing themselves to be superior beings; little regard for human life, and surrounding themselves with henchmen, but at the first sign of *disloyalty*, eliminating them. There is also hunger for supremacy and glory as part of their personality.

"Could there be a pattern? I wondered. *"Maybe there is a sinister correlation between the two. Maybe they had the same kind of upbringing, a common mental disorder or zodiac sign with the same planetary influence."*

I was trying to entertain myself but it took me some time to realize how close I was from the essence of what truly happened to Audrey.

OCTOBER 04, 2003
MIAMI, FLORIDA

The day after my arrival from Cabo, I received a phone call from *HBO's* producer, Michael Sullivan. They wanted to interview me again now that I was in direct conflict

THE LAST ATTEMPT

with Pipin. How Sullivan found out that I was back from Cabo, escapes my knowledge, but he was not the only one.

By October 6 I had received phone calls from *Telemundo* and *Univision*, the two most important Spanish television networks in the U.S. They wanted to interview me, too. I had told them that I would gladly talk to them after Pipin's record attempt because I didn't want to be blamed for affecting his psyche if something would go wrong.

Pipin, however, anticipating my move, went ahead and made public the letter I had read before; the one in which he blamed me for Audrey's death for being the *"event coordinator."* Consequently, and with Pipin now openly attempting to blame me for Audrey's death, I accepted to all the interviews. Few days later, Miami was heated with the controversy.

From reports on the prime time news, to a one-hour program on the issue flooded the air, and the controversy lasted for weeks.

Suddenly, I became some kind of celebrity. Even an older lady, a cashier at my local supermarket, who recognized me from TV, asked while I was paying the weekly groceries,

"That ugly son of a bitch killed his wife; didn't he?"

"I don't know," I replied. *"I know he left the tank empty."*

In *Don Pan*, a Venezuelan bakery where I regularly buy Venezuelan-style pastries for my son Alexander after picking him up from the daycare, the lady behind the stand said,

"Oh, I saw you on TV last night. Poor girl; she was so beautiful, but she also seemed to be so depressed."

Days later, at the parking lot of a local dive shop, a Cuban spearfisherman I've never seen before but with enough spearguns in his truck to give away his hobby, told me,

"Hey, compadre, well done. It takes some big cojones to denounce Pipin, you know. So many people have died but no one says nothing, man. Everyone is afraid because he's a big time brujo, bro! How come you're not afraid of witchcraft? We Cubans respect that shit, you know."

"I'm not Cuban."

"Oh, so you don't believe in Santeria, bro?"

"Nope, I don't."

"Not because you don't believe it doesn't mean it doesn't exist, bro."

"No offense, but if that's the case, why all the brujos in Miami can't get rid of Fidel in Cuba?"

"Ah! Because Fidel is a bigger brujo than Pipin, bro."

And after the one-hour special, the situation only worsened, making this newly acquired celebrity-status quite uncomfortable. The program, which translated to English means *Behind the News*, was produced by *Telemundo* and conducted by the network's most respected anchorman in Miami, Ambrosio Hernandez.

Pipin had already returned from Cabo and was invited to expose his side but didn't show his face. Now he was alone; he didn't have someone else to cover for him. Instead, he recorded his statement, which by the way, caused alarm among the viewers. In his edginess, he was deepening his name in the mud by giving incriminatory remarks. Only Wiky, Ricardo Hernandez and myself, assisted.

When the segment on *HBO's Real Sports with Bryant Gumbel* was aired on October 28 of 2003, the general commotion was overwhelming. Now Pipin, placed against the corner by Bernie Goldberg, admitted not having filled Audrey's tank.

The day after the show an irritated Pipin made another statement in the *IAFD's* website, now against *HBO*. But the harm was already done and there was nothing he could do to recoup his words.

Adding to Pipin's admission, I had provided the video that showed Audrey in her final and fatal dive. Now, with all the pieces together, I provide evidence on how Audrey's faith was sealed that tragic day by an empty tank; not by false allegations that she died because Wiky wasn't at depth.

In his statement, Pipin even threatened with another show that would tell *"the truth."* The show was a Spanish version of *CBS's 60 Minutes* aired by *Univision* and called, *"Aqui y Ahora"*. The segment was reported by a Colombian journalist acquaintance of Pipin and produced by a Cuban guy who used to work for Pipin, as well.

Therefore, Pipin expected the show to side with him, but even though the two friends attempted to diminish Wiky's credibility and twisted my real intentions by implying that it was all about money, they couldn't improve Pipin's image, at all. The truth was too evident and the reporter, along with the producer, would have risked their careers by attempting to protect Pipin any further. Actually, Pipin ended up loosing his temper with the reporter, on camera.

The worst part, however, is the objectionable failure of the program to address the key point on the whole dilemma; why was the tank empty? Instead, they presented Pipin declaring slander against Wiky and me, and eventually, they finished the segment with Audrey's mom repeating Pipin's own words; that she didn't want an investigation and the people condemning Pipin were *just jealous* of him.

The grave allegations made by the two closest persons to Pipin and Audrey when she died, being pitifully reduced to a mere case of *"jealousy"*.

After fourteen years of loyalty, risking his life as a safety diver for Pipin, and even covering the way he performs his so-called apnea records, Wiky was just jealous.

On the other hand, I had carried on with the company when money was gone, endured the most stressful times of my life, sided with Pipin, protected him, confronted the press, stood against absurd accusations of cover-up and voluntarily lost my source of income in a moment when Pipin's money worthiness was greater than ever with his movie deal . . . just because I'm jealous.

Once again, I was listening to Pipin speaking through somebody else. But by hearing Anne-Marie repeating Pipin's paranoid proclamation that the world is envious of him, something really awful and painful became overwhelmingly evident right there. A mother had just denied justice for her lost offspring and had kissed her daughter goodbye. And that truly sliced my heart in two.

THE LAST ATTEMPT

Even so, and despite the efforts to conceal Pipin's responsibility through an incomplete TV report, two vital questions remained unanswered:

Why Pipin didn't fill the tank?

Why Pascal didn't give Audrey a regulator?

Chapter 22

IN THE MIND OF A MASTER OF DEEP-CEPTION

OCTOBER 2003

On October 5th, two days after my return to Miami, I received a phone call from Cabo San Lucas; it was Pipin. It's needless to say that I went all out as I had discovered the entirety of his scheme. So I asked him not to call ever again and hung up. But he tried anyway.

Refusing to answer his second call, he left a message in my answer machine. To this day I preserve the tape along with all the documents (pictures, videos, emails, reports, documents, etc.) to prove the chronicle printed in this book, anticipating that one day, hopefully, this case will be investigated by a legal entity and perhaps brought to a court of justice.

The following is a translated (Spanish to English) but unedited transcript of the message left by Pipin:

"(Beep) Carlos, brother, let's think in a sensitive fashion what's going on. I don't know what happened, what they said in channel fifty-one, or what you are telling me that I accused you or much less, okay? The only thing that remains clear to me is that the only people that supported me and the only one for whom I have all the gratitude in the world is you, okay? So whatever thing they had twisted, altered or what do I know, let me know it before you cause a shitty situation for nothing, because for you I feel all the fondness that I have not . . . that I don't have for anyone, okay? Because you are the only person that has been like a family for me; because you are the only person that has been on my side in all this shit that happened. I know that you are going through difficult times; I'm going through difficult times, too. This thing we are doing is crisping the nerves of

THE LAST ATTEMPT

everyone. Breathe deeply; relax before you cause a shitty situation for nothing, because it won't take us anywhere. It would only take us to a shitty situation, which is what the whole world wants to see; that you and I end up fighting and destroying each other. And now is the moment that we should be more . . . closer. Think it well, I don't know, call me as soon as you can. (Beep)"

Now he was unlocking his sweet-approach on me, because after a year since Audrey's death, this is the first time he would state any type of gratitude.

My aunt Yvonne, who had come from Venezuela to help my wife with our three weeks old son, Christopher, while I was in Cabo, was listening to Pipin's message being recorded. As Pipin was giving his persuasive message, she looked at me with pity in her expression, but the pity face was not for me. The sympathetic face was for Pipin.

When Pipin uses the *sweet* approach, he's simply irresistible. Even through the telephone line, he can manipulate emotions with the ability of a Soap-Opera scriptwriter. Once Pipin hung up, my aunt, knowing the whole story already, had turned her pity face into a frown and said,

"*El hijo de su madre almost got me convinced!*"

Pipin's manipulative ways were in motion, once again, but unsuccessfully this time. And even though I had closely seen Pipin's dual nature, I could never imagine the extreme disparity of his reaction within days. Three days after calling me brother and expressing his immense gratitude, he made public a slander letter twisting facts and adding ghastly lies; a letter that by the way, he had it done days before my departure from Cabo.

So, by October 3rd he had the libelous letter already made; on October 5th he left his *loving-brother* message in my answer machine, and by October 8th he had the letter posted on the Internet; a rollercoaster of love and hate that defies logic.

"*How is it possible for a person to have such extreme duality?*" I asked my aunt. "*He's like two different and opposing persons in one.*"

"*Hey, mi muchacho, he's not normal. There is something wrong in his head,*" replied my aunt, with the wise simplicity that maturity brings. And she would be right.

Few days later, while watching a documentary on the *History Channel*, there was a psychologist giving a profile on Adolph Hitler, making me remember how I had compared the similarities between the megalomaniac German tyrant and Pipin. And the more the expert described Hitler's personality, the more my former partner was being described.

What resulted stunning was to hear the psychologist making a connection between Hitler's mental disturbance and his actions.

"*Of course,*" I said jumping off the couch. "*That's it. The motivation and answers to all of his apparently irrational and illogical actions must derive from his psyche. The final answer to what happened to Audrey must be in his mind.*"

Failing to realize that answers are not always material, I had kept looking for something logical and tangible to explain what happened. Until now I had been looking for answers from the standpoint of a normal and regular guy, but there is nothing neither normal nor regular about Pipin. Although I wasn't looking forward to, it was time to plunge into the abyss of his psyche to find the evasive final answers I had been looking for.

The next day I called my friend Daniel Gonzalez in Venezuela, a psychiatrist who after few minutes elucidating my experience, gave a remote; therefore, unofficial diagnostic.

"You are describing a person with a prominent case of Antisocial Personality Disorder," Daniel said. *"He's a sociopath, but to be more specific you should look into Narcissistic Personality Disorder, and mostly into Malignant Narcissistic."*

"What?" was my initial and uninformed reaction, *"I already know he's a narcissist . . . so, the guy's in love with himself. Come on, Daniel, what's the big deal?"*

"Carlos, do you know what Hitler, Mussolini and Stalin had in common?" Daniel asked probably utilizing my acknowledged interest in WWII history to make a point, and the fact that I had watched Hitler's profile on TV as I had commented him, prompting me to call.

"Yeah, they were all dictators; charming individuals but murderers. People feared them and revered them idiotically. They killed those who disagreed with them and established their own rules . . ."

"Exactly, and along with a couple other conditions, they were all Malignant Narcissistic. And if you want more contemporary examples, there you have Saddam Hussein, Fidel Castro and our very own Hugo Chavez."

Daniel expanded by saying that *Narcissistic Personality Disorder* or *NPD* encompasses some of the most malicious personality flaws in humans and its deeds affect everyone close, one way or another.

"But to have an official diagnosis," added Daniel, *"a test should be performed."* The test, he said, is applicable for patients with personality disorders, anxiety and depression. It's also used in cases of domestic violence ever since abuse and narcissism are, in many cases, intimately related.

"Daniel, the possibility of Pipin getting professional care, thus performing the test is as good as seeing Dr. Freud performing the test himself."

"Yeah, I imagine, but even without the test, I know he is a malignant narcissistic."

When Daniel mentioned the correlation between abuse and narcissism, he nailed it. That same night, with my wife and kids asleep, I decided to expand my research through the world's largest source of information; the Internet. With the computer desk next to my side of the bed, I was afraid of seeing the eyes of an owl staring at me through the darkness, but I was careful and noiseless this time.

I found numerous sites concerning mental health, and the information was both; enlightening and brutal. The repercussions of the illness are indeed much worse than what I have ever imagined.

With my eyes glued to the computer screen, I whispered in recriminatory tone, *"Oh my God, what a blind fool I've been."*

One of the most prolific websites in terms of information and elucidating the different avenues the syndrome may take is the one presented by Dr. Sam Vaknin, Ph.D., who kindly allowed me, after contacting him, to transcript his findings.

THE LAST ATTEMPT

According to the mental health community and Dr. Vaknin's website, a Narcissist is a person who presents five or more of the following nine traits:

1. Feelings of Grandiose and Self-importance; he demands to be recognized as a superior being. The person exaggerates accomplishments and talents; exaggerates his traits to the point of lying or cheating.
2. Is preoccupied with fantasies of unlimited success, power, brilliance, beauty, or ideal love.
3. Believes that he or she is "special" and unique and can only be understood by, or should associate with, other special or high status people or institutions.
4. Requires excessive admiration.
5. Has a sense of entitlement, i.e., unreasonable expectations of especially favorable treatment or automatic compliance with his or her expectations.
6. Is interpersonally exploitive, i.e., takes advantage of others to achieve his or her own ends.
7. Lacks of empathy; is unwilling to recognize or identify with the feelings and needs of others.
8. Is often envious of others or believes that others are envious of him or her.
9. Shows arrogant, haughty behaviors or attitudes.

It was a shocking surprise to read the above list. I was looking into the *Narcissistic Personality Disorder* to delineate Pipin's character, but it looked instead as if these sites had used Pipin to illustrate *NPD*.

In the silent darkness of my room, and while seated in front of the computer screen, I reclined my back, covered my semi-open mouth and said,

"Whoa, it's a perfect match!"

The following are expanded or alternative descriptions provided by Dr. Sam Vaknin's website and some other sites related to NPD to illustrate the disorder even further:

- His "achievements" can be imaginary, fictitious, or only apparent, as long as others believe in them. Appearance is more important than substance, what matters is not the truth, but its perception. His capacity to deceit, however, should not be underestimated.
- Fraudulently claims qualifications, experience, titles or connections which are unclear, misleading, or fake, but always ostentatious.
- Requires and demands excessive admiration, adulation, attention and affirmation; wishes to be feared and to be notorious (defined by the mental health community as *"Narcissistic Supply"*).
- Behaves arrogantly, feels superior, omnipotent, invincible, immune; he does not adhere to laws since he feels above the law and omnipresent (defined as *"Magical Thinking"*).

- Uses others to achieve his own ends (defined as *"Interpersonally Exploitative"*)
- He is constantly envious of others and seeks to hurt or destroy the objects of his frustration (defined as *"Devoid of Empathy"*).
- Suffers from paranoid delusions as he believes that the rest of the world is acting against him.
- Has a *Dr. Jekyll/Mr. Hyde nature*, with *Hyde* (the monster) being the real character while *Jekyll* (the nice character) is just a role playing. He is wicked, cruel and vindictive in private, but innocent-looking and charming in front of eyewitnesses; nobody can (or wants to) recognize this individual's vindictive nature—only the narcissistic's victim is aware of the aggression.

Here is where my surprise reached the pinnacle. I had always used, jokingly, the Dr. Jekyll/Mr. Hide analogy referring to Pipin's personality, and that's exactly how Dr. Vaknin refers to people with NPD. Only that, there was nothing funny about it this time.

As I continued to read into the illness, the astonishing signs kept mounting.

- Is a convincing and trained liar with histrionic or theatrical faculties.
- Exhibits abnormal and improper approach in sexual matters, sexual behavior and/or bodily functions. Underneath the charismatic façade there are often indications of sexual harassment and discrimination, perhaps even sexual dysfunction, sexual insufficiency, sexual violence or abuse.
- Is prejudiced and chauvinistic, especially against the opposite sex, people of a different sexual orientation, other cultures, race, religious beliefs, foreigners, etc.—but goes to great lengths to keep this aspect of his personality surreptitious. He uses cruel jokes as a way to disguise his offensive intentions.
- Is elusive and has a Magician-like aptitude to get away from accountability.
- Undermines, denigrates, discredits and destroys anyone who is perceived to be an adversary, a potential threat, or who can see through the narcissistic's pretense.
- Is clever at creating conflict between those who would otherwise gather incriminating information about him.
- Is quick to discredit and neutralize anyone who can talk knowledgeably about his antisocial behavior.
- Might pursue a vindictive vendetta against anyone who dares to hold him accountable.
- Gains gratification from denying people what they are entitled to.
- Highly manipulative, particularly of people's perceptions and emotions; especially guilt.
- Poisons peoples' minds by manipulating their perceptions about others.
- Is obsessed with fantasies of unlimited success, fame, fearsome power and glory. He's also obsessed with his own physical beauty and sexual performance (defined as *"the Somatic Narcissistic"*).
- He demands automatic and full compliance with his unreasonable expectations.

- He's unable to identify, acknowledge or accept the feelings, needs, choices or priorities of others.
- He is dishonest, intrusive, and unbelievably petty.
- In matters of money, is greedy, selfish, tightfisted, and financially unreliable.
- He is a robber of other people's ideas.
- He always takes and never gives, unless he's looking for retribution of some sort.
- Uses psychological, physical, verbal and sexual abuse as a form of dehumanization and objectification. The victim must become an object and lose humanity.
- He disregards consistency and planning; does not keep agreements, makes false promises and considers predictability a demeaning behavior.
- Rages when frustrated, contradicted, or confronted, particularly by people he considers inferior and/or unworthy.

ANOTHER ASPECT OF A SOCIAL PERSONALITY DISORDER

In addition to the *Narcissistic Personality Disorder*, something Daniel mentioned that fitted perfectly with actions and situations I had seen this far, relates to the *Histrionic Personality Disorder*. Here is the list provided by the mental health community and Dr. Vaknin's site:

1. Is uncomfortable in situations in which he is not the center of attention.
2. Interaction with others is often characterized by inappropriate sexually seductive or provocative behavior.
3. Displays rapidly shifting and shallow expression of emotions.
4. Consistently uses physical appearance to draw attention to self.
5. Has a style of speech that is excessively impressionistic and lacking in detail.
6. Shows self-dramatization, theatricality, and exaggerated expression of emotion.
7. Is suggestible, i.e., easily influenced by others or circumstances.
8. Considers relationships to be more intimate than they actually are.

Having a consistent pattern of 5 or more of the above list fits the individual as afflicted with the disorder.

Just like in the list for the *Narcissistic Personality Disorder*, one only wonder what happens when the person shows a consistent and undeviating pattern with *all* signs presented in the list above.

Dr. Vaknin's and other websites helped me a great deal. Suddenly, it all made sense, particularly those aspects of Pipin's erratic personality that until now, were just puzzling.

From the moment I met him in Caracas back in 1989, through Audrey's demise in October 2002, and up until I severed my ties with him in October 2003, there are countless stories, situations or events which I can connect with the abovementioned descriptions, but the motivations for his actions were suddenly clarified.

However, after finding out that Pipin deliberately plans and executes his deeds according to his own atypical motives, I wanted to go deeper into his brain (scary thought, I admit). But determining what could have gone through his mind that stormy October 12 was crucial. And then, step by step, recreate the entire event to find an explanation for each and every one of his until now puzzling procedures. Therefore, I continued the search through libraries, book stores and the Internet.

One of the books I checked is the one written by Dr. Vaknin himself. He is the author of *"Malignant Self Love—Narcissism Revisited"*, and his book is the number one seller on the subject. That's when I discovered the other disturbing aspect of the *Narcissistic Personality Disorder;* the one to which Daniel had made a reference to.

IN THE MIND OF THE ABUSER

According to Dr. Vaknin and the mental health community, the narcissist shields himself against abuse by becoming the abuser. He is unable to love or feel empathy for others, making his maltreatment easy to render.

He surrounds himself with people from whom he can feed his *Narcissistic Supply* of adulation, attention and affirmation. The narcissist is in conflicting needs, because on one hand he draws from others his sense of self-worth, but on the other hand he must feel superior, disdainful and depreciatory against the source of his nourishment. And if the source of nourishment becomes confrontational, he will then become unpredictably aggressive, cruel, disloyal and dangerously and treacherously impulsive; even reckless.

Abuse is a fundamental part of the *Narcissistic Personality Disorder*. The narcissist idealizes first and then diminishes and rejects the object of his initial idealization. This abrupt and heartless devaluation is the most common form of abuse employed by narcissists. All narcissists, without exception, idealize and devalue constantly and permanently throughout a relationship; the *sweet and sour* approach.

The narcissist is also a master of mental torture and psychologically frightful manipulations. He inflicts pain and suffering to his nearest people; particularly friends and family. The spouse becomes an immediate victim because his need for control can be continuously used on her.

The abuse can present its ugly face in any, many or all of the following methods: lies, insults, exploits, tactless interaction, denigration, ignoring the other part, disregarding anything meaningful to the spouse, the usage of sadistic or morbid sense of humor, or to be brutally honest like in regards of physical appearance.

Blaming, accusing, judging, criticizing, ordering around, name calling, and violent anger are also part of the narcissistic repertoire of psychological weapons. And in more serious cases, physical and sexual abuse is also common.

Whether the abuse is psychological, physical, emotional or sexual, there are hundreds of different types of abuse, however, the narcissist is a master of subtle or stealthily abuse.

Most people outside the relationship between the victim and the victimizer are not aware of the abusive pattern being used.

Outdoors, they are charming, loving, caring, giving and soft spoken, but in the privacy of their home, the narcissist is an intimidating, nerve-racking and overpowering monster. Again, deception is the most important aspect of their terrible game. At this point, unless the spouse stands firm against the act and the abuser, the narcissistic's control is unrestricted and absolute.

IN THE MIND OF THE ABUSED

On the other hand, it takes two to Tango and without the compliance—willing or unwilling—of the abused, there wouldn't be an abuser. An adoring, available, submissive, self-denigrating partner is the narcissist's perfect feeding ground; the ultimate source of sadistic satisfaction.

The initial phase of attraction encompasses normal emotions; infatuation and falling in love. First the narcissist's counterpart must have a poor or distorted grasp of herself or reality; otherwise, she would desert the narcissist early.

A person with appropriate or normal levels of self-respect would not put up with the narcissist's controlling behavior once he shows his real face. It may take a while for the spouse to realize it, though. The narcissist is a monster in disguise.

The abused person is at the receiving end of a *sweet and sour* routine; one moment the abuser is in rage, insulting and demanding, but minutes later he brings flowers, smooth-talk and tender, loving care. But for the most part he will not apologize unless it is the ultimate resort. He may even reflect guiltiness over his partner and the making-up is just because of his *benevolence*.

The abuser is perceived by the abused as the person with the right to demand sacrifices. This is fueled by the fact that he seems to be superior in many ways; skillfully, intellectually, athletically, emotionally, economically and/or morally.

The tardiness to realize the abusive behavior may take months or even years, but at that time it may be too late for the abused partner to depart; her sense of self-worth has been diminished; perhaps eliminated.

In many cases the abused is a professional victim. She has the predisposition to punish herself; thus, the besieged life with the narcissist is a punitive measure (defined as *Masochistic Supply*) and this encourages the abusive behavior even more.

The partner survives through self-denial. She disallows her hopes, ambitions and even her sexual and emotional desires. She perceives her needs as a threat because it may provoke the narcissist's rage.

Through this denial state she submissively accepts his superiority and the greater or superior the narcissist is, the easier the partner succumbs to his authoritative Godly figure. She degenerates into an appendix of the narcissist; a mere extension of his supremacy. It is a symbiotic relationship; they feed on each other.

In few minutes of reading, Doctor Vaknin's website and his book became the lighthouse's guiding beam after a long and stormy journey through the darkness of a moonless night.

THE NEXT STEP

After cutting my ties with Pipin, I spoke to the press and told them what I knew then, but I noticed how, perhaps in an effort to appear objective, they filtered much of the essentials provided.

Then I waited for months to see if Wiky's legal action suing Pipin and *Sports Illustrated*, and Ricardo Hernandez's litigation against Pipin would bring him to justice, somehow. But time kept running and nothing happened.

In the interim, Ricardo Hernandez and I settled our mutual dispute amicably as he continued to pursue his legal case against Pipin, alone. In spite of everything, he was right about Pipin and we were wrong about each other.

Meanwhile, Pipin came out with his book deal, *The Dive,* in July 2004; a book wrongly categorized as nonfiction. In it, he barely touches the event that caused Audrey's death, but when he does, he makes up a bogus story that not only is false, but contradicts videos, witnesses and even his own previous statements.

One false account involves the call Anne-Marie made the afternoon Audrey died. Pipin claims that once I answered the call, he spoke with her. That's not true, as Matt Briseno can also attest. It was Matt who answered the call on both occasions and it was me who not only spoke with Anne-Marie, but gave her the terrible news; two phone calls that I will never forget. Pipin adamantly refused to talk to her.

Another appalling fabrication is claiming that Tata had asked someone on board the catamaran before Audrey descended, *"If the tank had been filled,"* and a voice of "unknown" origin responded back affirmatively from the boat.

He simply twisted what I had told him from the beginning; that I had seen Tata asking him; not some "unknown" character. But by doing so, Pipin removes responsibility from himself for having responded that the tank was already filled, and places responsibility over a phantom, because in his book, Pipin claims that even to this date nobody knows who answered. How Tata allows himself to be part of such fabrication is beyond my comprehension, but it doesn't surprise me.

The fact is that I saw Tata asking Pipin if he had filled the pony-tank, just as I also saw Wiky bringing the scuba cylinder to make sure the pony-tank got filled. Instead, Pipin bawled him away and his reaction got stronger when Wiky insisted on having the pony-tank filled. Every person aboard witnessed this situation and even Pipin ended up admitting it.

In general, Pipin portrays an over-dramatic and unrealistic love story using overly fake dialogues and even claims that Audrey was extremely happy and optimistic that day. But as the old axiom says, *"An image is worth a thousand words,"* the images of an overwhelmingly depressed Audrey went around the world with headlines and captions stating her dejected mood. Pipin, of course, continues to believe the world is not only dumb, but blind. But maybe he's right.

"Audrey Mestre was sad before entering the water," says the headline of this Dominican newspaper. This is one of the tabloids stating Audrey's melancholic condition.

He refers to me as his *"brother"*, thanks me for the support and help, while his earlier and absurd accusations are nowhere to be found in his book, although they continue to pop-up all over the Internet. Then he states in the acknowledgement page something bizarre; *". . . at least we survived!"* I know I survived but sadly, Audrey didn't. Now the question is what's the hidden meaning of this reprehensible statement?

He even describes me as a person with the organizational skills he lacks and admits needing me. He definitively received advice from someone smarter; someone who more likely told him to avoid confronting the one person who could put the facts together. But facts are facts, and they are coming out even if I have to stand against the monster called *Hollywood* and their endless hit-list of crafted myths. I know that's a lost battle for me, and the blizzard of potential controversy may blow my residual sanity away.

But this is not about winning; this not about me keeping my sanity; this is not about what I may lose. In any case, I've already lost it all. This is about doing what is morally and ethically correct. And ultimately, this is about Audrey. This is about what truly happened to her, and to conceal the truth to protect an icon is like removing Hitler and his deeds, good or bad, from the history books.

Yes, Hitler did some good. Actually, he was a genius; an evil genius but a genius nevertheless. If a person drives a Volkswagen Beetle on a highway, that person is utilizing two of Hitler's inventions. And highways are today the arterial system that transports the blood and soul of society in the very same countries that fought against him. But the allies didn't fight Hitler for whatever good lived in him; the allies fought him because of the people who didn't live thanks to him.

Likewise, the specifics about Audrey's demise must surface, although some people may say that the analogy is incompatible in terms of proportions; that to match up 56 millions deaths in opposition to Audrey's, just one person, is an unmerited comparison. However, it was Josef Stalin, another egomaniac of the time, who said: *"A single death is a tragedy; a million deaths is statistic"*.

The point is that ego can kill, just one person or millions is beyond the point; still tragic for those who have lost a beloved one and we cannot continue to be sightless before the truth. Ego may not be a tangible murder weapon, but it can be a silent accomplice or motive. Ego is an illness, but the sad part is that the sicker the person, the more society idolizes those who are flamboyant about it.

Although James Cameron publicly declared having placed his movie project in standby until 2008 (no need to wonder why), it may still happen. After all, *Hollywood* and facts not always go together and they may want to perpetuate the fable in exchange for a ton of money.

I can only hope that the King of the World is an honest and caring person—as he seemed to be when I met him—who will honor Audrey's memory with the truth. Audrey deserves that much.

A movie directed by Cameron, however, is a sure money-maker and that is, perhaps, why Judith Regan, owner of *Regan Books* and employee of the Fair and Balanced *Fox News*, negotiated a producer status in the movie for herself.

So, as the editor of Pipin's book, this one came out in spite of the contract problems with *Televisa* and even when the fairy-tale is not doing much to honor the truth and Audrey's memory alike.

Actually, Linda Robertson was eventually "moved" aside before completing the manuscript, allowing another person to embellish the story and make it more appealing for the prospective script. Being a reporter for one of the biggest and more respected newspapers in the country, I guess Linda Robertson's narrative was too realistic, but a truthful chronicle, most certainly, wouldn't be too charming for the so-called author.

In consequence, and after reflecting on the ups-and-downs of writing this whole story, including a potential retribution against my person from a vengeful idol, I decided to complete an unfinished task.

With the specifics at hand, like: the vital input provided by prominent personalities; the unconditional support of those who want the truth out; after having listened carefully

THE LAST ATTEMPT

to Pipin's incongruent and self-incriminating statements; and with more than two years of excruciating investigation, I felt compelled to finish a duty.

On October 12, 2002, due to the chaotic situation brought upon us after Audrey's tragic end, my daily reports were abruptly interrupted. But having now the last pieces of the puzzle, including the one and determining factor everyone failed to notice, a final report must be made.

Chapter 23

THE FINAL REPORT— WHAT REALLY HAPPENED

After years of personal interaction with Audrey and Pipin; close dealings with the key people directly involved in her dreadful event; my fateful involvement in the tragic occasion; an in-depth analysis of Audrey's last attempt and Pipin's deeds, behavior and psyche, and with the cooperation of experts from the mental health arena, I can sum-up with confidence the following:

On October 12, 2002, in spite of many other irregularities, a single constituent sealed Audrey's faith; a near-empty tank impeding her safe ascent to the surface. Her coach and husband, Francisco "Pipin" Ferreras, the one and only person directly responsible for the tank should have filled it, but he did not. That's unambiguous.

What remained a mystery, however, is *why* he didn't. With mechanical malfunction ruled out, only two options lingered over the analysis of the tank's failure to fill Audrey's lift bag:

1. Pipin forgot to fill it . . . or
2. He consciously failed to do so.

The first option is the one I had initially considered, but the pieces of the puzzle didn't match up. The supply-tank and transfer-whip were brought up by Wiky to the port side of the ship just before Audrey's attempt, and Pipin shouted Wiky away refusing to follow Wiky's indications to fill the pony-tank.

Tata had also asked Pipin, minutes after the incident with Wiky, if the pony-tank had been filled and he responded affirmatively. Matt Briseno wanted to have the tank

THE LAST ATTEMPT

filled earlier that day, but was stopped simply because *"that is Pipin's responsibility,"* as he was told by Tata.

These three people, attempting in three different occasions to ensure the tank's filling, discard the first possibility. Even Pipin, who in his book provides a story that no one in his/her right state of mind would buy, admitted having yelled at Wiky and asking him to go away the moment Wiky brought up the supply-tank. This settles, for once and for all, if Pipin could have forgotten.

In addition, during the interview for *HBO's Real Sports with Bryant Gumbel,* pressured by Bernard Goldberg, Pipin admitted not having filled the pony-tank that day.

Inevitably, that brings us to the second possibility; the one I considered first not to be possible, at least for a while—that Pipin just decided not to fill the tank. But what's the purpose of something so potentially, and ultimately, tragic? Was Pipin, like many people claim, trying to kill her?

There is an enigma, however, that troubled me for a long time. If Pipin wanted Audrey dead, why would he attempt to do so in front of so many people? Why would he attempt a risky maneuver to retrieve her from the bottom? He had asked for a scuba unit to be prepared, before hand, to rescue her and nobody calls an ambulance before shooting someone. This last point, by the way, provides another puzzling element. How come he was expecting for something to go wrong?

But there is one other possibility which I had not contemplated before; that maybe the tank was left empty with intent, but not with the intention to harm Audrey.

If we presume for a moment that what Pipin had intended was a plan to maintain his supremacy in *No-Limits*, to punish his "absconding" wife, and to secure a forged heroic position in the sport after having saved Audrey, every single piece of the puzzle matches perfectly. Now his seemingly illogical and irrational deeds, supported by in-depth analysis of his mental attributes, would make a whole lot of sense.

The following is a summary of those apparently irrational elements, previously narrated in earlier chapters, but with a realistic and logical explanation for each one:

DELEGATING "RESPONSIBILITY" ON ME THE NIGHT BEFORE

By doing so he had planned for a way out of trouble in case of necessity. Pipin would have never delegated the most important event so far, involving his wife, after two weeks of absolute control over the entire operation, unless there is an ulterior motive.

What Pipin needed was a scapegoat and I fitted perfectly in his plan; someone to be blamed for what it was coming. He didn't use this *hidden ace* in the Dominican Republic because there was no need for, and because after Audrey's passing, he needed me once again. I had already dealt with the local authorities and apart from Wiky and Ricardo Hernandez, no-one considered foul-play at the time.

Coincidentally, immediately after I severed my ties with him twelve months later, he pulled this same ace from the sleeve by publicly claiming that I was responsible for

Audrey's death because I was the *"event coordinator"*. Only when he became desperate, the magic card came to light; the puzzling and mystifying last minute "delegation" that at the time made no sense. But like an old Brazilian adage says; *"A year has passed since the frog bit him, now he comes to show the swelling?"* So nobody bought the phony claim.

Yes, I coordinated the media presence, boats, airfare and lodging (the last two along with Audrey and our assistant Carolina, by the way), but the operational aspects of the event itself like the rescue team, the doctor (or dentist should I say), the placement of divers underwater and the sled itself, never left Pipin's control. Pipin still the only person—as always—who was in charge of the sled and for filling the tank, period.

Now the question is: Would he sacrifice his so-called brother, best friend and partner? Of course he would. By continuously contradicting him in front of the staff, stopping him from sending Audrey deeper, and avoiding him to become the safety diver at the end of the line, I became a nuisance, and contradicting Pipin is a dangerous adventure. That also explains why, in a potentially lethal maneuver, he pulled my regulator underwater. The experts call it *Devoid of Empathy*, and that brings up the next point.

DID PIPIN TRY TO KILL HIS BROTHER/PARTNER?

At the time, when Pipin pulled my air-supply underwater, I considered such act just another one of his cowboy-like and senseless actions. A person out of air may, indeed, remove the regulator from another diver's mouth. But a person out of air would never take the time to remove the tank off the back of that other diver before securing the air. When Pipin pulled my regulator, he already had my tank in his hand.

Furthermore, with many years of experience in the water, I've become highly sensitive with the surroundings and able to feel a feather's touch over my wetsuit. But When Pipin removed my tank, I felt absolutely nothing. Pipin not only did it harmoniously and carefully as I ascended, but his precision and craftiness suggest the premeditation that would never exists in a person genuinely out of air. Pipin's intentions were, as he did, to leave me down there with no air.

Some people may say that I'm paranoid, but the long-established deaths of Massimo Berttoni and Pepe Fernandez; the two safety divers who died with Pipin "around", give me dead-serious reasons to be. I could have become safety diver number three, an absolute and unbreakable world record.

DEPARTING TO THE CATAMARAN BEFORE ANYONE ELSE

Despite "delegating" on me the night before, Pipin took direct control immediately after the briefing. In other words, coordination was never, de facto, delegated. The day of the event I was left dealing with the press, being the judge and taking pictures. Moreover, just before going to the catamaran, Pipin asked me to remain behind along with most of the team, and had asked me to bring Audrey on board only after receiving his call via radio. Over an hour had passed when he called.

Was that Pipin's way to ensure that the tank wouldn't be filled by me or any other member of the team? One thing is for sure; if I would have been present in the catamaran with him, and with my extensive background as a diving instructor-trainer, I would have known if the tank was filled or not and I would have insisted, hardheadedly, on having it filled. Same applies for Wiky.

INCREDIBLY FAST ASCENTS AND DESCENTS DURING PRACTICE

During Audrey's practice dives, Pipin did many bounce-dives for no apparent reasons. I even took pictures of him underwater, during his descents and ascents, to show him later how incredibly and unwisely fast he was doing it; especially the ascent. A long-established and industry-wide accepted safe ascent-rate is eighteen meters a minute or one foot per second, for those attuned with the imperial system.

But a practical way to tag along with the aforementioned rule is for a diver not to pass the smaller of the bubbles he blows. Pipin doubled his ascent-rate and left his own exhaled bubbles way below him, as the pictures I took, confirm.

But what an odd coincidence that the day of Audrey's attempt, a day in which he wasn't even supposed to use scuba, he performed the very same fast descent and later ascent when he plunged to rescue her.

So, was he practicing the impending rescue dive that, indeed, *actually* occurred the day Audrey died? It makes perfect sense and this leads to the next point.

The descents here, from two different days of practice, are so fast indeed that his bubbles are left well above.

Due to the outrageously fast ascents, also from two different days of practice, Pipin is leaving his own bubbles below him.

HAVING A SCUBA UNIT READY

Here is another mystifying piece of the puzzle. For the first time ever, Pipin asked for a scuba system to be assembled and ready for him the day of the attempt. With PADI Instructors from the resort's dive shop allocated between twenty and sixty meters, plus Wiky in ninety meters, the first ninety meters from the surface were covered.

Since it's a requirement to become a trainer, those PADI Instructors are all certified rescue divers. Whether she was found conscious or unconscious, they all knew how to assist Audrey. That's exactly why they were there.

Therefore, why would Pipin have a tank ready? This particular element clearly suggests an impending rescue in mid-water with him as the rescuer, although that day it didn't make any sense. And this is why:

The most crucial and risky of places in freediving events are the end of the line (one hundred and seventy-one meters in this case), or near the surface due to the inherent risk of shallow-water blackout; *not* in mid-water.

The use of a single tank to descend all the way down to one hundred and seventy-one meters is impossible. Even Pipin, who in scuba is a mind-blowing calamity, knows that. It's like taking a four-seat *Cessna* plane for a trip to the moon. Therefore, Pipin didn't ask for the unit to reach the end of the line. By the use of plain logic this option is eliminated.

THE LAST ATTEMPT

In contrast, for a freediving expert like Pipin, the use of scuba equipment to rescue Audrey within the last thirty or forty meters before surfacing, is not viable. Scuba equipment limits the rate of ascent, and the bulkiness of the equipment reduces maneuverability, which are the most important aspects when rescuing a freediver in blackout. In consequence, Pipin didn't ask for the unit to rescue Audrey on the last few meters of her dive. Plain logic, once again, eliminates this option, as well.

As a result, the tank was solicited in *anticipation* of a mid-water rescue (between forty and ninety meters; precisely the depths to which he had practiced his bounce-diving before, over and over. Having the scuba equipment ready and having practiced the same type of dive he performed to "rescue" Audrey that day, evidently suggest anticipation.

THE VIDEO PLAN

Wiky said that he had seen Pipin manipulating the video housing in an attempt to shut it off. Since Wiky had made an improvised repair of the switch, he knew that once *on*, it was impossible to switch it *off*.

Based on what Wiky said and after my return from Cabo San Lucas, I rewind the tape from the sled's camera all the way to *before* Audrey's descent. Until then I had only seen Audrey's fatal plunge. And indeed, the video itself shows Pipin's hands all over the housing while he is, apparently, attempting to change the current setting of the camera. It was recording and it was in the right angle; for that reason there was no need for him to try anything else.

Besides, there is another video shot at the surface, in which Pipin is clearly seen manipulating the video housing before Audrey's descent. Again, the timing shows that the video was already running and the angle was right.

If the plan includes an empty tank, the video camera in the sled would present incriminatory evidence of Audrey struggling at the bottom with a tank left empty. So Wiky's allegation, although conjectural, makes perfect sense and coincides with Pipin's actions.

CONSCIOUSNESS OF GUILT

Besides the video, there is a person who validates Wiky's allegation as potentially correct; that person is Pipin himself. In a slander letter Pipin wrote on October 2003, he over-emphasized that he was *"fighting hard"* to make the video camera work, but interestingly enough, the camera was already working and no-one had said, back then, anything about trying to shut the video off. Wiky mentioned the video situation months later in a private conversation with me and had never made public his hypothesis.

Hence, was Pipin's mind betraying him? Police investigators use something called the *guilty mind* to determine a criminal's involvement in a crime, and more often than not, they fall. Let's take the following made-up and simplified dialogue between a cop and a suspect to elucidate how the *guilty mind* works:

> Cop: *I'm here to investigate the murder of a woman.*
>
> Suspect: *But, I barely knew Mrs. Smith and I don't have a gun.*
>
> Cop: *How did you know it was Mrs. Smith and how did you know she was shot?*
>
> Suspect: *Ah . . . uh, I read it in the newspapers this morning.*
>
> Cop: *It hasn't been reported to the newspapers yet.*

This defensive but self-incriminatory stand is the only logical explanation for Pipin to address the *"fighting hard"* situation when nobody had mentioned it before, neither publicly nor privately. Not to mention that turning the switch of a video camera *on*, doesn't take a *hard fight*. Turning it off, however, would have required a *hard fight* simply because it wasn't possible due to the nature of Wiky's repair.

Something that Pipin wanted, however, was for the anticipated mid-water rescue to be recorded. That's why he requested two of the safety divers from *Viva Diving* to videotape at thirty and sixty meters, respectively.

This range fits perfectly with a rescue plan, and by having it on tape, it would have shown to the world his "heroic feat".

This also explains the seemingly illogical action of switching these two divers from protecting Audrey to be videotaping instead, despite the fact that Audrey's plunge had been already filmed for the press the day before in a shallow-simulation dive. That's why it was done the day before; the press would have it right after the record was done and the divers could focus on protecting Audrey.

On one hand, the lack of video on the sled wouldn't show the empty tank, but on the other, having two cameras, one at thirty meters and another one at sixty meters, would definitively show Pipin rescuing Audrey and becoming a hero on the spot *(Narcissistic Supply?)*

SO, WAS IT A MURDER ATTEMPT OR A RESCUE ATTEMPT?

The paradox here is that Pipin didn't try to kill Audrey, not in front of so many witnesses and the press. On the contrary, that's when the international press became vital in Pipin's extraordinary appetite for notoriety.

When people from the press asked me if Pipin killed Audrey, my answer always surprised them:

"I don't believe he intended to kill her."

This is not a last jiffy of support for my former friend. It's not a perpetuation of blind loyalty toward my charming ex-partner; much less that he bought me out with a small fortune or by paying my mortgage, as he once intended. My conclusion is based on what the evidence shows and how perfectly all the links on the chain of events that concluded with Audrey's demise, perfectly connects with each other.

THE LAST ATTEMPT

The following scenario, based on proven facts, is what in all probability passed through Pipin's mind but it took a deadly and unforeseen turn. That would explain why, immediately after Audrey's passing, Pipin was more astonished than sad.

THE PLAN

Audrey makes it to the bottom. There is not enough air in the tank to come back up and Pipin had already made sure of that, so Pascal rescues her by providing a regulator. Under the circumstances, that's to be expected. Now Audrey becomes a scuba diver, meaning that the record is automatically invalidated and Pipin remains the official, at least for our own organization, world-record holder.

Pascal brings her up to ninety meters to transfer Audrey to Wiky. Wiky, now with Audrey, initiates his ascent towards the closest diver. This diver is at sixty meters (videotaping). So, with a video-housing in his hands, this diver can't help, and knowing Wiky, he would have continued with her to a shallower, thus safer depth for Audrey.

Meanwhile, Pipin is already descending fast with *his first-time-ever* prearranged scuba gear, and somewhere around fifty meters he takes Audrey away from Wiky to continue the ascent. He had been practicing this very same fast descent/ascent for days.

Then he raises Audrey out of the water with all the cameras clicking and recording the heroic action for the press, for the movie we were planning to produce, *Ocean Women*; and for posterity. That would have made him a greater legend than Jacques Mayol; his ultimate dream.

With Audrey failing to take the record away from him and becoming the undisputed hero, Pipin would have gotten a standing ovation; *Narcissist Supply* at its greatest.

The previous scenario coincides with something Pipin told me once just before parting to Cabo San Lucas,

"When I went down, I was expecting to see Audrey breathing off a regulator from Wiky in about fifty meters."

This not only confirms the reason for his prearranged scuba unit, but it sounds like the *guilty mind* showed up once again, because now the question here is, why fifty meters?

When I calculated the time frame of the hypothetical scenario in which Pascal would have brought Audrey to Wiky (with Audrey breathing off a regulator, of course), Pipin's *"fifty meters"* expectations were quite realistic. The calculation is quite simple to accomplish.

First, he could feel Audrey's dive through the vibrations on the cable, just as I did. So he knew the exact moment she reached the bottom. With a difference of only seconds, we had previously calculated Audrey's time to reach the end of the line and the entire dive, as well. Pipin and I had used a mathematical model before to determine a timeline for Audrey's attempt, and we even had an open contest on our website's forum to give a prize away to whoever predicted the closest time.

Second, Pascal and Wiky's ascent rate are predetermined by safety standards.

Third, another important element is that Pipin had swapped watches with me the days of practice; why?

Pipin wears a *Seiko* watch named after him, which cost one hundred and fifty thousand yens in Japan (US$1377 but not available in the U.S.) My watch is a diving *Casio G-Shock* for which I paid sixty dollars in *BJ Wholesale*.

For a perpetual show-off like Pipin, trading a Paso Fino Spanish Horse, for the coffee-carrier donkey of *Juan Valdez* doesn't make any sense. His watch, however, doesn't have a chronometer but mine does; and when it comes to timing, digital is far more precise than analog.

Interestingly enough, the day of the attempt he didn't ask for my watch. Instead, he had somebody else's *Casio*-like watch with a digital chronometer, as well. Since he was mad with me, and I was to be blamed for what it was to come, I guess he preferred to use someone else's and avoid having to return mine afterward.

Consequently, the hypothesis that he had planned a rescue operation in which he timed Audrey's dive before hand, to determine in which depth range he should find Audrey, is not only plausible but logical. Otherwise, how can he explain the *coincidence* of a mathematical model and his own words alike placing Audrey in just about fifty meters? How can he explain having the scuba gear already preassembled? Was one of the greatest freedivers of all times doubting his own capabilities to hold his breath for a potential shallow-water blackout? The answer is a definitive no.

TIGHT SECURITY AROUND AUDREY

In this rescue scenario nonetheless, something still missing; Audrey could have talked to the press afterward and say that she failed because of an empty tank; a tank left unfilled by her own husband. His heroic stunt would have become either a severe case of negligence or a sinister and egotistical act of treachery. Even though Pipin had absolute control over Audrey, and the chances of Audrey speaking publicly against Pipin were minimal, he had made plans to avoid such possibility.

She had defied him already with the divorce request; consequently, right after getting Audrey out of the water, with the entire world witnessing his "heroic" performance, he would have stopped Audrey from talking; no questions asked, no interviews given by her.

That's why Pipin had given specific orders to Eddie Matos and the boat crew to restrain anyone from speaking with Audrey. Eddie, innocently, would have done his job efficiently. Besides coordinating a Rescue Squad, Eddie is a former cop and security specialist for Santo Domingo's former Mayor and Merengue music legend, Johnny Ventura. With his training, he would have performed his duties competently.

Then Pipin would have taken Audrey immediately, lock her up in their room, just like he had done for the last two weeks, and strengthen his undermined control.

THE LAST ATTEMPT

Audrey's options at that moment would have been leaving him without breaking the record—assuming that she had finally conquered her *"victim syndrome"*—or swallow her pride and continue to accept Pipin's almighty control *(Masochist Supply)*.

In this last case she could have tried a second attempt two days later, the tank would have been full this time and I would have been back in Miami accused of being the person responsible for Audrey's failure the first time *(Interpersonally Exploitative)* because I was the mysteriously last-minute designated *"Event Coordinator"*. He would have rid himself of his greatest nuisance *(Devoid of Empathy)*.

In September 2003 Pipin made me realize his intentions in this regard when he said,

"If I would have been the safety diver at one hundred and seventy-one meters instead of Pascal, I would have forced Audrey to breathe from the regulator . . . she would have survived and two days later, I would have let her have the record."

Although with this second attempt—if successful—Pipin wouldn't possibly be the record holder anymore, his heroic feat saving Audrey the first time would have been by far greater and more credible than any of his records.

This is especially true since his last record in Cozumel, January 2000, was obscured with the uncertainty of his conscious level when he surfaced, plus the permanent stigma over his always-suspected cheating.

Although an evil scheme, Audrey's rescue would have been more pragmatic before the eyes of the world, and even the competitive freediving community, mostly the only ones not believing in Pipin's records, would have seen him as a true champ.

Pipin even made public a similar statement saying that with him as the deep safety diver in one hundred and seventy-one meters, Audrey would be alive. This statement also explains why he initially wanted to replace Pascal as the bottom safety diver; another seemingly absurd proposal.

In his mind, not filling the tank was part of his plan, but not been the safety diver at the end of the line made his plan failed and I was to be blamed for that because I'm the one who strongly rejected the idea.

Delegating on his *brother* the night before, and eventually placing the blame on me, was my punishment for contradicting him and get on the way of his initial plan. That's why I became a target. I had forced him to rely on Pascal to oblige Audrey to breathe from a regulator, and that's also why he initially blamed Pascal for *lack of authority*.

What's more, by carefully reviewing his words—even without the clinic eye of a psychiatrist—anyone can see his psychological profile, his guilty-mind, and how the statement perfectly fits with his rescue plan.

"If I would have been the safety diver at one hundred and seventy-one meters instead of Pascal . . ."

This denotes the *"Grandiose and Arrogant"* side of his personality. Pipin as a scuba diver is a disaster. He would have killed himself on the way down. Moreover, he is clinically-proven oxygen intolerant. In spite of his awful scuba skills, the high oxygen partial-pressure of that type of dive alone would have been enough to cause incontrollable convulsions, and ultimately, death.

Here is, by the way, another bewildering situation that now offers a logical explanation. During the decompression stops we made after the practice dives, he kept breathing pure oxygen instead of regular air. I even kept myself monitoring him closely just in case he would fall into convulsions underwater. Pipin even manifested afterward feeling good and claiming that, perhaps, he had developed tolerance for a high partial-pressure of oxygen.

Consequently, one can only ask if he was testing to see if he could eventually replace Pascal on a dive in which the partial pressure of oxygen is not safe for the oxygen intolerant. And why replace Pascal, anyway? Nevertheless, Pipin sees himself as *"invincible"* and a better diver than Pascal, who is one of the most technically advanced divers in the world *(Magical Thinking?)*

"I would have forced Audrey to breathe from the regulator . . ."

This part of his statement indicates the omnipotent *control* he deems he had over her, but it also conveys his expectation for Audrey to breathe from a regulator. It is just plain logic; without air in the pony-tank her only viable option was to breathe from one of Pascal's regulator, period. There's no way around that one.

"She would have survived . . ." Like an almighty God deciding over life and death. There is no need to say more.

"And two days later, I would have let her have the record."

This is the epitome of his superpower; *"I would have let her"* denotes his absolute control over Audrey, and to say *". . . have the record"* instead of *". . . attempt the record"* suggests the certainty on Pipin's part that the record was a done deal ahead of time.

In the end, assuming that's the way things would have gone, he would have used Audrey to accomplish his own end *(Interpersonally Exploitative?)*

IS THIS RESCUE PLAN JUST A THEORY?

It is Pipin who eventually confirms my previous statement when he publicly declared (and it doesn't get any more public than this) to CNN's Paula Zahn, on June 30, 2005, the following:

"The only thing that I really, really won't forgive myself is that I wasn't the diver down there that day."

As atrocious as it seems that's the real Pipin talking. Appalling statement but enlightening, all the same. While he is, subliminally, turning over the blame on Pascal; he is also, naively, confessing his original intention of rescuing her. Consequently, he is the one validating my point.

Pipin doesn't regret the empty tank, which is what ultimately caused Audrey's demise; the only thing that he *"really, really"* regrets is not becoming the wife-saving hero at the bottom. Therefore, the rescue plan is finally revealed by no other than Pipin himself.

With the pony-tank being full, there would be no need for him to be down there and Audrey would have made it safely to the surface in a record time. That's says it all.

In summary, in Pipin's valiant plot as a rescue diver at the bottom, he would have been the hero *(Narcissistic Supply)*. He could have regained control over Audrey and she would have become submissive once again *(Masochist Supply)*. And I, the object of Pipin's frustrations, would have gone back home after being conveniently used *(Interpersonally Exploitative)* and Pipin showing no remorse whatsoever *(Devoid of Empathy.)*

Only the closest members of the staff, perhaps, would have known the truth, but at that point they would be simply petrified. Attempting to confront Pipin on my behalf would be like lighting a campfire with jet-fuel. Plus, by feeling omnipotent, immune and above the law, the entire scheme fits into what the mental-health community defines as *Magical Thinking.*

Let's not forget that at least *FIVE* people have died—not counting Audrey or the ones we don't know about—with Pipin around, and he has never been investigated, much less prosecuted. Therefore, his *Magical-Thinking* has been fed with a simple fact; he always gets away from mysterious multiple deaths happening around him, without scrutiny.

What Pipin and his narcissistic thinking will never realize is that letting him replace Pascal at the bottom would have been like playing Russian roulette with a fully loaded Magnum-44. Either his lack of common sense, lack of respect for the laws of physics, the lack of appropriate scuba diving skills or his oxygen intolerance could have killed him, but the combination of all of the aforementioned factors, would have made a cocktail more lethal than drinking a whole glass of cyanide sweetened with rats poison.

So today I'm most certain that stopping him from replacing Pascal saved his life, but now we know why he had asked for the scuba gear to be ready for him before hand. That rescue would have been great for the movie-script we had planned to produce.

THE WITCHCRAFT RITUALS

For the skeptic or secular person this is the most bizarre and less credible aspect of this entire saga, but this is not about what the rest of mortals believe; it's about what Pipin believes. He rules his life by the basic principles of the Santeria religion, and particularly, its dark side called, *Palo*. This eerie bond between him and esoteric rituals is public and even promoted by Pipin himself. Furthermore, it was part of Pipin's introduction in the movie *OceanMen*.

The troubling aspect is that just before Audrey's event, many circumstances connect Pipin and his actions with his esoteric beliefs. The white shirt with the Aztec sacrificial Sun-god that Pipin wore the night before; the names of two dead people written in Audrey's wetsuit; the banana peel ceremony he asked Audrey to perform; the red bandana wrapped around Audrey's wrist marking her the epicenter of his ritual, and the well-known fact that he reveres the African descendant gods of the occult *Olokún* and *Shangó*, are all unambiguous indications of some ceremonial-like performance.

And yet, contradicting what most people from Pipin's inner circle believes, I don't think that he offered Audrey in sacrifice; at least not before her death actually occurred.

Instead, I'm more inclined to believe that Pipin was consulting his mythical gods and requesting their divine intervention to make his plan a success. And the center piece of his plan was Audrey. That's probably why she was "marked" with the red bandana.

The moment Audrey died; a shocked Pipin could not articulate a word as he, most likely, became more concerned about the potential consequences of his now failed rescue plan. But as the hours passed by, Pipin started to react as always, according to his guiding creed of satisfying his gods' unhealthy and wicked appetite for flesh and blood. That's when the tongue-tied Pipin, hardheadedly insisted on having Audrey cremated.

Back in Miami, Pipin took Audrey's ashes to his bedroom to allegedly "sleep" with her one last time, but the Santeria altar he has in his private quarters actually brings upon one of two eerie connections between Audrey's remains and his ceremonies. That's when Wiky, who closely knows Pipin's religious rituals, became agitated.

The following day Pipin wore a ceremonial gown; Audrey's twin wetsuit, the same one that he, oddly, refused to wear the day of Audrey's event. Now the question is if by wearing the same wetsuit the day of Audrey's attempt, the *gods* could have been confused and "taken" the wrong person. At least that's the explanation I received from an expert in Santeria in Miami while investigating this saga.

The other eerie connection happened when Pipin entered the water to spread the ashes in the ocean and surrounded himself with Audrey's remains. Whether it was the ultimate expression of love or the creepiest demonstration of bizarre behavior, the presence of the press made it all a spectacle of melodramatic characteristics with Pipin being the center of it. And by inviting the press, he made a public show of a ceremony inherently intimate in nature. What it was supposed to be a ceremony to honor and remember Audrey, it became instead another event; *Pipin's Show,* as Wiky fittingly pointed out. Not to mention the invisible but ominous presence of *Olokún* onboard the boat that honors his name.

THE LAST ATTEMPT

Credit: Angelo Cordero

Audrey's ashes are all around Pipin and whether this is an esoteric ritual or the most bizarre demonstration of love, this ceremony became another astonishing display; and why is he using Audrey's twin yellow wetsuit this time?

Days later Pipin told me—as he also declared it to the press—that he had taken all of his wooden statues representing his different gods and tossed them in the ocean. He had done it in open defiance *for having taken Audrey away from him*. But when I visited Pipin's house, only days after such statement, I sat down in the living room and saw the creepy sculpted figure of a bearded and skinny old-looking man holding a walking stick.

The figure is about three feet high and leans forward supporting its crippled body with the stick, while its piercing and spine-chilling eyes seems to follow you anywhere in the room. When I asked Pipin for the figure he simply said, *"That's Olokún."*

"I thought you had tossed them in the ocean?"

"Oh, no . . . I can't do that with Olokún. He's my spiritual guide. He protects me."

"FUCK, FUCK, FUCK!"

One last point is the use of the F-word in plain English. One may assume that right after Audrey left the surface Pipin perhaps recalled not having filled the pony-tank. That would make anyone yell whichever naughty word comes to mind.

But in a moment of stress, the brain would normally search for a word in the ruling language; for Pipin that will be Spanish, by a long shot. Therefore, it's reasonable to expect, *"Coño", "Mierda", "Carajo",* or some other Spanish colloquial expression; especially since we were in a Spanish-speaking country.

Even by giving him the benefit of the doubt, how come he did not remember having filled the tank after three different people had asked about it, but he would suddenly remember it when Audrey was already on her way down. Besides, when I asked him why he was cussing, he replied with a rhetorical question, *"Why is she going so slowly?"* But as my chronometers later showed, she wasn't.

There is a much more logical explanation for this. Everything Pipin does with cameras around is a *"Charles Bronson", "Dirty Harry"* or *Bruce "Die Hard" Willis* theatrical performance. In the hundreds of hours of tapes made in the company, he always presented himself on camera as an ultra-macho-tough-guy.

In *OceanMen,* Umberto Pelizzari is presented surrounded by his sister, his mom, his assistants, his friends and even swimming placidly with Dolphins, conveying this way the image of a nice and likable guy. Instead, Pipin told me that Pelizzari was seemingly gay in the movie.

But unlike Pipin, most people left the movie theater after the premiere in Miami, looking at Pelizzari as a nice and athletic individual who doesn't have any problems showing his gentle side; therefore, secure of his masculinity.

Conversely, there is a scene in *OceanMen* in which Pipin navigates with a center-console inflatable boat, alone, with a somber face, pulling-in his stomach, pumping-out out his chest and going at a rampant speed with the propeller screeching out of the water every time the boat bounced over the waves.

There is no reason for the scene, whatsoever, except for spraying machismo and testosterone all over the movie theater like water-sprinklers over grass. But the scene fits perfectly with the image he likes to promote, *el "Perro Solitario"* or *"The Lone Dog"* as Pipin calls himself. In that regard, director Bob Talbot did a superb job.

As a result, the use of the F-word goes along with that other side of Pipin's personality, the *Histrionic Personality Disorder*. Allow me to reintroduce point number 6 from the list of deeds of a person with this syndrome:

> *(6) Shows self-dramatization, theatricality, and exaggerated expression of emotion.*

And from the list of additional deeds to describe the Narcissistic, the mental health community says the following:

- *Is a convincing and trained liar with histrionic or theatrical faculties.*

That's why Pipin's *"Fuck, Fuck, Fuck,"* in plain English, is nothing but a theatrical performance; an anticipation to the rescue, because by yelling it in loud voice he elevated the tension and focused the attention over him, especially from the English-speaking international media; the ones who would later distribute his intrepidness around the world.

THE LAST ATTEMPT

Furthermore, when I asked Pipin what was troubling him, he expressed concerns about Audrey descending too slowly, but the video and McCoy's computer conclusively proves that Audrey was making a normal descent; slightly faster than normal, actually. Besides, once Audrey reached the bottom, and after telling Pipin that Audrey's time had been seven seconds faster than her last practice dive to one hundred and seventy meters, he kept cussing anyway.

Evidently, he wasn't concern about her rate of descent. Audrey's dive, until then, was quite normal and uneventful; so, why the cursing? That's because the only person anticipating a problem was him; no one else, and he was *acting* accordingly.

Pipin's plan to rescue Audrey, however, needed for Audrey to take a regulator from Pascal and breathe from it, but it didn't happen that way, and that brings us to . . .

THE FINAL QUESTION

Why wasn't Audrey breathing off a regulator?

Pascal initially assisted her by pushing the sled up with Audrey holding from it, and the video indisputably illustrates this fact. However, that was a totally unintelligent move from his part. Pascal is restrained by his own ascent rate; so what was he trying to achieve?

To ascend with her at eighteen meters a minute—almost twice as fast as he should actually ascend (for technical divers the ascent rate is half the norm)—all the way up to ninety meters, would have taken about 4.5 minutes to reach Wiky's depth. Audrey would have drowned way before that.

Additionally, when Pascal pushed Audrey up, the sled came to a full stop in one hundred and sixty four meters for exactly thirty seconds—this is a fact provided by McCoy's computer. That's when Pascal started to add his own breathing mixture inside the lift bag via one of his regulators, and that was another impractical maneuver.

Due to the crushing pressure of the ocean at that depth (17.5 kilos per square centimeter / 257.2 pounds per square inch or 18 times greater than at sea-level) and the low working-pressure a regulator can constantly release (between 120 psi to 145 psi), to inflate the lift bag with enough gas takes an awfully long time.

Therefore, the only option left for Pascal was to give Audrey a regulator. Pascal had a redundant system with many of them hanging all around his body and Audrey needed just one. The key question now is why Audrey didn't take one of them? Or did Pascal ever offer it to her?

In any case, an expert in scuba diving or any person who has been on the edge of drowning can say that out of pure instinct and self-preservation, Audrey should have taken a regulator to breathe from it, but why didn't she?

Some people have conjectured that she was under the influence of a severe nitrogen narcosis, and even though it is more likely to occur to a scuba diver, it can also happen to deep-water freedivers.

In the video Audrey can clearly be seen reacting immediately to the warning bang made by Pascal at 160 meters, and the way she manipulates the tank's valve and effectively disengaged the clip holding the two sections of the sled together, eliminates the possibility of being under the lethargic effects of nitrogen narcosis.

A noticeably retarded reaction and imparity to execute the most basic mechanical functions are the most distinctive signs of narcosis. Audrey was not even close and neither was Pascal. And despite whatever dubious statement Pascal may give today—especially after the mind-boggling and conflicting account he gave me in Cabo—he had offered a regulator to her. He declared it to the staff late at night the day Audrey died, and it makes absolute sense that he would have done just that, only that she refused it.

Pascal, on the contrary, declared months later to *Sports Illustrated* that he had a prearranged deal with Audrey; that unless she asked for a regulator he wouldn't offer it to her.

That's the most absurd statement I've heard from Pascal and I've heard few by now. Just imagine a lady bleeding profusely while trapped inside a crashed car. Without assistance, she will die within minutes. Meanwhile, an expert paramedic named Pascualino is standing outside the vehicle watching the woman bleeding her life away while he holds a First Aid kit in one hand and a cell phone on the other, but he would neither attempt to stop the bleeding nor to call 911 until she asks for help.

Accordingly, it's just plain logic that under the circumstances, Pascal would have offered a regulator; that's why he was there. Otherwise he would be a plain moron and his diving license should be seized and thrown into a meat grinder, because the other alternative left I can't even mention it. Even though he confers dutiful and well-paid loyalty to Pipin, I must believe that Pascal was a friend of Audrey, above all.

One way or the other, the main question remains; why didn't she takes a regulator which was either offered or hanged just inches away from her?

Some people also argue that breathing a compressed gas with the lungs filled with plasma (blood shift) could cause spasmodic coughing, suffocation and possibly, death.

Although no one has tried breathing compressed gas at one hundred and seventy-one meters while being in apnea, there are some studies stating that it might be problematic—even lethal to do so—but still all hypothetical.

In contrast, Pipin has openly contradicted that theory. He maintains that for an apneist to breathe gas at great depths is not only possible, but a proven fact. He had done it before and I'm not referring to his questionable records.

Pipin actually did an openly publicized stunt dive in the Cayman Islands in 1997, where he took a breath at depth from a miniature scuba system called *SpareAir*. He dove to one hundred and fifty meters holding his breath in that occasion, breathed compressed air at depth and went back to the surface. Was it a test for future records, perhaps?

All experts in the field would agree that at the ascent rate utilized in a No-limits event, breathing compressed air may cause an air embolism, but there is a trick to avoid such occurrence. The trick is to take only *one* breath and exhale it in the way up to avoid lung over-expansion. If the diver takes a second breath, he or she will force the compressed air from the first breath into the circulatory system in enough quantity to actually produce the air embolism. That's the explanation Pipin gave me once. Basically, according to Pipin's reasoning, it's like taking a sip of water to refresh but spitting it out (just like boxers do between rounds); taking a second sip would force the first one to be swallowed.

But whether the trick works or not, I must insist, for those freedivers dumb enough to even consider it, that this is for informational purposes only. To attempt such maneuver can cause paralysis and brain damage, among many other things, including death.

In any case, Audrey, who blindly followed Pipin's directions, was likely to believe Pipin over those theoretical studies. Besides, facing the certainty of drowning, why not give the regulator a try? Breathing off a regulator may mean death; not doing it will assure it, as it did.

Consequently, Audrey should have taken the regulator to preserve her life, right? Not really. The answer is in the video, but something so obvious, actually took me months to figure it out, even when the idea had crossed my mind as early as three days after her death.

REVISITING THE VIDEO

The videotape clearly shows the moment when Audrey opened the valve; there was a hissing sound coming from it that lasted only a second. That must have been a frightening sound for her, given that she was expecting a full blast of air ramming out to inflate the lift bag; the blasting discharge of 3000 psi of pressure when the tank is completely full.

Some air was still inside, though; the residual air left from the day before when Pipin filled the tank for the last time. This remaining air, however, was not nearly enough to fill the balloon.

That's when Audrey briefly opened her eyes in disbelief and disappointment, glancing forward to the sled. Audrey knew right there that it was Pipin, the person to whom she had given her unconditional love and trust, who failed to fill the tank. I can't even imagine her disillusionment.

She was on the surface moments before when Pipin bawled Wiky away from the supply-tank and the transfer-whip and replied later to Tata that the tank was *"taken care of"*. Audrey heard him. Besides, she also knew that the only person always taking care of the tank for her was Pipin.

Now under the crushing pressure of the ocean and the dead silence of the abyss, the hissing air became instead the hiss of the serpent before striking, inoculating the mortal venom with its fangs. And once perfidy showed its ugly face, she accepted her faith. It must have been an overwhelming and devastating feeling.

Then she closed her eyes in consternation, grabbed the sled with both hands and became submissive once again. She waited, but not for Pascal in a shiny armor of tanks and regulators to save her. She wasn't waiting for Pipin to fulfill his movie-script-like plan, either. More likely, she didn't even know that he had plans to rescue her in any case.

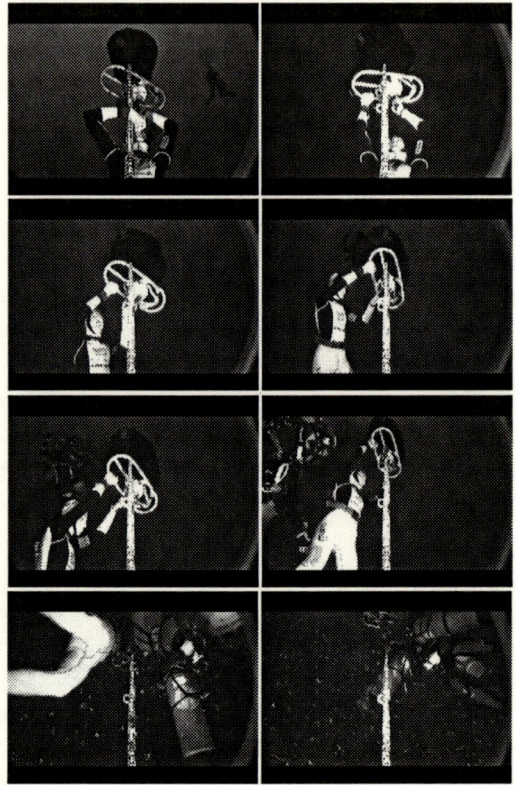

Images from the sled video shows Audrey realizing the emptiness of the tank.
She would attempt nothing else after that.

She didn't try to pull herself along the line and make it to ninety meters, where it would have been safer for her to breathe compressed air from Wiky. With her excellent condition, such ascent could have been possible. This type of action is called *Variable Ballast*, and the current female record is much more than the eighty-one meters separating her from Wiky.

Instead, she held the sled, and after closing her eyes in dismay, she passively waited for death to put an end to her suffering. Audrey was submerged in one hundred and seventy-one meters of depression, but if she had no control over her life, at least she could control her death.

Now, this is more than just a theory; it's actually based on my close familiarity with Audrey; long conversations with her; what the video shows; what the data provides and unquestionable facts about her life.

During her early teenage years she had overcome serious back problems that kept her in bed for months. For a long time she lived under the peril of becoming permanently paralyzed, and that's when she became familiar with depression, as her physical suffering

THE LAST ATTEMPT

not only affected her body but her self-esteem, as well. She had also endured some very private problems which I rather not disclose.

She recovered after years of therapy and struggle, but never fully; neither physically nor psychologically. Despite her latest extraordinary physical shape, her spinal column remained as fragile as a crystal chalice. And more recent emotional scars were added to the old ones after some personal affairs diminished her self-respect to a minimum expression; she was being forced to do things beyond description.

That awful day of October 12, just before entering the water, she remained motionless. She seated passively on the boat's platform with a pale face and languid expression. Like a sad puppy, her eyelids dropped halfway in consternation. That image was captured by reporters and went around the world with captions stating her palpable gloomy mood. Audrey was down in the dumps and even the press stated her condition in their headlines the next day.

Those French eyes, once flirtatious and vivacious, now lacked of *joie de vivre*. She had a thousand-yard stare, perhaps looking into her thoughts or searching for a way out. She was physically present, although her mind was on the edge of the universe. Looking like a virgin in the offering altar ready to be sacrificed, her spirit had long departed.

She was a troubled young woman with fluctuating states of untreated depression. She had attempted against her life, *twice,* by cutting her wrist open, and the scars left were the definite proof that she meant serious business when severely depressed.

Remarkably, Audrey had a cross tattooed on her left wrist, right over the scar. Paradoxically, the cross was called Ankh or Key of the Nile, and for the ancient Egyptians, it was a symbol of life.

Audrey was a devoted reader of Egyptian history and mythology, and over the scar of her left wrist, she had this cross tattooed which for the ancient Egyptians was a symbol of life.

In spite of her failed efforts to cut her days short, she loved life. She enjoyed travel, good eating, friendly gatherings, history (particularly Egyptian history) and arts, as she was a skilled artist herself. But on October 12, 2002, around 2:30 p.m., Audrey's self-preservation was overwhelmed by anguish. As if her life had been sucked away by a *Nosferatu* of emotions, she didn't fight for it because she felt she had none. And despite all the notoriety and glamour around, her hollow existence was filled with melancholy.

She was the co-star in a make-believe story for the world, while her real life was in discrepancy with the fable being crafted. Just like a French Marilyn Monroe of the abyss, she had a disturbed life in which glamour was only a façade and for which did not provide enough *raison d'être to live*.

It wasn't just the empty tank what wrecked her will. It was the drained heart, the empty promises, and the unfulfilled dreams. It was everything awful she had gone through until that moment. It was a long road of misery, neglect, mistreatment and pain.

She had finally come to realize that her once beloved husband was a lover of many but a friend of no one; a synthetic character whose life is rule by the perpetual breaking of freediving records and the laws of the human race, alike.

Audrey wasn't breaking records for herself; she was only proving her worthiness to her godly spouse. She only wanted to gain the love and affection of a loveless man. Everything must be for him, from him and about him. That's how she ran her life. But after the monumental effort, she ran out of energy; she ran out of will; she ran out of breath.

During the wee hours of Tuesday 15, while standing on the beach of the resort, at exactly 3:33 a.m. this is the awful possibility that crossed my mind. I already knew that she had refused to take a regulator from Pascal, and that made no sense; unless she didn't want to survive. After that, I kept seeing 3:33, constantly, on my watch, on the clock of my room, on the microwave's clock, on my computer and everywhere else, on a regular basis.

Was it a sign that three people had asked Pipin for the tank? Was it that I had asked Pipin thrice if he had filled the tank? Was it just a recurrent coincidence? Or was it a sign that Audrey had attempted for a third time against her life? I honestly do not know. Three threes keep on showing even to these days, and that's all I know.

But in any case, Audrey was emotionally, physically and athletically pushed beyond the limit, again and again. She kept breaking records in a category wrongly called *No-Limits*, because there is a limit, after all. Given the motives and opportunity, she attempted one last time but to bring her life to an end; a third and finally successful attempt. She had found her limit. She had found her peace.

WHAT THE MENTAL HEALTH COMMUNITY HAS TO SAY

The following aspects are presented by the *American Psychiatric Association* in their *"Practice Guidelines for the Assessment and treatment of Patients with Suicidal Behavior"*. This guideline can be found in their website.

It's important to emphasize that the *American Psychiatric Association's* report is not intended to serve as a professional medical care or to substitute it. In their statement the APA asserts that the parameters presented in the report should be considered as guidelines only. However, the guidelines were developed by psychiatrists who are in active clinical practice, as the report states.

THE LAST ATTEMPT

Among many others, the following are characteristics evaluated in the psychiatric assessment of patients with suicidal behavior:

- Evidence of hopelessness.
- Previous suicide attempts, aborted suicide attempts or self-harming behavior.
- Acute psychosocial and chronic psychosocial stressors, which may include actual or perceived interpersonal losses, family discord, loss of a child, domestic violence, and past or current physical or sexual abuse or neglect.
- The loss of the ability to tolerate psychological pain and satisfy psychological needs.

The report also establishes that even without a plan to commit suicide, having access to suicide methods—a gun, a knife, a bridge, or how about diving to one hundred and seventy-one meters to find an empty tank—increases suicide risk.

"Even in the absence of a specific suicide plan, impulsive actions may end in suicide if lethal methods are readily accessible," says the report of the American Psychiatric Association.

The same report establishes that compared to the general population, patients who attempted a previous suicide were thirty-eight (38) times at greater risk of committing a suicide successfully. Again, Audrey had attempted twice.

THE TRUTH ABOUT WHO AUDREY WAS

Despite Audrey's emotional roller-coaster, there was a constant in her personality. She was a shy, exquisite and lovely person, and that never changed. Only that internally, she was debating with conflicting emotions and paradoxically moral situations.

She was full of non-reciprocated love, or what it's worse; her love was distorted into something fake and morbid, and still is. Consequently, Audrey became emotionally hollow. As beautiful as her spirit was, her soul was vacant. She had traded love for fear, understanding for distinction, and support for submission. Involuntarily, she became the emotional equivalent of a black-hole in space trying to feed from stardom and glittery matter, yet unsubstantial. In vain, she only did it to reach him; the greatest star of all.

Giving unreturned affection is not enough, and although fame can feed the ego, it's only temporarily. It's all ethereal. Just look at some of the rich and famous of Hollywood—speaking of narcissists—and the erratic life many of them live filled with alcohol, multiple-failed relationships, child neglect and drug abuse. They are, just like Audrey was, playing somebody else's role; a life without a profound meaning. And if you fall victim of a high-priest of bizarre rituals madly in love with his picture-ID, you are doomed for life, a very short one in Audrey's case. She was twenty-eight.

Now Pipin continues to perform a melodrama with Audrey's memory as a counterpart, a love-story that would perpetuate his legend, while on the side he keeps another life; the real one. There is love in his story, though; a unilateral love affair in which he furnishes the entirety of that love to himself; a self-made man who finds his creator simply adorable.

As a *Dorian Gray* born in a Cuban city with an ironically suitable name, Matanzas, which means in Spanish lots of killings, he has the same troubles characterized in Oscar Wilde's famous novel. He sees his own picture as a legendary sport hero breaking deep-diving records for ever, but his ability to compete and be the greatest is succumbing to the inexorable time and to the damage that his brain and body have been enduring for years.

Not to mention the true champions of the sport these days; Carlos Coste, a Venezuelan athlete who surpassed the barrier of 100 meters in Constant Ballast with astonishing easiness; an impossible for Pipin.

There is also Patrick Musimu, the same athlete we had sponsored for a Constant Ballast record in the Dominican Republic in April 2002, who already exceeded the amazing barrier of 200 meters in *No-Limits*; another impossible for Pipin, unless he manages, once again, to avoid monitoring for a big section of the dive while ascending.

In addition, there are also the sacred legends of the sport like Tanya Streeter and Umberto Pelizzari. And the last one, by the way, has proved time after time again his superiority against Pipin, who logically, refused multiples challenges from the Italian to compete face to face.

In one occasion Pelizzari made a statement in which he claimed that Pipin, based on performances in all categories, not only wasn't the top freediver in the world as Pipin constantly claimed, but that he couldn't even be positioned among the top twenty. In defense of Pipin, I replied to Pelizzari's claim and ended up in a public exchange of opinion with the Italian champion.

"Your friend is not who you think he is," said Pelizzari in one of his responses, and now I know.

Pipin reacted and offered Pelizzari a boxing match and a challenge to measure their private parts. It happened through an Internet freediving forum in 1999 and the exchange was followed by thousands of freedivers worldwide.

"Maybe Pipin just wants to see Umberto's penis," I joked with Audrey once as she laughed out of control.

Maybe at one point Pipin was among the greatest. Perhaps his initial performances were done correctly. At least I hope so, yet his chain of records is as strong as its weakest link.

But besides his unilateral love affair, he has some other attributes. He has the charm to turn anyone to his favor. He can weep in front of a camera and break his voice with convincing pleads for sympathy. He has the ability to look straight into your eyes while bluntly lying and convince you otherwise.

His protocol to obtain allegiance from someone he needs, embraces smooth-talking first, which includes precisely what you want to hear. He may seduce you with an enticing offer that to refuse it, you must be an idiot; accept it and you will become one.

Then, slowly but surely, he would initiate his deceptive, calculating and overpowering behavior until one day you are no longer useful and the discarding can be harsh. So harsh indeed, that one second you are diving with a life sustaining regulator attached to your

THE LAST ATTEMPT

mouth, and the next second it's gone, ripped away by a vengeful underwater god who can't stand being contradicted by plain common sense.

I survived the abrupt action, but I can only wonder about Pepe and Massimo, the two divers who died in the water with Pipin and his buddies, *Olokún* and *Shangó*, being in the scene. What happened to them, no one truly knows.

For a long time I was wrongly convinced that he was just the byproduct of an erroneous upbringing, lack of education and an immoral role model imposed by a vicious dictatorship for which he privately admits his admiration. So I learned to love *Dr. Jekyll* and overlook *Mr. Hide*. I candidly offered friendship and support even after everyone had turned away from him.

Yet I was fighting a war deep inside my soul; a war of multilateral fronts; a battle between friendship and principles; a battle between loyalty and values; a battle between upcoming opportunities and a gut-feeling.

I struggled for a whole year to find the right answer. I searched for the truth although it was always in front of me. It eluded me, or perhaps, I eluded it, because truth was as big as a six-foot tall Cuban wrapped in imprudence, in crafted myths, in ego and self-promotion. I only had to expose the outer layers of deception to find it. But I finally did.

AN OFFICIAL INVESTIGATION IS NEEDED

Pipin's stunt dives are not as critical as the deaths surrounding him, and every single one happened with Pipin nearby. There are prisoners in jail with less than six deaths in their account and people refer to them as serial-killers. The question now is how many other deaths must occur before someone says enough is enough; let's investigate. If a proficient investigation clears him of wrongdoing, so be it. But if not, he should be placed where no harm can be conferred to others in the future; and that may include me.

Unfortunately, there was only a preliminary investigation in the Dominican Republic and the case was ruled-out as a drowning accident, but the reopening of the case could reveal otherwise. I'm ready and looking forward to it, because the amount of evidence, although circumstantial, is overwhelming.

Audrey's parents, though, are the only ones able to reopen the file. There is no jurisdiction over the case in the U.S. and even though I have publicly, but unsuccessfully, requested an official investigation on Audrey's tragic ending, nobody listened. I guess the world is also deaf; or perhaps it's just plain apathy.

"If there is a criminal investigation, they should investigate Carlos, because he was the event coordinator," said Pipin to the press in October 2003 in response to my request.

What is enlightening to see, however, is how the *guilty mind* came out once more. I had asked for an *official*, not *criminal* investigation, and there is a distinctive difference. A fire department starts an *official* investigation every time there is a fire, but it doesn't turn into a *criminal* investigation until foul-play becomes evident.

The case is that Pipin doesn't want an investigation and publicly demanding not to have one could be in itself an admission of guilt. But Audrey's mother publicly supports his request and that is incomprehensible. Pipin, however, started to call her *Mama* soon after Audrey's passing, and that's the kind of charm that a grieving mother can't resist.

Puzzling as it may seem, Audrey held her breath one last time only to become breathless for ever, and her parents don't want to know why?

Anne-Marie joined Pipin in his pleads to leave things as they are. It's bewildering but one day they should snap out of his influence, I hope; unless Pipin took Audrey's place in their hearts. But, was Audrey replaceable? Can Pipin truly take her place? Of course not, but I will never underestimate Pipin's capacity to subdue people.

But the one thing I do know is how much pain Anne-Marie and Jean-Pierre went through after Audrey's death and how much Audrey loved them. That's why I can't understand the lack of interest to find the truth. Wiky claims having tried to contact them in few occasions to tell them what happened, but they have refused to speak with him.

ANOTHER TAPE; ANOTHER APPALLING IMAGE

An added reason for an official investigation is found in the video taken by the sixty meter diver. I had watched this tape only once to verify Wiky's position at depth. But after observing Pipin literally bumping into Wiky, and Pascal few meters below, I turned the tape off and ignored it throughout the investigation; the same with the tape filmed by the thirty meter diver. I only looked to confirm what Wiky had said all along; that he hadn't left his post.

For an entire year I was focused on the sled's video, the equipment and Pipin's actions, but once my ties with him were severed, I brought all three tapes (the two recorded by the two divers and the sled's) to the studios in Miramar, FL of the twin networks *NBC 6* and *Telemundo*.

The sled's video would become public for the first time, showing how an empty tank and not the alleged absence of Wiky is what caused Audrey's tragic end.

Inside a dimmed area about the size of a living room of a middle-class house, three out of four walls were covered from floor to ceiling with sophisticated equipment. Multiple little screens encrusted within dozens of switchboards were playing the day's news when the network's news editor asked a coworker to move aside. Then he recorded and played all three tapes in its entirety on one of the screens. That's when one of the tapes unveiled literally out of the blue, what happened after Pipin had retrieved Audrey's inert body from Pascal, and the sight couldn't be more appalling.

DESCRIPTION

Far below Pascal is barely visible as he's holding Audrey at 90 meters. Unable to ascend any longer without risking his life, he attempts to place on her a small air-filled,

THE LAST ATTEMPT

sausage-like marker buoy. The device is about 1.5 to 1.8 meters (5-6 feet) in length but too slim to hold enough air to lift Audrey.

Unable to descend any further, Wiky is few meters above him observing the action. His originally planned bottom time has been exceeded four folds and his air-supply is barely enough to surface. By staying for so long Wiky was also risking his life.

Seconds later Pipin appears literally bumping over Wiky during his descent. Pipin is rushing; no doubt he's in a hurry, as expected. The rate and angle of descent are a replica of the plunges he did during the practice dives.

Due to the distance from which the diver is filming, it's hard to discern what's happening when Pipin reaches Pascal, so the diver descends even more. Now the diver is at Wiky's depth and Pipin is clearly visible. He had taken Audrey from Pascal and is now ascending. Pipin seems to circumvent Wiky and passes him leaving the sled's cable between them.

But now comes the shocking part. Pipin is positioned behind her back with Audrey facing away. His right hand is holding her by the right hip while his left hand comes around from under Audrey's left armpit, holding her by the throat. By doing so, Pipin is opening Audrey's airway, underwater!

The network's news editor, even by lacking the expertise of a professional diver, asked perceptibly disturbed,

"Why is he holding her from behind? And is he supposed to hold her neck that way?"

My response was none. Astonished, I couldn't react. My mind went back to the day when Audrey's bloody foam kept running down my left hand.

"Why does she have so much water in her lungs?" I asked myself that day. *"This is not normal."*

Indeed, about 15% of drowning victims actually suffer a "Dry Drowning", but in freedivers this percentage is much higher due to the intentionally activated mammalian diving reflex. Dry drowning happens when a water-induced spasm closes the airway preventing water from reaching the lungs. The diver suffers asphyxia but the chances of revival are much greater when water is not lodged inside. Due to this fact, the airway of an unconscious freediver *must*, as a first rule, always be protected during the ascent.

Suddenly, another puzzling situation is clarified; Pipin had either neglected or forgotten this crucial and widely known aspect among professional freedivers, and that's how Audrey's lungs got filled with water.

But the shocking images worsened. Pipin, during the ascent, switched from the regular kick to what we divers know as "suspension" or "frog kick". This is a sideways and circular motion of the fins performed when you want to hold ("suspend") yourself in the same place or reduce the speed of translation.

"Why is he slowing down?" asked the editor. *"If that was me saving my wife, I would be speeding all the way up, man!"*

Depth: about 80 meters. Pipin is holding Audrey away from him, holding her by the neck with his left hand. The other diver on the screen is Wiky; the person who Pipin publicly claimed wasn't down there. Also noticeable is to see the sideways or suspension kick. That's the first of three that can be observed on the video.

Even though the image is blurred, Pipin's holding is more evident. This holding method is allowing water to enter freely into Audrey's lungs.

THE LAST ATTEMPT

Here is the change in the kicking pattern, now from below, once again.

Actually, Pipin's ascent was quite fast but not on those initial meters. Kim McCoy had given me the graphic produced by the computer she wore, a diagram of Audrey's dive. In this image the line representing the ascent is wide and ample in the beginning to later rise almost vertically. That's when Pipin rushed to the surface.

In the illustration, Pipin's ascent goes seemingly slow in that initial phase, but when McCoy gave me the graphic I didn't dig much into. Having to break the inertia caused by the water pressure at depth, or the initial shock of having Audrey unconscious and on the verge of death, could have affected him in the beginning, or so I believed. But Pipin changing kick patterns not once, or twice, but as many as three times was something I could have never imagined.

Someone may seek for the logic of Pipin doing something so potentially incriminating in front of a camera, but his mask limits his peripheral sight and the video shows him facing in different direction at all times. Simply said, he's *not* aware of this diver, who ignoring Pipin's command, had descended almost twenty more meters from his post at sixty.

This latest tape showing the throat-holding, airway-opening technique and the kick-changing pattern may modify my data-supported rescue attempt to something else. If that's the case, it would give credit to the conjecture sustained by other people; or is it here where the two theories become one? Because there is no doubt, Pipin was expecting to see Audrey breathing from one of Pascal's alternate air sources.

Up until then, the evidence validates a rescue scenario; including Pipin's own statement; *"The only thing that I really, really won't forgive myself is that I wasn't the diver down there that day,"* as he declared to CNN.

But, did he change his mind after finding an unresponsive Audrey not breathing from Pascal's regulator? Was he trying, for his own sake, to ensure Audrey's fate, or was it just a mistake? Because whether he did it deliberately or unconsciously, by not keeping her airway sealed, Audrey's doom was.

Or maybe one should disregard his professional freediver status with ample experience and believe that he didn't know that the airway must be protected; that it was a mistake.

Maintaining the airway open is a technique actually utilized by compressed-air breathing divers but never by freedivers, and the holding is never by the neck but by the chin. The intention is to minimize the risk of lung injury due to the expanding air; a problem freedivers don't have.

So the question remains, and the answer may just be entrenched inside Pipin's mind. But what excuse will he provide now? Will he say that a "voice" told him to grab Audrey by the neck? Perhaps that voice also told him to initially slow down the ascent? Would that be the same voice of unknown origin he claimed in his book having said that the pony-tank was filled? Maybe the voice is real; perhaps it's *Olokún's* voice but only Pipin can hear it.

PRESENT TIME

Audrey is gone, and so is my friendship and business relation with Pipin—in case you wonder. Life got a little rough and that's an understatement, yes. I became jobless, and for over two years I couldn't get this whole episode off my mind. I think I never will. My partnership with Pipin destroyed my business, turned my life upside down and transformed my American dream into a nightmare.

Audrey's demise is one of the most emotionally painful passages of my life. Not because of her death, because in the end, and although she was taking the greatest risk of all, we were all living on the edge by pushing the limits with our dives. Death was always a latent possibility.

What really affected me is how it happened and why. It was a senseless fatality. That empty tank not only placed Audrey in the doorway of an early death, but it also killed my affection and devotion for someone, who despite his personality flaws, I admired for his athletic feats and cared for like a true brother.

Then I received advice from Daniel and from a friend of James Cameron named Joe McInnis, the author of *Aliens of the Deep*, a book based on James Cameron's IMAX movie of the same name.

"Get it off your chest, Carlos," told me Daniel over the phone. *"Write it down; it'll be a form of therapy . . . and you need it."*

Doctor Joe McInnis also suggested, when he paid me a visit on my home in Miami, *"You need to tell the story, but make sure you tell the truth and nothing else. Say it the way it happened and let people judge Pipin."*

Writing about this saga, nevertheless, was not an easy decision. People around Pipin do die, and by bringing the facts to light I may become the target of his wrath. But since everyone who perished around him lost their life in the water, my options were simple;

THE LAST ATTEMPT

tell the truth and don't get in the water with him, ever again. I don't want to become *coincidental* casualty number 7; unlucky number that would be.

Another apprehension I had was the public's reaction. Celebrities are protected by a mantle of leniency that commoners don't have. Even the most hideous of crimes may be exonerated as a recompense for past amusement and entertainment of the masses. Former football player O. J. Simpson and Pop-Star Michael Jackson could easily fit into the aforementioned situation.

O. J. now lives only a couple of blocks away from me, in Kendall, Miami, with a small crowd chasing him regularly. But it's not a lynching mob looking to hang the sport hero by the neck or some other parts of his body; they are in pursuit of his autograph. I saw that happening few years ago in front of the dive shop of an acquaintance of mine, next to a local *Home Depot*, where O. J. was doing some shopping.

Then there is Michael Jackson, who settled with a little fortune a first case of child molestation and was exonerated on a second case from similar charges; different kid, though. Outside the court, the crowd acclaimed with arms extended up to the sky praising *The Lord* for the freedom granted to their superstar. *"Screw the kids!"* a blind follower from the crowd may have said, and so did Michael Jackson, I guess.

Maybe he's innocent, but if I ever get to see Michael Jackson near my sons, I'll give him the *thriller* of his life and turn him black once again, with a beating. Then, more likely, I'll end up in jail detested by the masses just for protecting the innocence of my kids. After all, I haven't entertained the crowd, so leniency won't be on my side.

On the same page, one night I was debating my options while writing the initial pages of this book. Feeling overwhelmed by the prospect of becoming loathed by apneists all over, I took a break. I decide to read a book related in no way to diving or anything that would resemble this saga. Like anyone else, I was reading Dan Brown's Best Seller, *The Da Vinci Code*.

One night while on bed, I fell asleep and didn't place the bookmark on the last page I had read. So when I grabbed the book the following morning looking for that page, by coincidence, I opened it on page 231, Chapter 55, where the author cites two quotes from Leonardo Da Vinci. The first quote says:

"Many have made a trade of delusions and false miracles, deceiving the stupid multitude."

While the second quote, right after the previous one, says:

"Blinding ignorance does mislead us. O! Wretched mortals, open your eyes!"

That's when I said to myself, after recovering from the eerie feeling and the goose bumps layering my skin, *"it's time to write,"* and as Dr. McInnis said, *". . . let the people judge Pipin"*. And so be it.

FINAL THOUGHT

Everyone makes good and bad decisions, and like anyone else I have my own share. Having sold my dive shop in the Florida Keys to an unethical guy from Holland to partner

CARLOS SERRA

Pipin was not a wise one. And as a consequence of Audrey's tragedy, I gave up a fifteen year-long career in diving after having accomplished the highest level a professional diver can reach. That's my karma, I guess.

But looking back in time, evoking the people I've met while running the *IAFD* and the places we traveled, I don't entirely regret it. Getting to know Audrey was a bliss that lasted until the moment she exhaled those last breaths, right in my hands. Then the pain came.

Eventually, Adriana divorced me after sixteen years of marriage and I don't blame her; I wasn't the same anymore. The most depressing time of my life fell upon me as an imploding tower of multiple stories. Unexpectedly, I found myself in its lobby, alone, paralyzed with fear, seeing shattered glass cutting my dreams, splitting my soul but never my wrists. Like Audrey, the thought crossed my mind, but I'm not as brave as she was.

Each crushing floor represented some of the worst situations a person can go through in a lifetime, but it all happened within a couple of years; the loss of my long-dreamed enterprise; the collapsing of my marriage; the senseless death of someone I loved; the abrupt loss of income; the sudden departure of a much desired way of living and having to walkout empty-handed from the first home I ever bought; my American dream; my cozy castle.

But leaving my lake-front house, however, with private security, tennis courts and a resort-style pool, and digress to a rented one-room apartment, pales when compared to the oppressing restriction of not seeing my boys, everyday. Their welcoming open arms after a hard day's work were as revitalizing as a cold and crispy glass of water at the end of a marathon run. Now I live in thirst. I miss them so much.

On top of that, my mother was tardy diagnosed with cancer due to the ineptitude of a doctor. Her early death is now a certainty only delayed by the caring love of my stepfather and her incredible courage and determination.

Even so I accept it all with resignation. There must be a philosophical reason for all of these troubles. It doesn't mean I forgive Pipin, because forgiveness is a godly business and unlike him, I don't pretend to be a divine entity. But something positive had to emerge from Audrey's loss.

After her passing I've regained my passion for oil-painting, something she loved and encouraged me to pursue. In only few months after her death, I worked over forty canvases. Not even in the previous five years I had painted so many. It was a self-imposed psychotherapy to keep my mental sanity within acceptable parameters, and in spite of my friends' opinion, I think is working.

My dry-cut, British-style sense of humor seems to be returning and that must be a good sign, although I feel sorry for those in the receiving end of my newfound jokes. But I'm still missing Audrey's laughter.

Today I continue to emulate God's real masterpieces, laying down colors and shapes in the blankness of a canvas. The main subject is my other passion, the ocean and its dwellers, naturally. Mainly seascapes, exotic mermaids and the always good-natured whales, orcas and dolphins are the main theme. And that brings my memories back to that day at the airport, before departing to Santo Domingo, when with melancholy in her voice Audrey said,

"*I wish I could be a Dolphin*".

Maybe instinctively I'm painting her. Perhaps it's a way to save her; to keep her alive. If I, among others, couldn't save her in life, at least I can seek to preserve her memory and symbolically grant her wish.

Inspiration begins to flow mostly at dusk, when the serenity of the night takes over and its quietness helps me focus. Next to the easel is a picture of my boys; my inspiration; my life support; my motivation; my pride and joy. In that picture they are sleeping in tranquil purity, accompanying my everlasting nights. Their innocence and placid rest induces me to pour my feelings through the paint.

With music in the background instigating my memories, an old song from *Led Zeppelin, Stairway to Heaven,* plays. The first passage of its lyrics suddenly makes me wonder about relevant truths contained in simple songs:

"*There's a lady who's sure / all that glitters is gold / and she's buying a stairway to heaven*".

Believing, out of faith, that's where Audrey now dwells, the brushstrokes define over the canvas the shape of playful dolphins, as I can only hope that they also go to heaven, where Audrey must be freediving peacefully, in eternal happiness with them.

"Art, like morality, consists of drawing the line somewhere". G.K. Chesterton

END

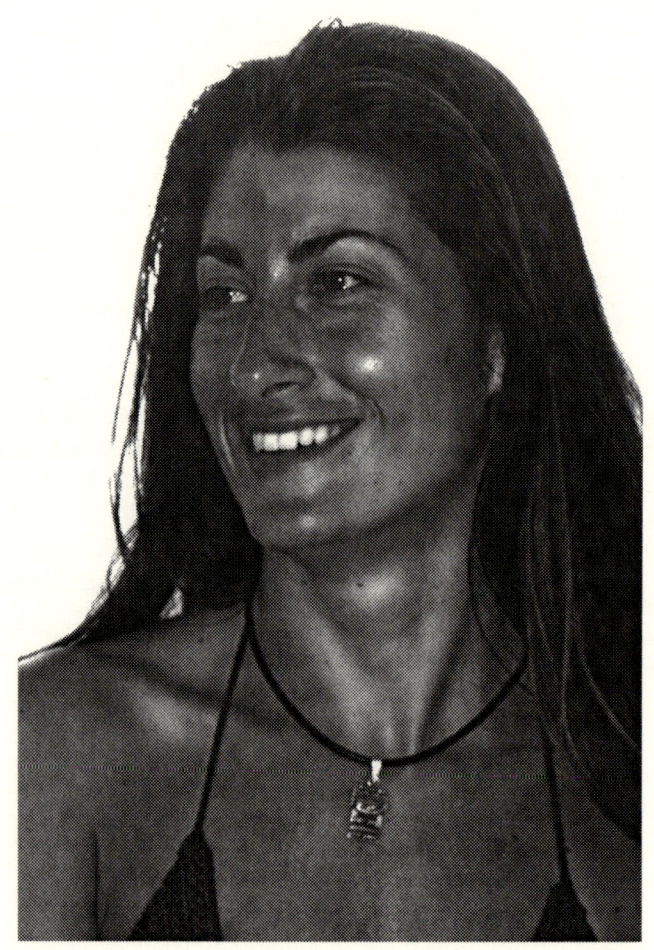

Credit: Angelo Cordero

Audrey Mestre
(August 11, 1974-October 12, 2002)

THE LAST ATTEMPT

UPDATE

Matt Briseno: Still lives in Kona, Hawaii, but travels often to the mainland to visit his six (so far) grandkids. His family-tree keeps adding branches. He has not maintained any contact with Pipin ever since Audrey's tragedy.

Bill Stromberg: Back home in Europe, he continued to participate in the world championship, either as a judge or as an athlete for AIDA. As the largest and strongest freediving agency, the association continues to sponsor events of international magnitude around the world with Bill as its president.

Angelo Cordero: Lives in South Beach, Florida, where he keeps capturing images of the rich and famous while maintaining a solid career as a fashion photographer. Although a professional in his realm, he kindly allowed the use of his pictures for this project without monetary compensation. He only wanted the credit as Pipin used Angelo's shots in his book but never gave him any credit.

Tata: Lives in Mexico and occasionally travels to Miami to meet Pipin. He suffered a great deal with Audrey's passing, but remains loyal to his boss.

Pascal: Lives in France but continues to travel around the world performing deep and cave dives. If he keeps supporting Pipin or not is unknown.

Wiky: Lives in Boca Raton, Florida. With his reputation initially damaged by Pipin's allegations, he couldn't work for a while. He attempted a legal case against *Sports Illustrated*, but the magazine had only repeated Pipin and Pascal's statements claiming that he wasn't at depth. The case never made it to court. With his name finally cleared, Wiky is now back into teaching scuba diving and established a corporation for underwater filming. To these days, he continues to get glassy eyes every time he speaks of Audrey, and as he promised a week after her death, he has never been in contact with Pipin ever since.

Jacques Mayol: The death of the great master of freediving is already known, but his prophetic words continue to reverberate stronger than ever. On September of 2006, while the final chapter of this book was being written, Carlos Coste, the most exceptional freediver nowadays, suffered an accident while attempting to set a world record in a category new to him, No-limits. *"Someone will suffer a serious accident one day or perhaps even die while attempting to break Pipin's record . . ."* said Mayol and it is happening. Carlos Coste suffered paralysis of his left side. Although a full recovery is expected, months of treatment and therapy will keep him away from competitions; hopefully not permanently.

Pipin: Still lives in Miami, Florida, attempting to pursue different venues; from promoting a teenager who sings in the Latin version of Rap music called *Regetón*, to emulate Angelo as a fashion photographer. He also produced a calendar (2006) with a pin-up Argentinean model named *Dorismar*, who soon after the calendar hit the stores, was deported from the United States by immigration. The model was arrested in her home in Miami and expelled within 8 hours as an illegal alien. Although the situation caused a public controversy, who actually gave the tip to the authorities for her unlawful long-stay in the U.S. remains a mystery.

CARLOS SERRA

Carlos Serra: Now divorced, he currently lives alone in Miami, Florida, but sees his children few times a week. He acquired a job as a manager with a big corporation and remains retired from professional diving; at least for now. Even so, he dives in scuba and freedives regularly. He continues to paint on a regular basis but still insecure about making a career as an artist. After severing his ties with Pipin, he dedicated the following three years to examine Audrey's event, its collateral issues and writing this book. *"I've made a promise,"* he says, *"to find out what happened to Audrey no matter what, and it's now fulfilled."*

Printed in the United Kingdom
by Lightning Source UK Ltd.
121717UK00001BA/21/A